Advance Praise for *When Our Light Is Tested*

"The abhorrent December 14, 2025 shooting at Sydney's Bondi Beach, that claimed fifteen innocent lives and injured dozens, was a shock—yet hardly a surprise. It was a result of years of rising hostility, expanding animosity, and amplified ignorance. The aim of this important book is to provide desperately needed context concerning the Jewish people and the Jewish democratic State of Israel. Colonel Michael Scott has known conflict and studied the perils of war, he has served throughout the Middle East and spent several years living in Israel, making this book so very relevant for understanding the far-reaching impact of the tragic Bondi attack."

—**Isaac Herzog**, president of the State of Israel

"Colonel Michael Scott offers readers a rare and powerful piece of moral clarity. The Book of Psalms 34:15 reminds us to 'seek peace and pursue it.' The pursuit of peace requires moral courage, finding your voice to stand up against hatred. Because hate of any kind leads to hate of all kinds. This is our nation's moment of moral reckoning. *When Our Light is Tested* could not have come soon enough."

—**Rabbi Levi Wolff**, chief minister,
Central Synagogue Sydney

"When I sat with Lissy Abrahams and other survivors of the Bondi massacre, I saw the human cost of an ideology that celebrates death over life and targets the innocent. What happened in Bondi is not an isolated Australian tragedy, nor just a headline about strangers. It reflects a reality that strikes at the heart of our shared humanity—a global sickness now manifesting across Western democracies.

"I stand with Israel, and I stand with people of conscience everywhere who refuse to surrender their societies to hatred, intimidation, and moral inversion. Colonel Michael Scott is right: This moment demands more than sympathy. It demands clarity, courage, and critical thinking from those who too often capitulate to the loudest voices instead of relying on their God-given moral compass.

"He is calling for action to confront antisemitism and violent extremism. We cannot afford to be bystanders while innocent lives are being taken."

—Phillip "Dr. Phil" McGraw, PhD,
television journalist and host, *Dr. Phil*,
#1 *New York Times* bestselling author;
founder, ENVOY Television Network

"*When Our Light Is Tested* is a confronting contribution to Australia's national conversation after Bondi. Colonel Michael Scott writes with clarity about how antisemitism corrodes social cohesion and democratic values. Whether or not readers agree with every conclusion, this book demands engagement rather than indifference."

—**Jeremy Leibler**, president of the Zionist Federation of Australia

"Colonel Michael Scott is a principled Australian and a good man doing important work at a difficult moment in our nation's story. His military service may have ended but he continues to serve our nation and the broader global community. He brings moral clarity, lived experience, and quiet courage to one of the defining challenges of our time, and leads with heart and an unshakeable commitment to truth. I'm proud to call him a friend and to support his efforts to stand against antisemitism and bring people together."

—**Erin Molan**, Australian television and radio presenter; host, *The Erin Molan Show*

"An incisive analysis of what led to the Bondi Beach Chanukah massacre. Normalising anti-Jewish hate speech in its multiple forms, against the background of a failure of leadership and western moral decay, led to its inevitable outcome. Colonel Michael Scott brilliantly connects the dots and provides an urgent warning. What starts with attacks on the Jewish people ends in the undermining of all democracies and traditional western values. Scott challenges us all to decide whether and how we will face up to the dangers and our responsibility to future generations."

—**Dr. Ron Weiser, AM**, former president of the Zionist Federation of Australia (1996–2006), board member of the Jewish Agency for Israel, and honorary life president of the Zionist Council of NSW, Co-Chair of the Jewish Agency's Task Force on Antisemitism

"We have watched with deep concern how much and how fast our country has changed—and not for the better. What once seemed unthinkable is now tolerated. What once united us is now fraying. Citizens cannot afford to stand by while hatred and division take root. *When Our Light Is Tested*, together with Michael's earlier excellent book, *A Light Still Burns: Israel and the Values Worth Defending*, helps us understand what is happening—and what each of us must do to correct this dangerous descent. This is a timely and necessary call to responsibility."

—**Evelynne and Jack Gance**, co-founders, Chemist Warehouse, philanthropists

"*When Our Light Is Tested* is a serious and necessary book! It is grounded in lived experience, not ideology, and written with moral clarity rather than rhetoric. My true and dear friend Colonel Michael Scott approaches Israel, antisemitism, and the wider civilisational challenge with sobriety, responsibility, and respect for complexity. This is not a book for those seeking slogans; it is for readers—particularly non-Jewish readers—who want to understand reality as it is, and to think clearly about what is at stake. At a time when confusion is widespread and judgment is often replaced by noise. This very important book helps restore proportion, context, and responsibility."

—**Lieutenant Colonel (Res.) Giora Levi**,
Israel Defense Forces, סיירת מטכ"ל

"The massacre at Bondi was not an aberration in an otherwise healthy global climate. It was a warning. As someone who has spent decades confronting violent extremism, I can say with certainty that the ideology driving such attacks does not recognise borders. Colonel Michael Scott is correct to frame this as a broader struggle affecting all Western democracies. When leaders hesitate to identify and confront radicalisation early, the cost is paid later by innocent civilians, and possibly by entire societies. Security, resilience, and moral clarity are not optional—they are prerequisites for preserving free societies."

—**Lieutenant Colonel (Res.) Jonathan Conricus**, former international spokesperson, Israel Defense Forces senior fellow, Foundation for Defense of Democracies

"Colonel Michael Scott brings the lived experience of a frontline soldier to the global challenge of antisemitism and has taken the valiant step of speaking out, first in his work *A Light Still Burns*, and now with *When Our Light Is Tested.*

"Importantly, Scott is not Jewish. He understands and is prepared to fight for the enduring morality and values which define civilisation. This is a serious book for serious times. It deserves to be widely read."

—**Piers Akerman**, veteran Australian journalist and commentator

"Just weeks after Australia's deadliest terror attack, baying mobs cheered as a raging protest leader urged them to 'Globalize the Intifada'—and in effect, to perpetrate another Bondi Beach Massacre. The Antizionist hate movement is less a threat to Israel than to the Western societies that are being swept away by conspiratorial hysteria, obsessive hatred, and violent scapegoating. In *When Our Light Is Tested*, Colonel Michael Scott offers a sober analysis of how the

Antizionist brain virus has brought political extremism to Western democracies—and how those democracies can save themselves before they are consumed."

—**Eylon Levy**, former spokesman for the State of Israel

"This book isn't just about antisemitism or the Bondi massacre. It's about what happens when a society slowly stops telling itself the truth. Colonel Michael Scott writes with lived credibility and moral clarity, showing that antisemitism is a warning sign for the health of the culture itself. What's at stake isn't one community, but the values that hold the democratic West together. *When Our Light Is Tested* makes that impossible to ignore."

—**Eitan Chitayat**, founder of I'm That Jew and CEO of Natie Branding Agency

"This is a must-read book for anyone who cares about the safety, cohesion, and moral future of Western society. *When Our Light is Tested* forces us to reckon with the historical truth that violence against Jews is symptomatic of something far deeper than the mere hatred of Jews and does not remain confined to Jews. No one is insulated from the forces we are reckoning with in this moment, and we must all stand up and fight back against them.

"Western values and our way of life are being compromised as Colonel Michael Scott so brilliantly explores in this book and failures in leadership must be called out and questioned so that we can clearly identify the forces of evil and secure a solid future on western shores advocated for collectively by each of us."

—**Marnie Perlstein**, Australian Jewish advocate, social media influencer

Also by Michael Scott

A Light Still Burns: Israel and the Values Worth Defending

WHEN OUR LIGHT IS TESTED

The Bondi Massacre and the Choices Ahead

MICHAEL SCOTT

A WICKED SON BOOK
An Imprint of Post Hill Press
ISBN: 979-8-89565-776-8
ISBN (eBook): 979-8-89565-777-5

When Our Light Is Tested:
The Bondi Massacre and the Choices Ahead

Cover Design by Jim Villaflores

This book is a work of nonfiction. It draws on publicly available information, personal experience, and contemporaneous reporting. Every effort has been made to ensure accuracy at the time of writing. Errors or omissions, if any, are unintentional.

The views expressed are those of the author and do not represent the views of any government, institution, or organisation with which the author is or has been affiliated.

This book is not intended as legal, military, or professional advice. References to individuals and events are made in good faith and for the purposes of commentary, analysis, and record.

Some names and identifying details may have been withheld where appropriate, in order to protect privacy or safety.

Post Hill Press
New York • Nashville
wickedsonbooks.com
posthillpress.com

Published in the United States of America
1 2 3 4 5 6 7 8 9 10

For those who stood when standing carried a cost.
For the innocent, and for those who refused to look away.

In memoriam of Paul Keen and Stanley Roth AM—two of my role models, mentors, father figures, and lions of Australia. Men who bore the accumulated weight carried by our finest: responsibility, moral clarity, and service rendered quietly over decades.

Like lead runners in a 4 × 400 metre relay, they took the opening—and hardest—lap: running the congested start, absorbing pressure, establishing rhythm, and carrying the baton with strength and discipline so others could run their legs well. They did not slow to seek applause, nor did they allow criticism or distraction to deflect them; they laboured to ensure the race could continue.

By their example, they showed us how to live with steadiness, courage, and purpose. The baton has now been passed. It falls to us to honour their legacy—not only by carrying forward what they so faithfully advanced, but by striving to be better, as they were, in the lives entrusted to us.

"Civilisations die from suicide, not by murder."
Arnold J. Toynbee

"A great civilisation is not conquered from without until it has destroyed itself from within."
Will Durant

"The most practical and important thing about a man is still his view of the universe."
G. K. Chesterton

"The tragedy of modern man is not that he knows less and less about the meaning of his own life, but that it matters less and less to him."
Václav Havel

TABLE OF CONTENTS

PART I: THE UNEASE

PART II: THE DECAY

PART III: THE CAPTURE

PART IV: THE RECORD

PART V: DANGER: WHEN HATE COMES HOME

PART VI: THE UPWARD PATH

APPENDICES

FOREWORD
(from Three Bondi Survivors)

Michael Scott

I have known war. I have known loss in war. But what happened at Bondi was different. It had announced itself—through language, intimidation, and tolerated escalation—but not its time or its place. It arrived instead in an intimate setting, in a space that should have been safe: for me, for my Jewish friends, and for the wider Australian public. What follows are the accounts of friends who were there.

They come from different walks of life, different roles, and different stages of life—yet their testimonies converge on a single, disturbing truth: this violence did not arrive unannounced.

Chavi Israel was there as a young mother, shielding her infant son with her own body at what should have been a children's festival. Her testimony is not political analysis. It is instinct, terror, and moral clarity in its rawest form—the moment when a parent understands that the most basic promise of safety has collapsed.

Lissy Abrahams was there as a mother and as a clinician, someone trained to recognise patterns, trauma, and the consequences of institutional failure. Her account situates Bondi within a longer arc—one that connects language, appeasement, and moral evasion to their inevitable outcome.

Larry (pseudonym) was there as a volunteer protector. A father. A professional. A member of the Community Security Group who understood—long before that evening—that Jewish life in Australia was being pushed into a narrowing corridor of risk. His testimony speaks to responsibility assumed where leadership failed, and to the cost borne by those who step forward when others look away.

These accounts are not offered to shock or to perform grief. They are offered to test us—to see whether we are capable of learning from what had already been signalled, and of applying that learning with enough seriousness to prevent what need not happen again.

Part of dealing with trauma, loss, and grief is turning it toward purpose. We cannot change what has already happened. What we can—and what we must—do is refuse to waste the knowledge it has given us: to learn, to act earlier, to name danger before it becomes catastrophe, and to choose responsibility over comfort and clarity over delay.

What follows is not an exercise in outrage. It is an insistence that testimony, when taken seriously, carries obligation.

Chavi Israel

I am Chavi. At the time of the shooting, my son Meir was seven months old.

My husband is a nurse. On the day of the attack, he was out of town, singing at a wedding. When the shooting began, he was helpless—unable to reach us, unable to protect us. That sense of powerlessness has deeply traumatised him, and it still does.

I am a twenty-seven-year-old Orthodox Jewish woman. I grew up in Melbourne, in Caulfield. I always felt safe—even though there was always security outside our synagogue. That was normal. Jewish normal. I moved to Sydney six years ago.

After October 7, we were all grieving. Still in shock. Still watching what was unfolding in Israel. Two days later, I saw on television the Israeli flag being burned outside the Sydney Opera House. We heard the chants—"gas the Jews."

Not overseas. Not on social media. In Australia. I will never forget it.

That moment shattered something fundamental. It was twenty minutes from my home. And I remember thinking: this doesn't look good. I know how these things start. It always begins with words—with lies, with tolerated language, with chants and justifications. And then it turns into violence.

The aim is to make Jews fearful. To isolate us. To create permission structures for antisemitism. To make us visible targets.

Zionism—a beautiful word—has been deliberately misappropriated and made to sound dirty. That is why I founded *The Empowered Jew*. Because our community needed it. Because we could see where this was heading.

I was at the Bondi Chabad Chanukah event on December 14. Every year I go. It is always beautiful. A children's festival. Bubble performers. Face painting. Chanukah music. Hot dogs and donuts. A joyful Jewish celebration on a hot Australian afternoon. I was with friends. Our children were laughing and running freely.

In one second, everything changed. I was shielding my baby with my body.

A children's carnival turned into a bloody massacre. Over forty people were injured. Fifteen people murdered. There were bodies all around me. I still don't understand how I wasn't a casualty. One moment: carefree joy. The next: sheer evil. Light to darkness in a heartbeat.

At first, I thought it was fireworks. Then I saw the Community Security Group officer screaming for people to get down. That was the moment I knew. I could not believe this was happening—here, in Australia.

Antisemitism is like cancer. If you do not treat cancer, it spreads. And if you do not stop it, it kills. This is not just about Jews. Antisemitism never stops with the Jews. When it is tolerated, society itself begins to rot.

What is happening is not simply the decay of Jewish safety in Australia. It is the decay of Australia as we have known it—a country built on fairness, order, and the protection of minorities under the law.

Australia is at a crossroads. It either turns for the better—or it continues down a path that leads somewhere very dark.

How many more people need to die before Australians wake up?

This did not need to happen. The government needed to step up—and it didn't. The federal government has blood on its hands. The prime minister has blood on his hands.

When a government fails to act after clear warning signs—after public incitement, after intimidation, after violence—that failure is not neutral. It has consequences. And those consequences were paid in blood at Bondi.

Jewish businesses are shutting their doors. Avner's Bakery. Goldstone's Gallery in Melbourne. Visible Jewish life is retreating because safety is no longer guaranteed by our government.

The Governor-General has powers. And yet nothing is said. Silence persists while Jewish Australians are told—implicitly—to accept fear as the price of belonging.

We have a prime minister who has not taken our concerns seriously. Who has not prioritised our safety. A leader who has failed in the most basic duty of government: to protect its citizens. For that failure, he should resign—or be removed. Because when a mother must shield her baby with her own body at a children's festival in Australia, something has already gone terribly—unforgivably—wrong.

Lissy Abrahams

I am a mother of two in my fifties, born and raised in Australia to parents who emigrated here from England. I am also a psychotherapist specialising in couple's therapy. I have spent my professional life helping people communicate, resolve conflict, and hold relationships together under strain.

I grew up freely. I always had non-Jewish friends and moved easily between communities. Integration was not something I was taught; it was something I lived. Difference was normal.

Then October 7 happened, and the stories I had grown up hearing—the ones you are told belong to history, never to be repeated—came violently back to life. The horror was not abstract. It was rape, torture, families hunted in their homes, people burned alive, hostages dragged away while the world argued over language.

I was about ten years old when a Hebrew teacher encouraged us to watch *Holocaust*, the miniseries starring Meryl Streep. It was brutal and confronting—my first real encounter with generational trauma, and with what human beings are capable of when systems fail and hatred is indulged. After October 7, I saw those same patterns again—not only in the violence itself, but in the responses to it: weakness, moral evasion, institutional failure, and a bias that treats Jews and the Jewish state as uniquely undeserving of protection.

Before October 7, I had rarely encountered antisemitism directly. The main exception was London. In 2011, swastikas were being painted on doors in Golders Green, a heavily Jewish suburb, and the prevailing response was one of appeasement and minimisation. I remember thinking then that something was wrong.

I had been in London during the 7 July 2005 bus and underground bombings. When I heard the sirens in Bondi years later, I recognised the sound immediately. It was the same sound.

After October 7, something else happened that is harder to describe. Save for the rare non-Jew who took a public stand in support of us, we were mostly all alone. We asked for help—clearly, calmly, and repeatedly. We said that Jews needed protection, and that those being targeted needed to be kept safe. There was no meaningful response from government, and little from much of the broader public. That absence, more than open hostility, was soul-destroying.

Then Bondi happened.

And what must be said plainly is this: Jews were hunted. We were hunted. Not overseas. Not in a history book. In Australia. In Bondi. In 2025. That is not rhetoric. It is description.

After Bondi, there was—for a time—an outpouring of love and solidarity. The Disaster Hub was extraordinary. The Australian Jewish community was extraordinary: mobilised, disciplined, compassionate, and focused on caring for the families of those murdered and those affected by the shootings. I stepped into the media, nationally and internationally, to give testimony. Adrenaline carried me for a while. Then it fell away, and the deeper question remained: Has Australia actually learned anything?

On 14 December 2025, I was at Bondi Beach attending a family celebration for dear friends. I was walking with my twenty-three-year-old daughter near the Chanukkiah when we heard what others first assumed were fireworks. I immediately knew they were not. They were gunshots—close, sharp, unmistakable.

I told my daughter she needed to run. I was in high-heeled shoes and told her to run ahead without me. She refused. She would not leave her mother.

My daughter decided we should run beachside and hide underneath the Bondi surf lifesaving club. People inside were confused. The danger had come from outside, but the fear followed us in. I took control and said plainly, "This is a terrorist attack. People are being murdered. We need to be careful." I told people to pull the roller doors down. Bring them down. Secure the space.

My daughter and I had different instincts about where to hide. I backed her decision to shelter at the end of a tunnel. I backed her call. If I was going to die, I would die on my daughter's terms. These instincts were not theoretical. They were inherited.

When it was finally possible to evacuate, we jumped into the back of a stranger's ute to get away from the scene. We had no idea whether there was one shooter or many. No idea whether others were nearby with knives or explosives. That uncertainty—the complete absence of reliable information—is something people who have never lived through an attack struggle to understand. In those moments, you move without clarity, guided only by instinct, responsibility, and the singular obligation to get your child to safety.

I returned two weeks later. I did not want to allow my enemies to live rent-free in my mind. I stood there and lost control as the terror I had hidden from my daughter finally surfaced. I cried.

Hope is not a strategy. Condolences are not a strategy. Platitudes are not a strategy. Community resilience cannot substitute for national responsibility. We need serious action, including a Royal Commission—not as symbolism, and not as a cure-all, but as a necessary first step to establish truth, accountability, and a strategic path forward.

I remain an optimist, but I am not naïve. I believe things will get worse before they get better unless we change course.

This is not over. What happened in Bondi will either be remembered as the moment Australia drew a line, or as the warning it chose to ignore. We are not heading in a direction that gives me confidence this was the last attack.

Matilda—the youngest victim of the Bondi massacre—did not die for a cause. She died because something is deeply wrong, and because the government failed to stop it. How many more children must be murdered before we are willing to name the problem honestly and confront it without euphemism or fear?

For the families who have already lost everything, the cost is immeasurable. The question now is whether that failure will be acknowledged and corrected—or whether more innocent people will be forced to pay, tragically and brutally, for our continued unwillingness to act.

Larry (Pseudonym)

I am an Australian, forty years old, married, and a father of two children—one aged five, the other four months. I am unable to use my name here owing to the ongoing risk to me and my family. I am a survivor of the Bondi Massacre.

My wife works in design; I work as an IT engineer specialising in medical software. I have lived and worked in Australia and Silicon Valley, and today we live in Sydney's Eastern Suburbs.

The reason for my anonymity is that I am a volunteer with the Community Security Group (CSG)—a community-led organisation comprising primarily professional Jewish Australians who supplement law enforcement in response to the threat faced by Jewish communities. Our volunteers include university students and mature professionals who provide security at Jewish schools, synagogues, and community events.

After 7 October 2023, I was angry. Like many, I wanted to exercise agency—to do something tangible rather than watch the world argue over language while Jewish communities absorbed the consequences. It was my wife who suggested I volunteer. Her reasoning was simple: If I wanted to make a real, positive impact, this was how.

I have now been involved for two years. I don't have spare time—few of us do—but I do what I can, when I can. I have gained a great deal personally from serving my community. I am a proud Jew, and I do not believe in living in fear. Yet since 7 October, I have also felt something I never expected to feel in Australia: moments of fear about being seen for who I am—a proud Australian Jewish man.

Whatever happens in Israel has ramifications here. Jews are routinely blamed. We do not see Russian churches firebombed because of the war in Ukraine, yet Jewish communities in Sydney and Melbourne increasingly bear the consequences of what people perceive is happening in the Middle East—often based on slogans, misinformation, and moral theatre rather than facts.

That is why organisations like the CSG exist.

On 14 December 2025, I volunteered at a Chanukah event at Bondi Beach. As I write this on 2 January 2026, the organiser from Bondi Chabad—whom I met that day—remains in hospital.

I had taken a short break from volunteering after the birth of our second child. But I knew December would be busy, and I knew the first night of Chanukah is a major event in our community. I also knew Bondi in summer—crowded, symbolic, and exposed—was a potential target.

That day, I even considered bringing my children. My wife took them instead to an equivalent event at Dover Heights. Thank G-d they were not at Bondi.

The event was designed to be open and inclusive—like Christmas in the public square. Families, music, face painting, a climbing wall, a petting zoo. Innocent, joyful, and public. My role was not to enjoy it, but to scan and observe—to be visible, calm, and alert.

There is a sentence that lives quietly in your mind when you do this work: Today could be the day.

About thirty minutes before the attack, I was positioned near the bridge. At one point I was directed to provide a presence elsewhere in the park. These adjustments are routine.

Then came an incredibly loud banging sound. I saw sparks. My brain tried to rationalise it—fireworks? Firecrackers? Balloons?

Very quickly it became clear: It was gunfire.

In Australia, in Sydney, you do not expect this. But it happened—and it happened fast.

The first instinct was fear. People ran. A wave of panic surged through the park. I had only a radio. I didn't know where the shooters were, how many there were, or what weapons they had.

Then instinct shifted. I was there to protect.

I ran into the event to take cover and orient myself—not blindly into danger, but into a position where I could assess and respond. I took cover on the stage that was meant to be used to light the Menorah.

It was still light—about 6:45 p.m. The Menorah was never lit.

Bullets flew overhead. The sound of gunfire was relentless—like a metronome. What I remember most vividly is the helplessness: I had nothing to respond with. A radio. A phone. Concealment, not real cover.

In my mind, 7 October played on repeat. I remember thinking: If police don't get this under control—or if they are overwhelmed—they will come in here and kill us.

I shouted for people to get down. I prayed.

I saw horrific sights—people murdered, badly shot, bleeding out. Police officers were present, but they were outgunned. This is not a criticism of individuals; it is a reality of capability. What is more confronting is that an event like this had been telegraphed for over two years. With profound disappointment, I reflect on the failure of Australia's federal leadership to act decisively in the face of escalating warnings.

When the gunfire stopped, we waited. We did not know whether the threat was neutralised or mobile, or whether this was part of a wider, coordinated attack.

Then we moved into response mode.

I provided first aid, applied pressure, and delegated where possible. Others performed CPR. Medical responders arrived quickly—lifeguards, community health workers, and Hatzolah. Over the radio I heard: "I'm shot. I need help."

Kelly Sloane MP arrived while the situation was still unfolding. I urged her to get to safety. She chose to stay. She was remarkable.

My family at Dover Heights went into immediate lockdown.

Afterwards, the scene was chaotic: blood, injured people, the dead, parents searching for children. Many faces were familiar. I asked detectives whether there had been other shootings at Jewish events. The answer was that there may have been. That uncertainty—combined with knowing my young family was nearby—was deeply unsettling.

Eventually, a properly equipped police response team arrived. The area was declared safe. We accounted for our team, debriefed, and began counselling. I did not sleep.

The hardest moment came later. My wife stayed with her parents that night. Our five-year-old son asked her, "Is dad dead?"

No parent should ever have to answer that.

In the days since, the community has rallied in extraordinary ways. We are bound now by shared trauma. Some suffered far worse than I did—friends were shot, murdered, or seriously injured. Support has come from across Australia and from Israel, including specialist psychological first-aid teams.

Returning to the site days later—walking the bridge—was unexpectedly therapeutic. The vigil was raw and emotional. This was a targeted attack against Australian Jews, but it was felt beyond our community too.

And yet, I also sense how quickly the wider world moves on.

That is why this matters.

I am proud of my service with the CSG. Proud of the volunteers—students, professionals, parents—who choose responsibility over comfort. And proud that, even after such darkness, our community continues to gather, celebrate, and live openly.

Chanukah is about light—but also courage. The refusal to surrender identity to intimidation.

On 14 December 2025, we did not light the Menorah at Bondi.

But the obligation remains.

To show up.

To protect life.

To live without fear—wisely, but without surrender.

Australia has long comforted itself with the belief that "she'll be right." But history teaches otherwise. Things are fine—until suddenly they are not. And by then, it is too late.

This did not happen without warning.

It is not "over there."

It is here.

From Testimony to Reckoning

These accounts are not included as prologue or ornament. They are evidence. They describe not only what happened on one evening in Bondi, but what happens when warnings are absorbed without consequence, when responsibility is deferred, and when the language of concern replaces the discipline of action. Chavi, Lissy and Larry speak from different vantage points—mother, clinician, and volunteer protector—yet their experiences converge on the same truth: This violence did not arrive unannounced. It followed a period of tolerated escalation, institutional hesitation, and a widening gap between what was known privately and what was acted upon publicly.

What follows in this book does not attempt to relitigate their trauma, nor to extract meaning from suffering for its own sake. It seeks instead to take their testimony seriously—as a moral and civic challenge. If testimony is ignored, it becomes memorial. If it is examined honestly, it can become instruction. The task now is not empathy alone, but discernment: to understand how a society that prides itself on safety, pluralism, and restraint allowed conditions to form in which such an attack could occur—and how easily those same conditions could be replicated elsewhere. The preface that follows turns from witness to analysis, not to soften what has been said, but to ensure it is not wasted.

PREFACE

This is the second book in a deliberate sequence.

A Light Still Burns: Israel and the Values Worth Defending, published by Wicked Son in October 2025, was written in response to a moment of forced moral clarity. The atrocities of October 7, 2023 stripped away euphemism and denial. They revealed—with brutal simplicity—both the nature of Israel's enemies and the values Israel continues to defend, often alone and at great cost.

That book looked outward. It examined Israel's conduct in war, the moral asymmetry it faces, and the civilisational principles that bind Israel's struggle to that of the democratic West. It was written as a refusal to avert the eyes—a call to clarity at a moment when antisemitism surged and Western moral confidence faltered, even as many in the West continued to believe that such pathologies were distant, containable, and safely "over there."

This book turns the lens inward.

The four quotations placed at the front of this book are not ornamental. They form the moral and intellectual frame through which everything that follows should be read.

Arnold Toynbee's warning that civilisations more often die by suicide than by murder speaks directly to the central concern of this book: that what threatens free societies today is not conquest from without, but erosion from within—through denial, indulgence, and the steady surrender of moral clarity. Will Durant's observation sharpens that insight further, reminding us that no civilisation is truly defeated until it has first participated in its own undoing.

G. K. Chesterton's insistence that a person's view of the universe is the most practical thing about them points to the deeper layer beneath politics, policy, and institutions. It is not simply what we do that determines our fate, but how we understand reality itself—what we believe is true, what we believe matters, and what we believe is worth defending. Václav Havel's lament completes the frame, warning that the gravest danger is not ignorance, but indifference: the moment when meaning itself begins to matter less, and responsibility is quietly displaced by comfort.

These four ideas—civilisational self-harm, internal decay, worldview, and moral indifference—are not abstract concerns. They are diagnostic. Together, they describe the conditions under which societies fail without ever formally collapsing.

In the months that followed October 7, something more unsettling than expected began to unfold. The threat did not remain distant. It did not confine itself to Middle Eastern battlefields or ideological abstractions. It moved inward—into Western institutions, media organisations, universities, workplaces, and eventually onto the streets of cities that had long believed themselves insulated from such violence. In Australia, that illusion collapsed on one of the nation's most iconic beaches in December 2025.

What demanded examination was no longer Israel's conduct, but our reaction to it.

Hatred itself was not the surprise. History offers no shortage of reminders that antisemitism never disappears; it merely waits for permission. What was new—and deeply confronting—was how quickly that permission was granted in societies that pride themselves on tolerance, reason, and moral seriousness. Violence was contextualised. Responsibility was displaced. Moral inversion was reframed as compassion. What should have shocked instead became managed.

The structure of this book reflects how such failures actually unfold—not in theory, but in lived experience.

It begins with **unease**: the early signals people sense before they can yet prove them—changes in behaviour, hesitation in conversation, the quiet recognition that certain truths now carry social cost. It moves from there to **decay**, as institutions stop correcting themselves and moral drift becomes measurable. It then confronts **capture**, the point at which language and narrative no longer clarify reality but actively obscure it. Only after that does the book return to **the record**—to history, law, and the realities of war—before tracing how indulgence abroad becomes **danger at home**. It ends by turning deliberately **upward**, toward agency and responsibility, asking what can still be done once illusions have collapsed.

This is a book written with a wide audience in mind. It is a book about Western fragility—moral, institutional, and cultural—and about how loudly proclaimed values can quietly erode. It examines how free societies lose confidence not in a single moment, but through drift, denial, and fatigue.

It is also offered deliberately as a tool.

Readers already immersed in these issues may find in these pages observations and analysis that sharpen, clarify, or reframe what they already sense. For Jewish readers in particular, the book is intended to serve an additional purpose: as something to be passed on. It is written with the expectation that it may be referred quietly to receptive friends—those open to reflection but not yet fully engaged—as a means of extending understanding beyond familiar circles.

For others, the book seeks to provide language where there has been unease without articulation. It is meant to be engaged with, tested, and returned to; used in conversation and shared deliberately within friendship groups—among colleagues, friends, and family members—as a form of quiet influence rather than public performance.

From small conversations come larger ones. From drops come ripples; from ripples, waves.

The good news—and there is good news—is that fragility is not the same as extinction. What is fragile can still be protected. What has been damaged can still be repaired. But only if we are willing to see clearly, speak honestly, and accept responsibility before catastrophe forces the issue.

If *A Light Still Burns* argued that some values are worth defending, *When Our Light Is Tested* confronts the reality that those same values, left unattended, can be lost—and that moments like Bondi, horrific as they are, can still serve as catalysts for correction rather than markers of terminal decline.

This book is offered in that spirit: not as a performance, not as a posture, but as an invitation—to think again, to speak plainly, and to choose differently while choice still exists.

PROLOGUE

Bondi: What We Know So Far—Written 24 December 2025

On Sunday 14 December 2025, Sydney experienced an attack that many Australian Jews had long feared was inevitable. For years, safety concerns had been raised, minimised, and too often dismissed. While the precise form and location of the violence could not be predicted, the risk itself was not abstract. What remained difficult to imagine was that it would arrive so brazenly, in such a public place, and in such a familiar setting. The target was a Jewish community Hanukkah gathering at Bondi—a place that symbolised safety, normal life, and the everyday freedoms Australians take for granted.

In the days since, the language has hardened into the necessary terms: mass murder, terrorism, antisemitic violence. The facts themselves are still being assembled. Investigators continue their work. Court processes have begun. Claims are being tested. Evidence is being sifted. Some details will change.

Any responsible account written at this stage must therefore be explicit about its limits.

What follows is a snapshot, not a verdict: what has been publicly reported, what police allege in court documents, and what has been confirmed by major outlets to this point.

The Event

The attack occurred during a Jewish community Hanukkah gathering in parkland at Bondi Beach, mere metres from the golden sand and blue water that define one of Australia's most recognisable public spaces. The first shots were fired at approximately 6:47 p.m., with emergency services called shortly before 7:00 p.m. Families, children, and elderly members of the community were present.

According to police allegations, two men—a father and son—arrived at the scene and launched a coordinated attack. They are alleged to have thrown multiple improvised explosive devices toward the gathering before opening fire. The devices did not detonate but were later assessed as viable.

One of the alleged perpetrators died at the scene. The other was seriously injured, survived, and was later charged with multiple offences, including murder and terrorism-related charges.

The Accused

The alleged perpetrators have been identified in reporting as Sajid Akram (father) and Naveed Akram (son). The surviving accused, Naveed Akram, has been charged with multiple counts of murder. Media reporting has indicated that the pair were of Pakistani origin. Questions of citizenship and residency form part of the material now before the courts.

What Police Allege About Preparation

Reporting based on court documents and police statements describes preparation and planning in the weeks and months leading up to the attack.

Police allege that in October 2025, the pair recorded extremist material and undertook firearms-related activity. In November, they reportedly travelled overseas, spending several weeks in the Philippines. The nature and purpose of that travel remains under investigation.

In the days immediately before the attack, police allege a reconnaissance visit was conducted in the Bondi area. On the day of the attack, CCTV footage is reported to show the pair leaving an Airbnb in Sydney's southwest carrying long, bulky items. Police allege these included firearms, components for improvised explosive devices, and extremist propaganda material.

This combination of alleged reconnaissance, travel, preparation, and equipment is why investigators and commentators have repeatedly described the attack as meticulously planned, while stressing that investigations remain ongoing.

The Victims

Fifteen people were murdered in the attack.

Among those killed were elderly members of the community, parents, and a ten-year-old child. Rabbis, community volunteers, and ordinary Australians attending a religious celebration lost their lives. The names of the victims have since been published, accompanied by tributes that speak to lives of family, service, and contribution.

The loss is not abstract. It is intimate and enduring—carried by families, congregations, and a community that had every reason to believe it belonged safely within the Australian story.

Motive and What Remains Uncertain

Police allege that the attack was ideologically motivated and connected to extremist Islamist beliefs. Material described in court points clearly to antisemitic intent.

To the ordinary reader—and to the Jewish community that was targeted—this was not an ambiguous act requiring interpretive caution. It was an antisemitic attack on Australian Jews, carried out at an iconic public beach, during a religious celebration, on the first night of Hanukkah. Sydney's affluent, waterside eastern suburbs are home to one of Australia's most visible and well-established Jewish communities—a demographic reality that gives the choice of location an unavoidable communal resonance.

That legal processes must still determine questions of individual culpability does not alter the nature of what occurred. Jews were attacked because they were Jews, in a place chosen precisely because it represented openness, public life, and belonging. The violence was directed not only at individuals, but at the idea that Jewish Australians could gather openly, safely, and without fear.

What remains for the courts is the full accounting of responsibility: the precise motivations of those involved, whether others assisted or encouraged the attack, and the detailed sequence of decisions that led to that night. What does not remain uncertain is the character of the act itself.

Why This Matters

In the immediate aftermath, one phrase appeared repeatedly in commentary: that this was "every Jewish person's worst nightmare."

That phrase captures something essential. The attack did not occur in a remote or marginal setting. It took place in open public space, in a suburb associated with leisure and ordinary life, at a community celebration. It shattered the assumption that such violence belonged elsewhere—to other countries, other histories, other people.

The Bondi massacre is not offered here as spectacle, nor as the sum total of what this book examines. It is the rupture that explains why this book exists at all.

If *A Light Still Burns* asked what Israel reveals about the values of the West, this book begins at the moment when that same moral test arrived on Australian sand.

What follows is not written in haste or outrage. Some of the essays that follow were written before Bondi; others in its aftermath. Together, they reflect a period in which facts began to settle, denial became harder to sustain, and a question could finally be asked with honesty:

What do we do now—once the illusion has collapsed?

INTRODUCTION

When the Illusion Shattered

On the afternoon of 14 December 2025, I was at a private residence in Sydney with my wife and close friends when my phone vibrated. The time was 6:57 p.m. The message was from my daughter. She was twenty years old and four hours away.

"*Dad, are you ok?*" she wrote. "*There's been a shooting at Bondi.*"

Like many parents, I felt that brief, disorienting pause—the moment when the mind struggles to reconcile an ordinary afternoon with the intrusion of something unthinkable. I was barely two kilometres away, less than ten minutes after the first shots. Yet it was my daughter—hundreds of kilometres away—who knew first. Such is the compression, and inversion, of distance in the information age.

We turned on the television.

What we saw, and what has since become clearer, was not random violence or a tragic aberration. It was the realisation of a danger that had long been sensed but insufficiently acknowledged: that a hatred rationalised, minimised, or dismissed as rhetorical would eventually arrive in physical form—in a place chosen precisely because it symbolised safety, normality, and national ease.

Bondi Beach is not a distant frontier or a contested zone. It is one of the most familiar stretches of sand in the country—a place where parents take children, friends gather, and Australians have long believed themselves insulated from the darker currents shaping the wider world. That belief ended there.

For Jewish Australians, the shock carried a particular weight. Since October 7, 2023, many had already been living with heightened vigilance—not hysteria, but recognition. The signs had been present for years: intimidation normalised, threats tolerated, antisemitism reframed as discourse. History suggests that when such patterns turn lethal, they do so quickly. Bondi confirmed what had been felt privately but too often dismissed publicly: that the boundary between overseas ideologies and domestic safety had dissolved.

But the impact did not stop with the Jewish community.

For many non-Jewish Australians—people of goodwill who assumed extremism was someone else's problem, somewhere else—Bondi marked a rupture. It stripped away the comforting fiction that antisemitism is marginal, or that it can be indulged rhetorically without consequence. It revealed, with brutal clarity, that ideas travel, narratives metastasise, and moral permission crosses borders faster than institutions are willing to admit.

This book begins there—not because Bondi was the first warning, but because it was the moment denial became untenable.

The essays that follow were written across a period of growing unease, institutional failure, and moral confusion in the West. Some predate Bondi; others were written in its aftermath.

Together, they form a record of a society that mistook comfort for stability, tolerance for wisdom, and silence for virtue.

The central argument is not complicated, but it is confronting: Our light—the habits, values, and moral reflexes that underpin a free society—is real, but not self-sustaining. It is tested under pressure, and it can weaken without ever formally failing. It does not go out all at once. It dims gradually, as clarity gives way to euphemism, as responsibility is endlessly deferred, and as violence is explained away until explanation itself becomes a form of complicity—unless enough are willing to stand up, to rise to the challenges of our time, and to pass the test.

Much of the modern Western conversation about antisemitism has been conducted at a safe distance. Violence is contextualised. Agency is blurred. Responsibility is redistributed until it disappears altogether. When Jews are attacked—whether in Israel or in the diaspora—the reflex is rarely to name hatred for what it is, but to search for explanations that dilute intent and absolve ideology.

Bondi exposed the limits of that reflex.

There was no occupation to invoke on that beach. No checkpoint. No settlement. No geopolitical grievance capable of bearing the moral weight placed upon it. There was only murderous intent, shaped by ideas that had been normalised, excused, or sanitised long before the first blow was struck.

This is not a book about Israel alone, nor is it a catalogue of outrage. It is a book about proximity—what becomes visible when abstraction collapses and consequence arrives at home. It examines how lies acquire moral authority, how institutions charged with truth abdicate their role, and how the costs of that abdication are ultimately paid by people who had nothing to do with the arguments conducted in their name.

The essays are arranged deliberately: from unease to decay, from narrative capture to consequence, and finally toward responsibility. Some are analytical. Others are personal. All share the same intent—to replace moral fog with clarity, and passivity with agency.

No reader is asked to adopt a political identity, join a movement, or outsource their conscience. What is asked is something both simpler and more demanding: to resist the comfort of distance, to reject the safety of euphemism, and to recognise that the defence of a free society is not delegated upward, but carried outward—by citizens willing to stand before they are forced to.

Bondi was not an aberration.

It was a test.

Whether it becomes a turning point depends on what we choose to do with what it revealed.

PART I

THE UNEASE

How danger announces itself

PART I
Introduction

Societies—or ways of life—rarely collapse without warning. What they lose first is not safety, but sensitivity.

Long before laws fail or violence appears in daylight, something subtler shifts. Conversations narrow. Certain subjects begin to close people off rather than open them up. Patterns emerge that are felt before they are fully understood.

Over the course of my life—first in uniform, and more recently as a civilian—I have learned to pay close attention to these early signals. Not because I am prone to alarm, but because I was trained to distinguish threat from noise, and intuition from imagination.

This part is about that early phase: the period when danger remains deniable, when those who notice are often told they are overreacting, and when fear—if it exists at all—is quiet, rational, and learned.

Unease is not hysteria. Properly understood, it is information.

1

Terminal Drift: It's Time to Defend Our Way of Life

Introduction

This essay was written in the shadow of mounting unease—before denial became impossible, but after warning signs were already everywhere.

"Terminal Drift" is not about a single event, policy, or institution. It is about a condition: the slow moral movement of a society that confuses motion with progress and tolerance with wisdom. Drift is seductive precisely because it feels benign. Nothing appears to collapse all at once. Norms erode quietly. Boundaries soften. Language changes before behaviour does.

What is described here is not extremism, but the absence of resistance to it—a failure of attention rather than intent. This essay asks the reader to consider how often societies recognise danger only after momentum has carried them past the point where easy correction is possible.

***

Just when I think I have cried my last tears after 7 October, more are found.

These are not tears of passivity, idleness, or helplessness. They are tears of resolve—and of unambiguous solidarity with Jewish Australians, with Israel, and with the Australia I knew before we succumbed to an "end of history" delusion.

At least a dozen people have been murdered at Bondi Beach. People I know. Families shattered in a place that should have symbolised freedom, joy, and safety. Instead, it has become another entry in a growing ledger of Western complacency paid for in Jewish blood.

Grief is a human response. But grief that ends in paralysis is a luxury we can no longer afford.

There are moments in history when a civilisation must decide whether it still believes enough in its own values to defend them. Across the Western world—Australia included—that moment has arrived. Many remain distracted, wilfully ignorant, or convinced that this is someone else's problem. It is not. It never was.

In 1989, political theorist Francis Fukuyama famously argued that humanity had reached "the end of history"—that liberal democracy had triumphed, that the great ideological struggles were over, and that the future would be managed, peaceful, and largely technocratic. It was an intoxicating idea. It was also catastrophically wrong.

We have been here before.

After the horrors of the First World War—the war to end all wars—the good citizens of Europe, represented by their governments, resolved to make war illegal. In 1928, the Kellogg–Briand

Pact was signed by dozens of nations, solemnly renouncing war as an instrument of national policy. It was earnest. It was moral. And it was utterly disconnected from human nature.

Within a decade, Europe was in flames again.

The folly was not the desire for peace. The folly was believing that peace could be wished into existence without vigilance, strength, or moral clarity. History does not end because we are tired of it. Evil does not retire because we pass resolutions. It adapts, it waits, and it exploits the naïveté of those who mistake comfort for progress.

Today, we live with the consequences of a similar delusion.

We have hollowed out the moral and spiritual foundations that once anchored Western societies. Many now walk through life with a god-sized hole in their hearts—unmoored, searching for meaning, and vulnerable to ideologies of grievance, victimhood, and rage. Into that void has poured a toxic fusion of identity politics, historical illiteracy, and moral relativism—what some have aptly called the woke mind virus. As George Orwell warned, "To see what is in front of one's nose needs a constant struggle." That struggle is now unavoidable.

At the centre of this civilisational stress test stands Israel—imperfect, embattled, resilient, and alive. Israel is not merely a strategic ally of the West; it is a moral lighthouse. The hatred directed at the Jewish state is not about borders or policies. It is about what Israel represents: memory, continuity, responsibility, and refusal to disappear.

It was in this context—not for personal or commercial benefit—that I wrote *A Light Still Burns: Israel and the Values Worth Defending*. It was written as a framing exercise: to help citizens of good will, Jewish and non-Jewish alike, understand the environment we are now living in before we are fully consumed by it. In this season of Chanukah and Christmas—festivals that each, in their own way, speak of light, endurance, and moral inheritance—it is essential reading not because it offers easy answers, but because it insists on clarity where confusion has become fashionable.

What happened at Bondi Beach did not emerge from nowhere. It is downstream of years of indulgence—indulgence of extremist rhetoric, of academic malpractice, of media gaslighting, and of community leaders unwilling to confront the worst elements in their midst. Words matter. Lies metastasise. And eventually, violence follows.

We are now confronted with a simple binary choice—in Australia, as across the West.

Either we stand up and defend our families, our values, and our way of life. Or we live with the consequences of complacency and cravenness.

I do not perceive a third option.

I choose the first.

I stand with Jewish Australians who now live with fear layered onto grief. I stand with Israel, not because it is perfect, but because doing so is necessary. And I stand with the Australia we knew before moral confusion became fashionable and cowardice masqueraded as compassion.

I will not be a bystander.

Grief must lead somewhere. Tears must harden into resolve. History has taught us—repeatedly—that civilisations do not fall because they are conquered. They fall because they forget what they are, what they owe their children, and what they are prepared to defend.

The light still burns. But only if enough good people decide—clearly, consciously, and courageously—to tend it.

2

Hacking the Human Brain: The Sixth Operational Domain

Introduction

Modern conflict is no longer confined to land, sea, air, space, and cyberspace.

Increasingly, wars are fought in a sixth domain—the human mind.

In this domain, victory is measured not in territory seized or forces destroyed, but in perception shaped, legitimacy eroded, and restraint reframed as guilt.

This chapter examines how cognitive warfare operates, why democratic societies are particularly vulnerable to it, and how narrative dominance has become a decisive weapon long before the first shot is fired.

***

In 2012, while serving as a lieutenant colonel in the Australian Army, I worked within the Chief of Army's think tank—the Directorate of Army Research and Analysis. My task: to imagine what the Army's future land force might look like in 2035. It was an opportunity to think strategically, unconstrained by budget cycles or rank. My brief was clear: challenge assumptions, think creatively, and—above all—look around corners.

At the time, military operations were commonly understood to occur across five recognised domains: land, sea, air, space, and cyber. Each had distinct tools, tactics, and strategic implications. More than a decade later, in Operation Rising Lion, the Israel Defense Forces delivered a masterclass in how to synchronise effects across all five. But even back in 2012, I suspected something was missing. So I posed a provocative question to our group of civilian scholars: If there were to be a sixth operational domain—one we're not yet prepared for—what might it be?

Several days later, a consensus emerged: the next frontier of warfare would be the human mind.

Back then, we speculated on how minds might be manipulated. Could nanotech alter cognition? Could neural implants hijack thought? Would social media fracture societies from within? At the time, it all felt speculative—almost sci-fi.

But that future has arrived.

Since the atrocities of October 7, 2023, when Hamas terrorists brutally attacked Israeli civilians, it has become clear: The sixth domain is no longer theoretical. It's real. And we are already fighting—and losing—within it.

The irrational hatred of Israel and Jews that erupted in the aftermath was not spontaneous—it was cultivated over decades. Our enemies—radical Islamists, anarchists, and social Marxists—have played the long game. Not by building bombs, but by infiltrating minds, classrooms, and institutions.

Social Marxism is a cultural offshoot of classical Marxist thinking. It replaces class struggle with permanent grievance—between race, religion, gender, and identity—where every hierarchy is oppression, and victimhood becomes a weapon. In this twisted worldview, Israel is recast as a colonial aggressor, and terrorists as liberators.

This isn't drift. It is Orwellian inversion: Rape is resistance, self-defence is genocide, truth is hate speech. Over the weekend, I was horrified to witness a performer at Glastonbury Music Festival chant "Death, death to the IDF"—and worse still, a crowd of Westerners echoing it back without hesitation. How on earth have we come to this?

What we are witnessing is not criticism of Israeli policy—it is the systematic dismantling of truth.

One book that shaped my thinking—both framing the problem and pointing to what the solution may look like—is *The Islamist* by Ed Husain, published in 2007. The son of Bangladeshi immigrants to the UK, Husain was radicalised as a teenager in East London. Alienated and angry, he found comfort in extremist circles. But when he travelled to the Middle East, he saw first-hand the corruption, moral decay, and hypocrisy of the regimes he once romanticised. That experience changed him. He walked away—and has since dedicated his life to deradicalisation.

His story is a potent reminder: Minds can be hijacked—but they can also be reclaimed.

And nothing reclaims the mind like lived personal experience. That's why getting the right people to Israel matters. Competing in the sixth operational domain won't be won over cappuccinos in Sydney, New York, London, or Toronto—or through tweets and slogans. It will be won by exposing tomorrow's leaders to truth on the ground, in Israel itself.

That is precisely the mission of The 2023 Foundation, the charity I founded after October 7. Our aim is to combat antisemitism through lived personal experience. Where the BDS movement seeks to lock people out of Israel so its lies go unchallenged, we bring people in. We let emerging non-Jewish leaders see the country with their own eyes, meet Israelis of all backgrounds, and draw their own conclusions.

Our vision is to grow tomorrow's non-Jewish upstanders—not bystanders. In many parts of the world, Israel isn't even seen as a destination for non-Jews. I plan to change that.

Einstein once said, "We cannot solve our problems with the same thinking we used when we created them." If we are to push back, we need better ideas and fresh eyes and faces working the problem. We need courage, clarity, and cultural confidence to win the war for the human mind.

That war is already upon us. And Jews in the diaspora are losing—outflanked in classrooms, newsrooms, and global institutions by those who glorify terror and distort truth.

Israel cannot fight this alone. She needs allies.

Gentiles like me. But I cannot do it alone either.

We must build the next generation of upstanders—the Douglas Murrays, Richard Kemps, and Erin Molans of tomorrow. That means meeting people where they are, building trust across communities, raising funds with urgency and purpose, and stitching together a global network of principled, courageous voices. People who will not flinch when the truth is under attack. A grassroots movement. Because from drops come ripples. From ripples, waves.

Only together—Jews and gentiles—can we rewire the corrupted minds of so many across the fortunate West.

Together, we will prevail. יחד ננצח

3

Orientalism: A Theory That Outlived Its Usefulness

Introduction

Long before violence arrives, before institutions fail visibly or streets become unsafe, societies are shaped by the ideas they absorb without questioning. Frameworks adopted in good faith can, over time, harden into habits of thought—guiding instinct, shaping language, and narrowing the range of what can be said aloud.

"Orientalism" was one such framework.

When Edward Said published his work in 1978, it offered a necessary corrective. It challenged cultural arrogance, exposed lazy generalisation, and warned against the moral blind spots of power. For a time, it sharpened Western self-awareness and restrained excess.

But ideas have design limits. Used beyond them, they stop clarifying and begin to distort.

This essay argues that Orientalism did not simply encourage humility; over time, it trained suspicion as a reflex and hesitation as a virtue. It taught institutions to doubt their own judgment, to treat clarity as domination, and to confuse explanation with moral seriousness. In doing so, it quietly disarmed Western societies—not militarily, but intellectually.

What follows is not a rejection of self-critique, but an examination of how a theory that once illuminated genuine blind spots has come to obscure responsibility, agency, and pattern. It seeks to explain why so many institutions sensed danger yet struggled to name it—and why unease persisted even as correction failed to arrive.

***

Few books have exercised as much influence over Western intellectual life while escaping sustained re-examination as *Orientalism*, published in 1978 by Edward Said. For more than four decades, it has shaped how generations of students, journalists, diplomats, and activists have been trained to see the world—particularly the relationship between the West and the non-West.

People don't argue about Orientalism very much anymore because they no longer feel they need to. Its ideas have been so thoroughly absorbed that they now operate in the background, shaping how people think and speak without being consciously referenced.

That alone warrants scrutiny.

Orientalism did not arrive in an intellectual vacuum. It emerged at a moment when Western self-confidence was already weakening—after Vietnam, during the unravelling of European empires, and amid growing suspicion toward claims of objectivity, authority, and tradition. Said offered what appeared to be a corrective: a way of interrogating power, exposing bias, and restraining cultural arrogance. For a time, it served that purpose.

But ideas, like tools, are not immortal. Used beyond their design life, they cease to clarify and begin to distort.

This essay argues that Orientalism is one such idea—a theory that once illuminated genuine blind spots but which, left unbounded and uncorrected, has outlived its usefulness and quietly trained Western institutions to mistake suspicion for insight, paralysis for humility, and moral hesitation for sophistication.

Edward Said: The Man and the Worldview

Edward Said was a literary scholar and public intellectual, born in Jerusalem in 1935 and raised largely in Cairo. Educated at elite Western institutions, he spent most of his academic career as a professor of comparative literature at Columbia University. Fluent, erudite, and politically engaged, he moved comfortably within the highest levels of Western intellectual life.

Said was born into a Christian Arab family. His father, Wadie Said, was a Palestinian Christian who emigrated to the United States, served in the US Army during the First World War, and later established a successful stationery business in Egypt. His mother, Hilda Said, was born in Nazareth and raised in Lebanon before settling in Cairo. Said himself was raised Anglican and educated in English-language schools, most notably Victoria College in Cairo, before studying at Princeton and Harvard.

Said's intellectual formation was thoroughly Western, even as his political sympathies aligned strongly with the Palestinian nationalist cause, which he championed publicly and persistently. This background matters not to question motive, but to understand the paradox at the heart of his work: *Orientalism* was written from within the Western academy, using Western critical tools, to indict Western civilisation as uniquely corrupting.

That posture would later prove influential precisely because it came from an insider, fluent in the language of Western moral self-critique.

The Argument, Stated Fairly

At its core, Orientalism advances a relatively simple claim. Western scholarship, literature, and political thought about the "Orient"—a broad and ill-defined category encompassing the Middle East, North Africa, and parts of Asia—was not neutral or descriptive, but deeply implicated in systems of power. According to Said, Western representations of Eastern societies consistently portrayed them as exotic, backward, irrational, and inferior, thereby justifying domination, intervention, and control.

Knowledge, in this view, was never merely knowledge. It was an instrument of empire. Even apparently benign academic disciplines—philology, history, anthropology—were implicated in a civilisational project that positioned the West as rational and progressive, and the East as static and subordinate. The problem, Said insisted, was not simply error or prejudice, but structure: a way of seeing that reproduced hierarchy regardless of intent.

This argument resonated powerfully. It appealed to moral instincts sharpened by the excesses of colonialism. It flattered the self-image of a generation eager to demonstrate ethical seriousness by interrogating its own inheritance. It promised a form of critique that was not only intellectual, but virtuous.

Read generously, Orientalism was a call for humility—a warning against cultural arrogance, lazy generalisation, and the presumption that Western categories were universal. Few would object to that in principle.

Read less generously, Orientalism did more than correct excess. It replaced confidence with suspicion, judgement with hesitation, and explanation with moral reflex. What began as a challenge to arrogance hardened into a habit of doubt—one that treated clarity as domination and restraint as virtue. In that shift, something essential was lost.

The problem lies not in what Orientalism questioned, but in what it replaced.

Early Warnings, Widely Ignored

From the beginning, serious scholars raised concerns about Said's method and conclusions. These were not reactionary defences of empire, but substantive critiques grounded in history, language, and evidence.

One of the earliest and most prominent critics was the historian Bernard Lewis, who argued that Said collapsed centuries of diverse scholarship into a single, malign motive. Lewis noted that many Western scholars of the Middle East were not agents of empire at all, but often worked in tension with political power, sometimes at personal cost. To treat them as a monolithic class serving domination was not critique; it was caricature.

Others reached similar conclusions. Scholars such as Maxime Rodinson, Albert Hourani, and Malcolm Kerr pointed to Said's selective use of sources and his preference for literary polemic over empirical historical scholarship. Large bodies of philological, linguistic, and archival work that complicated his thesis were marginalised or dismissed. Complexity was flattened into moral symmetry.

Perhaps the most devastating critique came from Robert Irwin, whose archival research demonstrated that Said routinely misrepresented the intellectual traditions he condemned. Irwin showed that many so-called Orientalists possessed deep linguistic fluency, cultural respect, and genuine curiosity—qualities difficult to reconcile with the charge of systematic dehumanisation. The alleged conspiracy of knowledge, he argued, dissolved under scrutiny.

Importantly, critique of Orientalism did not come only from the political Right. Marxist scholar Aijaz Ahmad exposed deep incoherence in Said's framework, noting that it oscillated between materialist claims about power and idealist claims about discourse without resolving the tension. If all knowledge is power, Ahmad asked, how is Said's own work exempt?

These criticisms were neither obscure nor unserious. Yet they failed to alter the trajectory of Orientalism's influence. The reason is instructive: The book had ceased to function as a hypothesis subject to testing. It had become a moral posture.

From Critique to Cynicism

The most consequential move in Orientalism is not its critique of bias, but its treatment of intent. In Said's framework, intention is largely irrelevant. Outcomes, representations, and structures are what matter. A scholar's sincerity does not mitigate the charge of complicity. Claims of objectivity become suspect in themselves—evidence not of neutrality, but of unacknowledged power.

Once intent is discounted, disagreement becomes morally fraught. To challenge the framework is no longer simply to argue a point, but to invite suspicion: whose interests are being served? What power structure is being defended? Debate shifts from evidence to motive, from substance to position.

Over time, this produces a distinctive intellectual climate. Analysis gives way to scepticism. Judgement is reframed as domination. Clarity becomes arrogance. The safest position is hesitation; the most sophisticated posture is doubt.

This is not humility. It is cynicism masquerading as wisdom.

Institutions trained in this mode learn to explain rather than evaluate; to contextualise rather than distinguish; to suspend judgement indefinitely lest it reveal bias. Violence is treated as discourse. Agency is blurred. Responsibility diffused. Moral asymmetry is normalised.

The result is not neutrality, but paralysis.

Defenders and Their Limits

Defenders of Orientalism often argue that its purpose was never to offer a complete theory of the world, but to correct an imbalance—to give voice to those marginalised by Western narratives. Postcolonial theorists such as Gayatri Spivak and Homi Bhabha have argued that Said exposed hidden assumptions in Western scholarship and widened the range of perspectives considered legitimate.

There is truth in this defence. Western scholarship was not immune to prejudice, and voices from the non-West were too often excluded or patronised. Orientalism contributed to a necessary broadening of the conversation.

But correction is not the same as replacement.

What began as a call for reflexivity hardened into a doctrine of suspicion. The expansion of voices became the elevation of grievance. The critique of power metastasised into the presumption of guilt. Over time, the framework trained its adherents not to weigh claims, but to sort them—assigning moral value based on identity rather than argument.

This is not pluralism. It is inversion.

The Consequences We Now Live With

The legacy of Orientalism is visible not in footnotes, but in reflexes.

It can be seen in the reluctance of Western media to name ideological motivation when violence erupts, preferring sociological explanation to moral judgement. It appears in academic settings where certain forms of hostility are excused as "resistance," while others are pathologised as hatred. It surfaces in the instinct to locate blame everywhere except where agency resides.

Most of all, it reveals itself when violence arrives without an available colonial pretext—when abstraction collapses and consequence intrudes into everyday life. At that point, the explanatory machinery falters. The language trained for suspicion is ill-equipped for clarity. Context becomes explanation, and explanation becomes excuse.

This is not an argument that Orientalism caused violence. It is an argument that it helped disarm societies intellectually—training them to look away from pattern, motive, and responsibility in favour of endless interpretation.

Balance Without Amnesia

None of this requires a return to cultural arrogance or intellectual complacency. Self-critique remains essential. Awareness of power is not optional. But there is a difference between humility and self-erasure.

A civilisation that loses confidence in its capacity to distinguish good from evil does not become neutral. It becomes permissive. A society that treats judgement as violence will eventually find itself unable to respond when violence arrives unambiguously.

The problem with Orientalism is not that it asked difficult questions. It is that it trained generations to stop answering them.

Conclusion

Ideas do not expire automatically. They persist by habit, institutionalisation, and moral inertia. Orientalism remains influential not because it continues to explain the world well, but because questioning it has come to feel transgressive.

That is precisely why it must be revisited.

The unease many now feel did not emerge spontaneously. It was cultivated—through frameworks that elevated suspicion over judgement and explanation over responsibility. Recognising that inheritance is not an act of rejection, but of maturity.

A theory that once illuminated genuine blind spots has outlived its usefulness. The task now is not to discard self-reflection, but to recover clarity—before hesitation hardens into incapacity, and before ideas trained for critique leave us unprepared for consequence.

4

Cumulative: The Quiet Reshaping of Everyday Life

Introduction

Before violence erupts, before statistics accumulate, before explanations are summoned and narratives hardened, something quieter takes place.

A way of life adjusts.

This essay is not about a single attack, nor a single ideology. It is about the slow, largely unremarked transformation of everyday life in the West—how behaviours change, spaces harden, and expectations narrow long before catastrophe forces recognition. It is about how danger rarely arrives announced, but instead embeds itself through accommodation, procedure, and habit.

Long before Bondi, long before shock and grief, the signs were already present: in airports, at sporting events, in public squares, in the architecture of our cities and the assumptions we taught our children. Each adjustment felt reasonable. Each concession seemed temporary. Together, they reshaped normality.

"Cumulative" examines that process—not to induce fear, but to restore clarity. To show how societies drift into a permanent defensive

posture without ever consciously choosing it, and how what feels like resilience can, over time, become resignation.

What follows is not an argument about the past. It is an attempt to make visible what has already been normalised—before the next adjustment is required.

The World We Assumed Was Stable

When I was a child in the late 1970s and 1980s, the greatest threat perceived at a sporting event was illicit alcohol. Bags were checked not for weapons, but for bottles and cans. Stadium security was a mild inconvenience, not a necessity—more about rule-keeping than risk mitigation.

Airports were much the same. They were places of anticipation and movement, not ritualised suspicion. You could walk a loved one to the gate. You could arrive late and still expect to board. Security existed, but it was largely invisible—a background function, not a defining feature of travel. The idea that passengers themselves posed a lethal threat to everyone on a plane or in an airport would have seemed absurd.

That world is gone.

Adaptation Without Debate

Its disappearance did not come with a declaration. It arrived incrementally, wrapped in procedural language and justified by necessity. Humans are remarkably adaptable creatures.

We normalise what surrounds us, particularly when change is neither announced nor debated. It happens below the threshold of conscious attention, absorbed incrementally—like flotsam carried downstream by a steady current, moving not because it chooses to, but because everything else is already in motion.

We adjusted.

We complied.

We moved on.

At sporting events, the adjustment came slowly at first. Bag checks became routine. Police presence increased. Concrete bollards appeared where grass and open walkways once sufficed. Entry points narrowed. What had been designed for welcome was redesigned for control.

The visible posture of policing shifted as well—from note-taking and crowd management, to layered protective equipment and expanded use-of-force options. In the aftermath of Bondi, the presence of long arms at public gatherings will no longer feel exceptional, but expected.

Air travel changed more abruptly. Shoes off. Belts off. Liquids surrendered. Bags searched and re-searched. Armed officers stationed where once there were airline staff and volunteers. Arriving hours early became expected. Each measure was introduced as a response to a specific threat. Each was then retained, standardised, and embedded.

This is how danger announces itself—not in panic, but through gradual accommodation, until the moment it is no longer gradual at all.

The Inflection Point

The inflection point is not difficult to locate. On 11 September 2001, nearly three thousand people were murdered in coordinated attacks using civilian aircraft as weapons. What followed was not simply a security response, but a civilisational adjustment.

Air travel was transformed overnight. Intelligence agencies were reorganised. Wars were launched.

But perhaps more enduring was the quiet recalibration of everyday life in the West.

In December 2001, Richard Reid, a British Muslim radicalised in the UK and later trained by al-Qaeda in Afghanistan, attempted to detonate explosives concealed in his shoes on a transatlantic flight from Paris to Miami. He failed—subdued by passengers and crew when his device malfunctioned. But that failure permanently altered how hundreds of millions of people would move through airports for decades to come. To this day, travellers remove their shoes—not because most pose a threat, nor because the risk is statistically meaningful, but because one man once did. A single act, carried out by one ideologically motivated individual, reshaped global behaviour in the name of precaution.

That pattern repeated.

A Recognisable Pattern

For Australians, one early warning came in October 2002. The Bali bombings killed 202 people, including eighty-eight Australians—many young, on holiday, and far from home. It shattered complacency about global terrorism and made clear that Australians were not immune to ideologies that target civilians. But Bali was still overseas. It was horrific, intimate in loss, yet geographically distant. Bondi would later remove even that final buffer.

The years that followed reinforced the lesson.

In March 2004, coordinated bombings on Madrid's commuter trains killed 193 people. In July 2005, suicide bombers attacked London's transport system during the morning rush hour, killing fifty-two commuters. In November 2008, gunmen carried out coordinated attacks across Mumbai, targeting hotels, a railway station, and a Jewish centre. In January 2015, the offices of *Charlie Hebdo* were attacked. In November that same year, Paris was struck again—at cafés, a concert hall, and a stadium—killing 130 people.

Each event differed in method and setting.

The common thread was ideological.

The perpetrators did not act anonymously, nor did they act from private grievance alone. Their violence was justified by an ideology that treats civilians as legitimate targets and elevates murder into symbolic action. The result was not limited to the immediate loss of life, but a lasting shift in how free societies assessed risk—drawing public life into a more permanent defensive crouch.

And we obliged.

When Defence Becomes Design

Markets were fortified. Public squares were ringed with concrete. Christmas markets acquired armed patrols. School drop-off zones were redesigned to mitigate vehicular attack. Architecture hardened. Movement was channelled.

The language shifted too. What had once been called terrorism was increasingly described as extremism, radicalisation, or grievance. Motive was contextualised. Agency was softened.

Still, the measures multiplied.

In 2016, a truck was driven into Bastille Day celebrations in Nice, killing eighty-six people. In 2017, Manchester Arena was attacked at the conclusion of a concert attended largely by teenagers. In 2019, coordinated suicide bombings in Sri Lanka targeted churches and hotels on Easter Sunday, killing more than 250 people.

By then, the pattern was unmistakable.

Pattern and Outlier

Yet even as the threat remained overwhelmingly Islamist in origin, Western discourse grew increasingly reluctant to say so. Attention shifted. Focus blurred. New equivalences were drawn. Lone actors and statistical outliers were elevated to suggest symmetry where little existed.

The massacre of Muslim worshippers in Christchurch in 2019 was rightly condemned. It was an act of racial hatred and mass murder. But it was also what serious analysts recognise as an outlier: a lone individual, without organisational backing, without a replicable global infrastructure, and without ideological endorsement from a transnational movement commanding allegiance across continents.

The same is true of rare, ideologically incoherent attacks in parts of Scandinavia—tragic and reprehensible, but not components of a sustained global campaign.

To note this distinction is not to minimise any loss of life.

It is to preserve analytical clarity.

Pattern matters.

The Cost of Silence

For more than two decades, the most consistent driver of mass-casualty terrorism in the West has been Islamist ideology—not Islam as a faith practised peacefully by millions, but a politicised, absolutist interpretation that rejects coexistence and sacralises violence. This is not controversial among security professionals. It becomes controversial only in cultural and academic settings where naming patterns is treated as prejudice rather than responsibility.

The cost of this reluctance is paid not only in blood, but in erosion.

Consider what now passes for normal.

Major public events are designed as security exercises. Architecture is defensive. Behaviour is conditioned. Children grow up knowing how to identify exits, avoid unattended bags, and comply instinctively with armed authority. The abnormal has been normalised so thoroughly that its absence would now feel strange.

And still, the escalation continues.

Knives replaced guns in jurisdictions with strict firearms laws. Vehicles replaced bombs where explosives were harder to obtain. Improvised devices filled the gap. Each countermeasure generated adaptation. Each adaptation demanded further control.

How far does this go?

The question is no longer whether everyday life will continue to change, but how far.

How long until suicide vests and pipe bombs are a routine assumption rather than an exceptional horror? How long until ordinary gatherings require screening not only for weapons, but for intent? How long until the line between public life and controlled space dissolves entirely?

These are not questions born of hysteria.

They arise from observation.

The unease many now feel is not ideological. It is empirical. It comes from recognising that a way of life once defined by openness now requires protection from those who despise it. It comes from noticing that concessions made in the name of tolerance rarely satisfy those who reject tolerance altogether.

Most people did not vote for this transformation. They did not debate it. They adapted to it because adaptation felt easier than confrontation. The alternative—naming the problem clearly and insisting on consequences—carried social and professional cost.

And so the bollards stayed.

The shoes came off.

The guards multiplied.

Agency and Course Correction

This essay is not a call for panic, nor for the abandonment of liberal values. It is a recognition that a free society cannot indefinitely absorb hostility without consequence. Security measures are not neutral. They reshape culture. They teach children what to expect. They condition behaviour.

The loss is not always visible.

But it is cumulative.

George Bernard Shaw observed that progress depends on unreasonable people—those unwilling to adjust themselves endlessly to the world as they find it, and prepared instead to insist that the world live up to what it claims to be. Perhaps Shaw was right in reverse as well. At certain moments, it is the "unreasonable refusal to accept drift" that forces societies to pause, reflect, and course-correct.

Such "unreasonableness" need not be radical. It may simply require holding a mirror up to society and saying: Look at where we are. Look at what has become normal. Look at where this path leads if left unchallenged.

Course correction does not begin with panic.

It begins with recognition—and with the exercise of agency.

When unease becomes ambient—when vigilance replaces ease, and procedure replaces trust—something fundamental has already shifted. The question facing the West is not whether terrorism has changed us. It has.

The question is whether we are willing to acknowledge how, and why—and whether we will act in the present to shape the future we bequeath to our children, and to those not yet born.

5

Theological Terror and the West's Blind Spot

Introduction

Unease deepens when patterns stop feeling accidental.

For years, Western societies reassured themselves that antisemitic violence was driven by marginal actors, social grievance, or rhetorical excess. Ideology was treated as noise rather than motive, and religion—when mentioned at all—was framed as distorted, peripheral, or irrelevant to the real causes of conflict. That framing offered comfort. It also obscured intent.

This essay examines what happens when that comfort collapses. It looks at the re-emergence of openly articulated theological sanction for violence against Jews—not expressed by lone preachers or fringe cells, but issued collectively by clerics and institutions claiming religious authority. The significance lies not in novelty, but in clarity: Violence is no longer justified obliquely or euphemistically, but named as duty.

This chapter explains why the unease described in earlier essays is rational rather than alarmist. It shows how moral permission is constructed before violence occurs, how belief hardens into obligation, and how a refusal to take theology seriously leaves liberal societies blind to dangers that announce themselves long before they arrive.

Inside the Istanbul Charter That Endorsed October 7—and What It May Mean for the West

In the shadows of public discourse, a manifesto has emerged—one that challenges not just Israel, but the very ideals of liberal civilisation.[1]

On 27 June 2025, hundreds of Islamic scholars gathered in Istanbul and issued a deeply troubling 11,000-word theological manifesto endorsing the Hamas-led atrocities of 7 October 2023—what they euphemistically call "Operation Flood of al-Aqsa." Far from a marginal rant, the document seeks to codify total war against Israel, declaring it a religious duty for Muslims worldwide and branding neutrality as betrayal.

This is not the work of a lone cleric or fringe extremist group. The *Charter of the Scholars of the Ummah* was signed by 385 religious figures and institutions from across the Islamic world—many with ties to Hamas, the Muslim Brotherhood, or state-linked networks in Turkey, Qatar, and Yemen. It was launched in Istanbul, where President Erdoğan's government has increasingly positioned itself as a global centre of pan-Islamist influence.

Read plainly, the charter is not a call for peace or negotiation—it is a theological endorsement of unending jihad. It

---

1 For the full text of the charter, see: Y. Yehoshua and N. Mozes, "Charter Signed by Hundreds of Muslim Scholars ..." Memri, Inquiry & Analysis Series no. 1857, accessed January 26, 2026. https://www.memri.org/reports/charter-signed-hundreds-muslim-scholars-supports-hamas%E2%80%99-october-7-attack-israel-it-was-jihad.

makes no distinction between Israeli civilians and soldiers, nor between political actors and ordinary citizens. It declares any recognition of Israel's existence to be religiously null and void and demands resistance "by all means" until total victory is achieved.

It is, in many respects, the clearest contemporary expression of a militant political theology rooted in the ideas of Sayyid Qutb, the Egyptian thinker whose writings helped shape modern jihadist ideology. Like Qutb, the charter views the world as a battleground between truth and falsehood, Islam and *Jahiliya* (ignorance), where divine justice can only be realised through violent struggle. It also draws from the rigid absolutism of Wahhabi doctrine, allowing no space for coexistence or religious pluralism. These are not mainstream Islamic ideas—they are revolutionary interpretations advanced by those who reject centuries of jurisprudential moderation.

That the charter was launched in Turkey is no coincidence. Under President Erdoğan, Ankara has become a hub for Islamist scholars and ideologues who seek to redefine Islam not merely as a religion, but as a totalising political project. From hosting Hamas leaders to funding clerical conferences, Turkey has played a pivotal role in shaping the global "resistance" narrative. The Istanbul conference was not symbolic—it was strategic. It formalised a transnational ideological movement cloaked in religious authority.

This movement is not confined to mosques or madrasas. The charter outlines a broad, coordinated strategy to delegitimise Israel on every front—legal, economic, cultural, and military. It urges lawyers to challenge normalisation in the courts, calls for global boycotts of Israeli-linked companies, and encourages academics and journalists to propagate its narrative. It is, in effect, a whole-of-society campaign to recast the Palestinian struggle as a global Islamic obligation—where martyrdom is sanctified, and compromise equated with treason.

To understand the broader significance, we might turn to Samuel Huntington, who first proposed his *Clash of Civilizations* thesis in 1993 and expanded it into a landmark book in 1996. He warned that future conflicts would increasingly be driven not by ideology or economics, but by deep cultural and civilisational divides—particularly between Western liberalism and resurgent religious identity. The charter fits squarely within this frame. It is not merely a document about Gaza—it is a direct ideological challenge to the liberal international order and the very notion that coexistence among diverse peoples is possible.

But to characterise this as a clash between "Islam" and the "Judeo-Christian West" would be dangerously simplistic. Many Muslims around the world reject the ideology advanced in this document, and some risk their lives in opposition. The problem lies not in Islam as a faith, but in transnational networks of clerics, institutions, and regimes that instrumentalise it for absolutist, anti-democratic ends.

The real clash may be within civilisations—between those who uphold dignity, pluralism, and shared humanity, and those who do not. Islam, like Christianity before it, may be on the cusp of an internal reckoning. The Christian world experienced its Reformation in the sixteenth century—a time of upheaval that gave rise to new voices and renewed moral clarity. One wonders whether a Muslim Martin Luther will emerge—someone with the courage, scholarship, and reach to challenge the theological monopolies that dominate discourse in parts of the Muslim world. If such figures do arise, they must be supported—not only by fellow Muslims, but by tolerant Jews, Christians, and others of goodwill who understand that a better future depends on empowering moderates to overcome extremism from within.

Encouragingly, the leadership of the United Arab Emirates, Bahrain, and other Abraham Accords partners have already taken bold steps to reshape regional dynamics in favour of coexistence and reform. These states offer a vision of Islamic modernity that challenges the fatalism embedded in the Charter. Their leadership—and the educational, cultural, and diplomatic links they have forged with Israel—could provide a model for others. For countries like Syria, Lebanon, Saudi Arabia, and Indonesia, the stakes are high. A decision awaits: whether to succumb to ideological rigidity or to join a regional and civilisational renaissance in which religion serves peace rather than war.

In Australia, the Muslim population has grown from 340,000 (1.7%) in 2006 to an estimated 850,000–900,000 (around 3.3%) by 2025. Among its most respected voices is Dr Jamal Rifi, a Lebanese Australian GP based in Sydney. For decades, he has been a powerful advocate against extremism and a bridge-builder across religious and cultural divides. Dr Rifi has repeatedly condemned religious violence and sectarian hatred, calling instead for social harmony, civic responsibility, and mutual respect—values that stand in direct opposition to the worldview promoted in the Charter.

As part of a broader solution, The 2023 Foundation—which I founded in the wake of October 2023—is working to create long-term, lived-experience pathways to understanding. One of our goals is to support the placement of Australian students, including Muslim students, into Israeli universities on scholarship. Living and studying in a land sacred to the three great Abrahamic faiths cannot help but deepen a scholar's perspective. Carefully selected and supported, these students return with firsthand understanding of Israel and its people—something no classroom, protest slogan, or national broadcaster can replicate. In a time of polarisation and misinformation, such initiatives are not merely helpful—they are essential.

This charter must be widely read and understood—not because it reflects the beliefs of all Muslims, but because it captures a powerful and growing current that is shaping minds, fuelling conflict, and justifying atrocities. The West must not only condemn its message—it must also support the many Muslims who resist it. Reformers, scholars, journalists, and citizens of conscience deserve our solidarity.

Because the real battle isn't only on the streets of Gaza—it's unfolding in courtrooms, universities, media studios, and policy forums, where ideas are weaponised and legitimacy itself is under siege. At recent rallies in Melbourne, chants of "Death to the IDF" have been heard—even amid synagogue firebombing and an Israeli restaurant assault—while the slogan has reverberated at Glastonbury and London gigs. This war—one that many in the comfortable West remain largely oblivious to—is not only real. It is being lost.

Last Best Chance: Chances Missed

Introduction

The mythology of missed opportunity has proven remarkably durable.

Again and again, Israel is said to have been offered peace—only to squander it through obstinacy, ideology, or bad faith. Each retelling reassures Western audiences that the conflict persists not because of rejection, but because of refusal.

This chapter interrogates that story. It examines what was actually proposed, what was rejected, and why the phrase "last best chance" has been endlessly recycled—even as evidence accumulated that it bore little resemblance to reality.

***

In my first career, I served as an Australian Army officer, rising to the rank of Colonel. From July 2019 to September 2021, I was seconded to the United Nations as a senior unarmed military observer with the United Nations Truce Supervision Organisation (UNTSO). For much of that period, I served as Acting Head of Military in the absence of the Major General, operating across

Israel, Lebanon, Syria, Jordan, and Egypt. I resided in Jerusalem throughout that time—Israel's eternal capital—and, as has been my custom across the entirety of my adult life, I read widely while deployed to the Middle East.

One such book was *Our Last Best Chance*, written by King Abdullah II of Jordan and published in 2011 by Viking (Penguin Group), with customary acknowledgements to his diplomatic advisers, international partners, and successive American administrations engaged in Middle East peace efforts. I read it not as a casual observer, but as a soldier, a peacekeeper, and a resident of the region—someone who had spent long hours on the ground assessing borders, ceasefire lines, security arrangements, and the fragility of assumptions made far from the realities they were meant to govern.

In *Our Last Best Chance*, King Abdullah presents a sober, often sincere appeal for peace between Israelis and Palestinians. It is a book written not in the language of rage or rejectionism, but of frustration—frustration at missed moments, squandered goodwill, and a conflict that seems eternally one diplomatic push away from resolution. In that sense, the book is both admirable and deeply tragic. Admirable for its optimism; tragic for its failure to fully confront the strategic realities that have repeatedly rendered such optimism untenable.

King Abdullah's core thesis is clear: that a viable two-state solution, broadly aligned with the 1967 lines and accompanied by land swaps and security guarantees, represented the last best chance for peace. He argues that time, settlements, extremism, and political cowardice have conspired to close a window that once stood open. Read generously—and it deserves to be read generously—this is not an anti-Israeli polemic. It is a lament. A plea to freeze time, rewind history, and recover a moment when peace still seemed achievable.

There is much in this proposal that is genuinely inspiring. It echoes, in substance if not in tone, the offers made by Israeli leaders who are rarely acknowledged for their seriousness or courage. Ehud Barak at Camp David in 2000 and Ehud Olmert in 2008 both advanced proposals that went further than anything previously imagined: near-total withdrawal from the West Bank, the division of Jerusalem, international custodianship over holy sites, and a Palestinian state with territorial contiguity. These were not token gestures. They were historic concessions offered by leaders acting in good faith, backed by the Israeli public's enduring—if cautious—desire for peace.

Yet this is where *Our Last Best Chance* begins to falter. For all its moral clarity, it treats the 1967 borders not as what they were—a ceasefire line born of vulnerability—but as a morally self-evident baseline for peace. History, however, has been less kind to that assumption. The lines of 1967 left Israel nine miles wide at its narrowest point, with its population centres exposed and its defensive depth virtually non-existent. They were not borders designed for permanence; they were armistice lines awaiting the next war. To insist on their resurrection today, after decades of regional upheaval, state collapse, and jihadist ascendance, is to mistake nostalgia for strategy.

The tragedy is that when such plans were proposed—by Barak, by Olmert, and in parallel by Arab and international actors—they might genuinely have led to a better tomorrow. That moment has now passed. The region that exists today is not the region of the late 1990s or early 2000s. Gaza remains dominated by Hamas, a genocidal Islamist movement. Lebanon functions in large part as a Hezbollah-dominated proxy arena rather than a fully sovereign state. Post-Assad Syria is shattered, governed by a former Sunni Islamist figurehead while rival regimes and militias engage in ethnic cleansing, including against Druze and other minorities. Iran has, for decades, sought to project power through militias and terror networks arrayed along Israel's borders. To pretend that a Palestinian state birthed under these conditions would be stable, demilitarised, and at peace with its neighbour is not optimism; it is strategic denial.

Crucially—and this must be said plainly—this failure cannot be laid at the feet of the Jews, the Israeli government, or the Israeli public. The majority of Israelis have, for decades, demonstrated a willingness to trade land for peace. They evacuated Sinai. They left Gaza. They supported Oslo. They backed leaders who promised painful compromise. What they have learned, through bitter experience, is that territorial withdrawal without durable security arrangements does not end conflict; it relocates it closer to their homes, schools, and hospitals.

Israelis do not reject peace. They reject proposals that would leave their country weakened, exposed, and dependent on guarantees that history suggests will not hold. A sovereign Palestinian state that cannot control its borders, disarm militias, or resist external manipulation would not be a partner for peace—it would be a launchpad for the next war, at a time and place of an implacable enemy's choosing. No responsible Israeli government could accept that risk, and no serious analyst should expect them to.

In that sense, *Our Last Best Chance* reads less like a roadmap than a eulogy—for a diplomatic era that assumed rational actors, shared end-states, and a mutual interest in coexistence. The Abraham Accords hint at a different future: one built not on unresolved Palestinian maximalism, but on pragmatic regional alignment, shared security interests, and incremental normalisation. They may lack the moral romance of the two-state vision King Abdullah champions, but they reflect the world as it is, not as we wish it to be.

Where to From Here? A View from 2025

From the vantage point of 2025, the path King Abdullah urged the region to take has all but vanished over the horizon. That ship has sailed. Not because Israel refused peace. Not because Jews rejected compromise. But because when a hand is extended in a genuine and sincere gesture—and that hand is not embraced, is spat upon, or more honestly, is grasped only so the other party can lunge with a knife—the hand is withdrawn. At that point, the initiator does what all rational actors must do: neutralise the threat or remove themselves from it.

This is not a moral failing. It is a law of human affairs.

Peace cannot be imposed on a people who do not yet want it. A Palestinian state will not come into being simply because the international community wishes it so, because more good money is poured after bad, or because maps drawn in 1967 are treated as sacred texts. The world does not work in such ways. States are not created by slogans or resolutions. They are created when a people decides—culturally, politically, and morally—that sovereignty is preferable to grievance, and responsibility preferable to perpetual struggle.

History offers instructive contrasts. The American colonies broke from Britain through violent revolution, followed by the painstaking construction of institutions capable of sustaining independence. India, by contrast, emerged from empire through a largely non-violent struggle under the leadership of Mahatma Gandhi, at a moment when Britain itself was exhausted by war and prepared to relinquish control. Both achieved statehood—but only because there existed leadership, internal cohesion, and a clear vision of what independence was for, not merely what it was against.

The Palestinian national movement, tragically, has not yet crossed that threshold. Violence remains not a last resort but a recurring political language. Corruption within the Palestinian Authority corrodes legitimacy from within. Hamas rules Gaza not as a liberation movement, but as a terrorist regime that feeds on despair and weaponises civilian suffering. None of this is Israel's doing. Nor can it be wished away by well-meaning diplomats.

If Palestinians truly want a state, they may yet have to fight for it—but not against Israel. They may need to confront and dismantle the worst elements within their own society: corrupt elites, kleptocratic officials, war profiteers, and ideologues who benefit financially and politically from perpetual conflict. History suggests that national liberation movements often fail not because of external resistance, but because of internal decay.

There are early, tentative signs—such as recent discussions involving local sheikhs in Hebron, or proposals for devolved governance models resembling small emirates—that alternative pathways might exist. These ideas are imperfect and controversial, but they reflect a growing recognition that centralised, revolutionary nationalism has failed, and that locally grounded, pragmatic, secular governance may offer a more realistic foundation for peace and prosperity in discrete areas.

Before borders can be negotiated, peace must be wanted. Before a state can be recognised, the idea of statehood must be preferred over the idea of resistance. Until Palestinians turn decisively against terror directed at Israel, reject the glorification of martyrdom, and demand accountable governance from their own rulers, no durable settlement is possible—on 1967 lines or any other.

There is, perhaps, a deeper historical rhythm at work. The biblical image of a people wandering in the wilderness for forty years before entering the land of milk and honey was not merely about punishment or delay. It was about generational change. The old generation—shaped by fear, trauma, and grievance—could not build a future. Only a new generation, formed by different assumptions and expectations, could do so.

It may be that the Palestinians are not there yet. Not ready for peace. Not ready for statehood. Not ready to choose life over struggle. If that is so, then the most honest course—for Israel, for its Arab neighbours, and for the international community—is not to pretend otherwise, but to stabilise, contain, and wait. To encourage reform where possible. To support economic dignity without subsidising violence. And to recognise that peace, when it comes, will not look like a reheated plan from the late twentieth century.

King Abdullah's vision was humane and sincere. But history is unsparing. Peace does not arrive because it is deserved, or because it is overdue. It arrives when the conditions for it exist.

The tragedy is not that the window closed. It is that too many still insist on reopening it without first rebuilding the foundations beneath it.

7

Hunted, Harassed, and Harangued

Introduction

Intuition is often dismissed as unscientific—something to be corrected by data or disciplined by process.

But in environments shaped by risk, intuition is rarely the enemy of reason. It is often its early-warning system.

There is a particular kind of fear that does not announce itself loudly. It does not panic or posture. It sharpens awareness. It alters behaviour quietly. Routes change. Eyes scan. Words are chosen more carefully.

In my first career, I learned to distinguish paranoia from prudence—and to respect fear that emerges from pattern rather than imagination. In recent years, I have watched that same kind of fear settle into the lives of people who never expected to feel it in Australia.

This chapter is about that fear. Not as an emotion, but as information.

A Quiet, Rational Fear

There is a particular kind of fear that does not announce itself loudly. It sits quietly in the chest. It sharpens awareness. It alters routes home, posture in public, the way a glance is interpreted, the way a word is weighed before it is spoken. It is the fear of being hunted, harassed, and harangued—not metaphorically, not historically, but now.

In Australia in 2025, many Jewish Australians are living with precisely that fear.

This is not the anxiety of political disagreement or social discomfort. It is the fear that arises when a society, through omission and inaction, appears to have quietly withdrawn its protection. When warnings are dismissed, patterns minimised, threats contextualised away. When those responsible for law, order, governance and moral leadership fail to grasp what is unfolding in front of them—or worse, grasp it and choose silence.

What has changed is not merely the intensity of fear, but its texture. For many Jewish Australians, fear no longer arrives in a single form. It is experienced through overlapping pressures that reinforce one another and, taken together, shape daily life.

Three Forms of Pressure

The experiences described in this essay fall into three related but distinct categories. Each matters on its own. Together, they explain why fear within the Australian Jewish community has deepened so markedly in recent years.

To be hunted is to face a credible risk of physical harm—to know that violence is not hypothetical, distant, or symbolic, but possible here and now. It is the fear that arises when threats escalate from words to action, and when recent events demonstrate that lethal violence against Jews is no longer unthinkable in Australia.

To be harassed is to be subjected to repeated, targeted hostility that may fall short of overt violence but is intended to intimidate, exhaust, and constrain. Graffiti, vandalism, verbal abuse, public intimidation, and the slow erosion of safe spaces all belong in this category. Harassment works not through spectacle, but through accumulation. Its power lies in persistence and deniability.

To be harangued is to be confronted, lectured, or browbeaten into silence—to have one's fear dismissed, minimised, or reframed as misunderstanding, oversensitivity, or political inconvenience. It occurs when individuals are verbally pressured, denied their own lived experience, or told that what they see and hear is not what it appears to be. Haranguing does not require shouting; it often arrives clothed in authority, credentials, or moral certainty.

These pressures are not sequential. They operate simultaneously and reinforce one another. Harassment normalises hostility. Haranguing suppresses recognition and response. And when both are left unchecked, the conditions in which people are hunted take root.

What follows is an account of how these dynamics are now being experienced by many Jewish Australians—not as theory or abstraction, but as lived reality.

A Soldier's Eye for Pattern

I write this as someone who spent more than three decades as a professional soldier. I have served in multiple theatres, including

Iraq and Afghanistan. I have lived and worked among populations where grievance, ideology, and violence intersect in dangerous ways. I was trained to distinguish coincidence from pattern; background noise from threat indicators; paranoia from prudence.

That experience taught me something simple and uncomfortable: Fear is often rational long before it is publicly acknowledged.

The Day After Bondi

The day after the Bondi massacre, I was at the beach with friends—the site of the attack the afternoon before. Among them was a Jewish woman with whom I had shared a meal the previous evening, together with my family and hers: resilient, accomplished, deeply attached to Australia, yet visibly carrying the accumulated weight of the past two years.

What we witnessed that afternoon was not dramatic in isolation. It did not involve weapons, shouting, or physical violence. And yet it landed with chilling force.

An unknown, solitary military-aged male moved through the area wearing clothing and markers that, taken together, identified him—to me and to others present—as an adherent to the Islamic faith. These included religious dress elements commonly associated with observant Muslim men, combined with combat cargo pants and military-style boots. To most observers, the ensemble may have appeared unremarkable. To those with relevant experience, it was immediately familiar. I have seen the same combination repeatedly in the Middle East, worn by contractors, auxiliaries, and militants operating in permissive civilian environments.

I make no claim about this man's affiliations, intentions, or criminality. Nor do I take issue with his presence at the makeshift shrine of flowers that had formed at Bondi in the hours following the murder of innocent Australian Jews by Islamic terrorists. I describe only what I observed, and how it registered through the lens of my professional experience as I reflected on the interaction after the fact.

He was speaking into his phone, expressing hatred he appeared to believe was private, yet loudly and unmistakably enough for my friend to hear. My Jewish friend challenged him—calmly and directly—and asked him to stop and to leave. This occurred at the site of a massacre of Australian Jews less than twenty-four hours earlier. In that moment, the calculus changed. He shifted from a mourner, respectfully and solemnly paying his respects, to a perceived threat.

What followed was a sequence that has become increasingly familiar in contemporary Australia: denial, minimisation, reversal. He insisted he was misunderstood. He denied saying what she had heard. He suggested she was mistaken. It was a choreography Australians have since seen repeatedly—including in other public incidents where inflammatory remarks, once challenged, are met not with accountability, but with repudiation.

She stood her ground.

And then she broke. She burst into tears—not because of what he said, but because of what it confirmed. This was no longer abstract; no longer confined to online spaces or distant protests. The threat felt present, proximate, and embodied. And when she looked around, she saw no authority intervening, no bystander stepping forward, no indication that anyone else fully grasped what had just occurred—or what it signified. In that moment, her fear was not only of the man before her, but of the realisation that she—and many within the Australian Jewish community—were standing alone in a society that had not yet registered the danger she had been warning of for over two years.

This is what it means to be harangued: to be confronted, denied, and pressured into silence, even at a place of mourning, even within hours of the dead being grieved.

Presence Without Protection

For months, helicopters have regularly circled Sydney's eastern suburbs—unrelated to this specific incident. But as this unfolded, aircraft again moved across the skyline of Dover Heights and Bellevue Hill.

The symbolism was hard to ignore: visible force, audible reassurance—yet no intervention where it mattered.

Presence without protection.

For communities already being harassed and harangued, the absence of intervention is not read as neutrality, but as exposure—a signal that if violence follows, they may face it alone.

Where Australian Jews Do—and Do Not—Feel Safe

Of the Jewish people I know, only those who once operated clandestinely in hostile environments in the Middle East have felt sufficiently confident to enter areas such as Lakemba.[2]

We hear increasingly from overseas that there are districts in London and Paris where even police tread cautiously, and

---

[2] Lakemba is a suburb in south-western Sydney, approximately 15 kilometres from the CBD, within the City of Canterbury-Bankstown. It has one of Australia's highest Muslim population concentrations (around 60%), with strong Lebanese, Bangladeshi, and Pakistani heritage communities

where Jews—and often native British and French residents—no longer move openly. Australia reassures itself that it is different. But the pattern is familiar: When intimidation is tolerated and authority retreats, no announcement is required. People simply learn where not to go.

Australia is moving in that direction.

Many of my Jewish friends are reluctant to spend time in the Sydney CBD, let alone the western suburbs.

This is not class-based.

It is threat-based.

And the fear is not imagined. It is learned.

In the military, terrain is often assessed as controlled, contested, or hostile. I use this only as analogy—a way of describing how civilians experience space when security becomes uneven and authority uncertain. Through that lens, what is striking is not where Jewish Australians now feel unsafe, but where they no longer feel secure.

Even long-established Jewish neighbourhoods—places where families have lived peacefully, raised children, educated them, and worshipped for generations—no longer feel reliably protected. Suburbs such as Caulfield in Melbourne and parts of Sydney's eastern suburbs have, over the past two years, been marked by arson attacks, repeated graffiti, and increasingly brazen public displays of hostility.

This is the texture of harassment: not a single dramatic event, but the accumulation of insults, threats, vandalism, chants, gestures, and warnings—each individually dismissed, collectively corrosive. Harassment works precisely because it is deniable. It exhausts rather than explodes.

This is how environments shift—not through sudden collapse, but through gradual erosion of confidence. When intimidation goes unanswered, it creates permission. And when permission is sensed, escalation follows.

It is against this backdrop that acts such as the horse-riding incident at Bondi must be understood: not as harmless provocation, but as public tests of boundaries—demonstrations of what will be tolerated, and what will not.

The Man on the Horse

On 8 September 2025, a twenty-year-old man, Ehtesham Ahmad, rode his Arabian horse, Khalil, along Bondi Beach while waving a Palestinian flag. The incident occurred in the early evening, was deliberately filmed, widely circulated, and reasonably understood by observers as a political act designed to attract attention. Beachgoers were startled. Safety concerns were raised. Police were called.

What followed matters.

NSW Police attended and spoke with Ahmad. He was issued a move-on direction, which he complied with. No fine was imposed. No charge was laid. No court appearance followed. The incident concluded not with consequence, but with completion.

Subsequent public commentary suggested enforcement options were limited—that because horses were not explicitly prohibited on Bondi Beach at the time, police had little power to act. That explanation does not withstand scrutiny. The law was not absent; it was available but not applied.

Police already possessed multiple statutory and common-law powers. Under the Summary Offences Act 1988 (NSW), conduct in a public place that a reasonable person would regard as offensive or disorderly is chargeable. Riding a half-tonne animal through a densely populated public beach while displaying a political symbol—particularly in an environment marked by heightened communal tension—plainly meets that threshold. The offence turns on impact, not intent.

The Act also addresses obstruction of free passage in a public place. Bondi Beach is a shared civic space. Members of the public were required to divert, retreat, and accommodate the rider's movement. That interference engages public-order provisions.

Beyond statute, police retain common-law powers to intervene where there is a reasonable apprehension of a breach of the peace. A horse among beachgoers presents an obvious and foreseeable risk. The threshold was met.

None of these avenues were tested.

Only later did Waverley Council amend signage and rules to explicitly ban horses on the beach—a tacit acknowledgement that enforcement failed first, and regulation followed only after public criticism.

The contrast has not gone unnoticed.

Disruption is policed.

Intimidation is contextualised.

Hatred is explained away.

Without consequence, there is only encouragement.

Some Tough Choices

When a community is simultaneously harassed in daily life, harangued in public discourse, and hunted by those willing to escalate to violence, the question is no longer whether the state should act, but how responsibly it will do so.

There are reasons certain forms of profiling exist in security and law-enforcement contexts. They are neither ideological nor racial. They are empirical. They exist because, when properly constrained and intelligently applied, they work.

This is not profiling against Muslims. It is profiling against jihadist violence—an ideological phenomenon with identifiable behavioural, linguistic, symbolic, and operational markers. Failing to maintain that distinction harms not only Jewish communities, but the vast majority of Muslims who are assimilated, secular, agnostic, atheist, or quietly devout and who wish to live ordinary lives free from intimidation and extremism.

Well-applied profiling is not about race. It is about indicators—patterns of behaviour, context-specific symbolism, rhetoric, and situational awareness. Used correctly, it is a safeguard: a means of protecting pluralistic societies, including mainstream Muslim communities, from those who seek to weaponize religion to justify violence.

What might this look like in practice, without fundamentally altering Australia's way of life?

It begins with visible, active policing in environments assessed as higher-risk. Lawful stop-and-question encounters, supported by identification checks and limited searches where justified, are standard tools in any serious security posture.

Where indicators warrant it, enhanced identity verification—including biometric recording—and, upon the establishment of probable cause, detention and examination of electronic devices should be available within existing legal safeguards and oversight.

At an institutional level, venues and organisations that function as incubators of hate must attract sustained scrutiny. This is not an attack on religion; it is a defence of public safety.

Finally, where non-citizens repeatedly transgress Australian law through incitement, intimidation, or support for violent extremism, deportation should be treated not as exceptional, but as a lawful consequence.

None of this requires abandoning Australian values. It requires enforcing them.

Prevention Is Not Punishment

Preventive security is not a cure-all. It cannot—and should not—be used to address every manifestation of antisemitism. Some offending is not ideological extremism but criminal abuse—conduct that the law treats differently, though no less seriously.

In Sydney's eastern suburbs, a seventy-one-year-old Rose Bay woman, Shona Barker, was charged on 2 December 2025 with multiple counts of intentionally marking premises without consent in relation to repeated antisemitic and anti-Israel graffiti over several months.

Her alleged conduct, still before the courts at the time of writing, is not a counter-terrorism issue; it is criminal behaviour under property damage and public-order laws. Barker is scheduled to appear in Downing Centre Local Court on 16 January 2026 in relation to those charges. In such cases, the appropriate response is not profiling or surveillance but consequence.

Custodial sentences—even brief ones—serve a signalling function: Compassion does not negate accountability, and deterrence still matters.

Permission Structures and Public Voices

On 30 August 2025, Professor Peter MacDonald, a senior cardiologist at St Vincent's Hospital in Sydney, publicly speculated—without evidence—that Israel's intelligence agency, Mossad, may have been responsible for arson attacks on Jewish institutions in Australia. His remarks were made at a public forum, widely circulated, and reported.

Following those comments, a formal complaint was lodged by Jewish medical practitioners. St Vincent's Hospital subsequently placed Professor MacDonald on leave and initiated an internal inquiry.

This controversy illustrates harassment by another name—not shouted in the street, but delivered from positions of authority. When senior professionals indulge conspiratorial attribution implicating Jews, even indirectly, it normalises suspicion. Words from figures of status do not need to incite violence to cause harm. They need only legitimise contempt.

Jewish Patients and Vulnerability in Healthcare Settings

The broader climate matters because many Jewish Australians report feeling compelled to mark "No Religion" on hospital admission forms, fearing that disclosure of their Jewish identity might affect how they are treated. This is not an allegation of misconduct, but a reflection of perceived vulnerability.

A dear friend in her seventies told me that when she required a general anaesthetic for a heart condition, she feared her care could be compromised if staff knew she was Jewish.

In Australia.

In 2025.

Safer in a War Zone

Other friends have travelled to Israel several times since October 2023. Many Jews report feeling safer there than in Australia—even amid rocket fire, active conflict zones, and existential threat.

When citizens of a liberal democracy feel more secure in a war zone than in their own suburbs, something has gone profoundly wrong.

A Tipping Point

Jewish Australians are not imagining this. They are not catastrophising. They are responding to lived experience—to harassment normalised, fear dismissed, and violence no longer unthinkable.

They are being hunted—not necessarily by conspiracy, but by a climate that emboldens hostility and constrains response.

Listening Before It Is Too Late

What played out on that beach at Bondi was not exceptional. It was illustrative.

At a micro level, it reflected what many Jewish Australians now experience at a societal level: being harassed in daily life, harangued when they speak up, and increasingly hunted by those willing to turn hatred into violence—while much of society fails to register the danger.

For Jewish Australians, the threshold has already been crossed.

Fear, when grounded in evidence, is not weakness.

It is intelligence.

Australia would do well to start listening.

8

The Lemon-Face Test

Introduction

Before people argue, they react.

Over time, I have learned to watch for the moment when curiosity gives way to something else—a tightening of the face, a withdrawal, a subtle but unmistakable signal that a conclusion has already been reached.

Since October 7, 2023, I have seen this reaction appear with increasing frequency when certain topics arise. Israel. Jews. Antisemitism. War. Responsibility.

This chapter is not an argument. It is an observation. Because in the work I am now involved in, recognising who is open—and who is not—is not academic. It determines whether engagement reduces harm or simply accelerates it.

Reading People, Not Positions

Across a professional lifetime—and, tellingly, over the past two years—I have learned to pay close attention to small human signals.

Not voting history.

Not ideology.

Not education or professional standing.

Just faces.

Non-verbal communication.

This instinct—perhaps inherited from my mother's quiet emotional intelligence—has proven unexpectedly useful in my current, slightly improbable role: a non-Jewish, apolitical, secular veteran involved in founding a charity focused on harm minimisation in the fight against antisemitism.

It is not a popular calling. But it aligns neatly with three of the four elements of *ikigai*: doing what you are good at, what you care about, and what the world needs.

Why Faces Matter More Than Words

There is a body of research that helps explain why this instinct matters.

In the 1960s, psychologist Albert Mehrabian examined how people interpret meaning when words and emotions are misaligned. His work is often lazily reduced to the so-called "7–38–55 rule": that 7 percent of meaning comes from words, 38 percent from tone, and 55 percent from body language.

Mehrabian himself repeatedly warned against this oversimplification. His findings apply narrowly—to situations of emotional incongruence, where what is said conflicts with how it is said. But within that limited frame, the insight remains powerful: When subjects are emotionally charged, people trust faces and posture more than language.

Long before someone tells you what they think, their body often already has.

After October 7: Moral Reflex Failure

Since 7 October 2023, a large and noisy cohort across the Western world appears to have lost both its instinct for danger and its capacity for judgment.

Moral reflexes that once operated automatically—distinguishing aggression from defence, fanaticism from grievance, civilisation from barbarism—now hesitate, invert, or fail altogether. In their place has emerged a flattening moral language, one that treats intent, context, and consequence as interchangeable, and insists on certainty where humility is required.

In that environment, the work to combat antisemitism can feel futile—like trying to slow a rising tide already at your shoulders. Public debate hardens quickly. Positions calcify. The louder the argument, the less listening seems to occur.

Still, the work continues, as it must.

Where Progress Actually Begins

Because experience has taught me that progress rarely begins with grand arguments or public victories. Those come—if they come at all—much later.

Real movement starts earlier, and much smaller, in the intimate terrain of human interaction.

In the first few seconds of a conversation—often before a word is spoken—you can usually tell whether someone is open to learning, quietly uncertain, or already closed.

That moment matters. It determines whether engagement is possible at all.

Antisemitism today is rarely undone by argument. It is reduced—if at all—by exposure, experience, and humility.

The Lemon-Face Test

I have come to call this informal assessment the Lemon-Face Test.

It is not scientific.

It is not judgmental.

It is simply observational—the kind of instinct that develops in people who have spent years reading rooms, not manifestos.

When Israel, antisemitism, or Gaza is mentioned, some faces tighten almost instantly. Lips press together. Eyes narrow. Posture shifts. Something closes.

That expression—the lemon face—tells you the conversation is unlikely to be productive. Not because the person is unintelligent or malicious, but because their conclusion is already fixed. The subject is not being considered; it is being filtered through pre-loaded assumptions.

When Minds Are Already Closed

I encountered this recently while studying alongside a diverse cohort in the MBA program at the Australian Graduate School of Management at the University of New South Wales.

One colleague—let's call her Amy—was progressive, articulate, and socially engaged. A white, Anglo-Saxon atheist with a strong sense of moral alignment. When Israel entered the discussion, the reaction was immediate.

Lemon face.

As if she had just sucked on a lemon.

There was no curiosity. No questions. Just a subtle but unmistakable withdrawal. The assumptions were familiar: power imbalance, colonial framing, moral certainty delivered without lived experience. It was not hostility so much as closure.

I have learned not to push in these moments. Harm minimisation sometimes means knowing when to disengage. You cannot reason someone out of a position they did not reason themselves into. Pressing harder does not open minds; it hardens them.

When Curiosity Appears

But not every reaction is like this.

Another colleague—a young Muslim woman from Indonesia, whom I will call Jane—responded very differently. When the same topics arose, her expression changed not with resistance, but surprise.

Her eyes widened.

Her posture leaned forward.

Her jaw dropped.

Where I cannot work with a lemon face, a jaw-drop is an opening.

It signals surprised curiosity rather than agreement—a recognition that something does not quite align with what one has been told. It creates space. And space is everything.

Don't Tell, Show

I was careful in how I proceeded.

I did not sugar-coat reality: Much of what passes for "knowledge" about Israel in mainstream media—and especially in the sewers of social media—is scurrilous. Often outright false.

But I was equally clear about what I was *not* doing.

I was not opining in a café in Sydney about what she ought to believe about the Jewish state. I would resent that myself. I would not do it to her.

Instead, I shared facts she had never encountered: that nearly 21 percent of Israel's population is Arab; that the overwhelming majority of those citizens are Muslim; that Arab Israelis serve as doctors, judges, parliamentarians, and senior professionals—including in the Israel Defense Forces.

She paused. This was not part of the story she had been taught.

That openness allowed me to explain what the charity I am involved with actually does—and just as importantly, what it does not do.

It is not about persuasion from afar.

It is not about slogans or scripts.

It is not about telling others what to think.

It is about letting people see for themselves.

Exposure as Harm Minimisation

We bring reasonable, open-minded non-Jews to Israel. We allow them to ask questions in context. To meet people across communities. To encounter complexity up close—not through abstractions, but through lived experience.

We turn over rocks.

We look under Band-Aids.

That, in our view, is harm minimisation.

Because we were studying innovation and entrepreneurship together, I suggested a themed visit focused on Israel's start-up ecosystem—water recycling, clean energy, medical innovation.

One proposed stop was Hadassah Hospital near Ein Kerem, just outside Jerusalem.

There, she could meet an Arab Israeli medical professional—let's illustratively call her Fatima. A Muslim woman. A doctor. An Israeli.

I told her I would step away.

"Ask Fatima anything," I said. "I have nothing to hide."

Her response was immediate.

"Michael, I'd love to do that."

Then, quietly:

"Please don't put my picture on social media. I don't want reprisals against my family back in Indonesia."

That moment stayed with me.

It captures a reality many now inhabit: where seeking first-hand understanding of Israel carries risk, while repeating approved narratives carries social safety.

A Word to My Jewish Friends

Many of my Jewish friends have been abandoned by swathes of their former friendship base since October 7. This has been particularly pronounced in artistic, academic, and progressive circles.

The instinctive response is to debate. To argue harder. To engage the loudest and most unreasonable voices.

I understand the impulse. But I would urge caution.

Trying to reason with unreasonable people is like converting your superannuation to cash, pouring it into a barrel, dousing it with petrol, setting it alight, and thinking, *that will earn me 20 percent per annum.*

It won't.

You've just destroyed your principal.

Emotional energy is finite. Spend it wisely.

Reinvest Where Returns Compound

Social connection, like capital, compounds when invested well.

Better to disengage from lemon faces.

Better to reinvest in those who show curiosity.

Better to nurture the silent majority.

When people are amenable, do not tell them.

Show them.

That is how minds change.

That is how harm is reduced.

That is how progress—quiet, incremental, and real—actually occurs.

Sometimes, all it takes to know the difference is a face…

…and five seconds of attention.

PART I
Conclusion

Unease is an uncomfortable place to linger.

It offers no villains yet, no clear lines of responsibility, no events dramatic enough to command headlines. It is made up instead of small adjustments—pauses before speaking, changes in behaviour, places that no longer feel quite the same.

Because it lacks spectacle, unease is often dismissed as irrational. Those who articulate it are told to wait for evidence, to trust institutions, to believe that if danger were real, someone in authority would say so.

History suggests the opposite lesson.

Unease is often distributed intelligence—many individuals responding independently to the same signals long before they are officially acknowledged. By the time danger becomes undeniable, people have already adapted.

What matters next is whether those adaptations are met with protection—or with indifference.

PART II

THE DECAY

When drift becomes damage

PART II
Introduction

Drift, left unchecked, does not remain abstract.

When systems fail to correct themselves, decay sets in quietly. Responsibilities blur. Standards lower. Failures that should prompt intervention are reclassified as unfortunate but inevitable.

Over time, the language of urgency is replaced by the language of management. Problems are "monitored." Crises are "contextualised." Atrocities become statistics, and statistics become background noise.

This is the phase in which societies often reassure themselves that nothing fundamental is wrong—even as evidence mounts that something essential has already been lost.

What follows is not an argument about intent. It is an examination of outcomes. Because when decay takes hold, what matters most is not what institutions claim to value, but what they tolerate—repeatedly, publicly, and without consequence.

9

Replacement Rate

Introduction

Before examining ideology, identity, or conflict, it is necessary to confront something more basic and more unforgiving: arithmetic.

Much of the instability now visible across Western liberal democracies is discussed in moral, political, or cultural terms. Rarely is it examined through the lens that ultimately constrains all societies—demography. Yet long before institutions fail or social cohesion frays, nations weaken in a quieter way: They stop replacing themselves.

Birth rates are not an abstract statistic. They determine whether welfare systems remain viable, whether economies can sustain growth, whether intergenerational trust endures, and whether a society retains confidence in its future. When fertility falls well below replacement level for prolonged periods, the consequences are not ideological. They are structural.

The essay that follows explores this reality directly. It traces the long decline in birth rates across Australia and the broader Western world, examines the unspoken assumptions underpinning modern welfare states, and contrasts this trajectory with a country that has chosen a different path—not through natural resources or geographic fortune, but through people.

This is not an argument about race, nor a call to nostalgia. It is an examination of whether societies that no longer reproduce themselves can remain stable, prosperous, and free.

***

For most of human history, population growth was not a policy question. It was a fact of life, governed by biology, mortality, faith, family, and necessity. Children were born because societies required them—economically, socially, and morally. Today, across much of the Western world, that assumption has quietly collapsed.

The consequences are profound.

Across Australia, Europe, the United Kingdom, North America and East Asia, birth rates have fallen well below replacement level—the approximate 2.1 children per woman required to sustain a stable population without immigration. This is not a marginal deviation. It is a structural failure that, if left uncorrected, will hollow out economies, strain social contracts, and ultimately destabilise liberal democratic societies from within.

The Long Arc of Decline

The post-war decades offer a useful baseline.

In the 1950s and early 1960s, Western nations experienced what is now termed the baby boom. Australia's total fertility rate (TFR) peaked at around 3.6 in 1961. The United Kingdom and France hovered between 2.7 and 3.0. The United States reached 3.7 in 1957. These were not anomalies; they reflected a cultural consensus that family formation was normal, desirable, and socially supported.

By the 1970s, that consensus began to fracture. The widespread introduction of reliable contraception, the sexual revolution, second-wave feminism, rising urbanisation, and the decoupling of sex from family formation all played a role. Australia's fertility rate fell sharply, dropping below replacement by 1976. Similar patterns emerged across Western Europe.

The 2000s offered a brief reprieve. Australia rebounded modestly, peaking at around 2.0 in 2008, aided by economic growth and targeted family benefits. But the recovery was short-lived.

By the 2020s, the picture had darkened considerably. Australia's fertility rate fell to approximately 1.6, with some states dipping lower. The United Kingdom declined to around 1.5. France—long considered Europe's demographic outperformer—fell to roughly 1.7. Denmark hovered near 1.6. These are not temporary fluctuations; they represent entrenched demographic trajectories.

A Quiet Ponzi Scheme

Modern Western welfare states rest on an implicit bargain: A large, productive working-age population supports the young, the sick, and the elderly through taxation and social insurance. This model functions only if each generation is sufficiently large to carry the next.

When birth rates fall and life expectancy rises, the arithmetic breaks.

Without enough new entrants into the workforce, governments face three unpalatable options: raise taxes sharply, slash services, or accumulate unsustainable debt. None are politically attractive. All erode social cohesion. What has emerged instead is a form of demographic denial—a hope that productivity gains, immigration, or perpetual economic growth will indefinitely mask the imbalance.

That hope is misplaced.

Australia has been unusually fortunate. For much of its modern history, it has ridden successive resource and commodity booms—from wool and wheat to iron ore, coal, and LNG. These windfalls have delayed hard demographic reckoning. But commodities do not reproduce. People do.

Strip away the boom cycles, and Australia faces the same structural problem confronting every ageing Western democracy.

The Israeli Contrast

Israel offers a striking counterpoint.

With few natural resources and constant security pressures, Israel has built its national resilience not on commodities, but on people. Its total fertility rate—approximately 3.0—is the highest in the developed world and more than double that of many European nations.

This outcome is not accidental, nor is it reducible to any single religious or ethnic explanation. It reflects a cultural environment in which family formation is normalised, supported, and socially valued. Parenthood is not treated as an inconvenience or a lifestyle regression, but as a contribution to the collective future.

Crucially, Israel demonstrates that high female workforce participation and high fertility are not mutually exclusive. The supposed trade-off so often assumed in Western policy debates is not inevitable.

Composition Without Accusation

Any honest discussion of birth rates must confront differences across sub-populations. In most Western societies, fertility varies significantly by religious observance and cultural norms. More secular populations tend to have fewer children. More observant Christian, Jewish, and Muslim communities tend to have more.

This is not an argument about race. It is an observation about behaviour and belief.

The uncomfortable reality is that societies which lose confidence in their future tend to stop reproducing. Where family is deprioritised, postponed indefinitely, or framed as a personal sacrifice rather than a social good, fertility collapses. Over time, demographic weight shifts—not through conspiracy or malice, but through arithmetic.

Ignoring this dynamic does not make it disappear.

A Culture Hostile to Family

In much of the West today, having children is subtly—but relentlessly—discouraged.

Media narratives frame children as environmental liabilities or lifestyle constraints. Even language has shifted: Children are increasingly spoken of as choices, rarely as responsibilities or gifts.

The result is a pervasive social stigma—particularly among educated urban elites—attached to early or larger families. This stigma has consequences.

At the same time, policy settings often send mixed signals. Abortion is defended as healthcare; adoption is under-promoted and under-resourced. Family tax benefits are means-tested or politically fragile. Childcare is subsidised, but parenthood itself is treated as a private indulgence rather than a public good.

What Incentivisation Looks Like

If governments are serious about demographic sustainability, they must move beyond slogans.

Effective pronatalist policy is not coercive. It is enabling. It reduces the friction between the desire to form a family and the practical ability to do so. This includes affordable housing, stable employment, genuine parental leave for both parents, and a cultural narrative that treats family formation as socially valuable.

Equally important is honesty. Societies cannot indefinitely outsource reproduction, nor can they rely on migration alone to solve demographic decline without consequences for cohesion and consent.

The Civilisational Stakes

Demography is destiny—not in a deterministic sense, but in a cumulative one. Nations that fail to reproduce themselves do not simply shrink. They age, ossify, and lose confidence. Their institutions become defensive. Their politics turn brittle.

This is not alarmism. It is arithmetic.

The replacement rate is not a moral judgement. It is a biological threshold. Fall below it for long enough, and no amount of rhetorical commitment to progress, rights, or prosperity will reverse the outcome.

The question is not whether Western societies will confront this reality. It is whether they will do so deliberately—or be forced to do so later, under far harsher conditions.

A God-Sized Hole in the Heart

Introduction

Societies do not hollow out all at once.

What erodes first is not law or order, but meaning. The shared moral grammar that once anchored responsibility, restraint, and judgment thins quietly, leaving behind language that sounds familiar but no longer binds.

In the absence of that deeper structure, concepts such as justice, compassion, and rights persist—but untethered from obligation. What remains is moral assertion without moral weight.

This chapter examines that vacuum. Not as theology, but as civilisational diagnosis. Because when something foundational is removed, whatever rushes in to replace it rarely carries the same capacity for restraint.

***

Walk through almost any suburb in Australia and you can feel it: Something foundational has thinned. It's not simply that fewer people attend church or synagogue. It's that the deeper grammar of Judeo-Christian civilisation—duty, restraint, forgiveness, covenant, the equal moral worth of the individual, the idea that freedom requires responsibility—is no longer assumed.

We still speak the language of *human rights*, *dignity*, *justice,* and *compassion*. But increasingly we try to live on those moral fruits while forgetting the root system that grew them.

The demographic shift is real, and it is measurable. In the mid-twentieth century, Australia was overwhelmingly Christian in affiliation. In 1954, roughly nine in ten Australians identified as Christian (about 89 percent). By 1991, Christianity was still dominant—around 74 percent—but the secular tide was clearly rising. By 2021, the picture had changed dramatically: 43.9 percent identified as Christian, while 38.9 percent reported no religion.

These numbers are not trivia. They track a civilisational transition from a society where faith and its institutions set a default moral horizon, to one where faith is increasingly private, optional, or viewed with suspicion—even as the social functions faith once served (community, meaning, moral formation, intergenerational continuity) remain stubbornly necessary.

The Inheritance We Pretend Not to Need

Modern Western societies often speak as though values such as equality before the law, the sanctity of life, human dignity, and freedom of conscience emerged spontaneously—or worse, inevitably. They did not. They were argued into existence over centuries, shaped by Jewish moral law and Christian theology, refined through painful historical experience, and institutionalised imperfectly but sincerely.

The idea that every individual has equal moral worth regardless of power or status is not a natural human instinct. History suggests the opposite: Hierarchy, domination, and tribalism are far more common defaults. The Judeo-Christian tradition disrupted that logic by insisting that every human being is made in the image of God, accountable to a moral law higher than kings, mobs, or states.

We are now attempting a civilisational experiment: retaining the moral conclusions while severing them from their metaphysical foundations. We want the inheritance without the inheritance tax. We want the ethic without the Author.

Can We Keep the "Good" and Discard the Rest?

Here is the hard question: Can we keep "the good" of the Judeo-Christian inheritance while discarding what some perceive as the "bad"—or discarding belief altogether?

Many modern Westerners want to answer yes. They want the moral framework, but not the metaphysics. They want the ethic, but not transcendence. They want the vocabulary of sin and redemption transmuted into politics and therapy, without the inconvenience of worship, accountability, or restraint.

But the "good" and the "bad" are often two sides of the same coin. The same tradition that can be abused by hypocrites also forms the conscience that condemns hypocrisy. The same faith that has been corrupted in history also created a moral architecture capable of self-critique, reform, and repentance.

Remove transcendence and you rarely get neutrality. You get replacement religions—ideology, identity, nation, self, pleasure, status—each demanding loyalty, each punishing heresy, each offering belonging in exchange for submission.

Replacement Religions and the New Sacred

The post-religious West has not abolished faith. It has redistributed it.

Politics becomes salvation. Identity becomes destiny. Victimhood becomes moral currency. The self becomes sovereign. These belief systems come complete with saints and sinners, rituals and taboos, confessions and excommunications.

What they lack is restraint.

Unlike the Judeo-Christian moral tradition, which insists on human fallibility, these secular faiths often operate with absolute certainty. Unlike religious traditions that developed concepts of forgiveness and repentance, modern ideological systems offer permanent moral exile.

Judgement has not disappeared. It has simply become harsher.

Faith as Community Moral Formation

This is why the erosion of faith is not simply the loss of "religious practice." It is the loss of a particular kind of community moral formation.

Rabbi Jonathan Sacks put it plainly: "Morality lives in communities and the traditions which sustain them." He also observed that you do not need to be religious to be moral—but it makes a profound difference to belong to a community consciously committed to being a blessing to others.

That is not a sectarian boast. It is a social observation.

Faith communities train habits: showing up when you don't feel like it; serving without applause; giving anonymously; visiting the sick; forgiving those who have wronged you; binding yourself to obligations you did not invent and cannot easily escape. These habits shape people long before they shape opinions.

Fear, Trauma, and the Return of Old Questions

And yet—this is where the story becomes more interesting—I am hearing anecdotally that interest in community and faith is surging in parts of Sydney, including the eastern suburbs. People who spent years treating religion as irrelevant are now asking older questions again: *What is worth living for? What is worth sacrificing for? What anchors a family? What protects children? What holds a nation together when it is frightened?*

I have seen a similar pattern among friends in Israel since the atrocities of October 7: a renewed seriousness about identity, peoplehood, tradition, and spiritual stamina. Not everyone becomes observant. But many become less casual about what they are and what they owe.

Trauma does that. When history snaps awake, shallow stories stop working.

Stories We Cannot Live Without

Yuval Noah Harari, writing in *Sapiens*, approaches the problem of social cohesion from a very different angle. He argues that large-scale human cooperation depends on shared "imagined orders"—the stories we collectively agree to treat as real: money, nations, laws, even human rights. Without shared belief in common meanings, societies fragment into tribes.

Whether one agrees with his conclusions or not, the underlying insight is difficult to escape. Societies cannot function without a shared moral grammar—a common understanding of who we are, what binds us together, and what obligations flow from that. A house divided against itself cannot stand, not because disagreement is forbidden, but because foundations must be shared.

Modern Western thinking increasingly assumes cohesion can be engineered by process alone—by law, policy, or procedure—while neglecting the deeper cultural inheritance that once made those systems intelligible and legitimate. We confuse pluralism with homogenisation, assuming that if we blend enough traditions, values, and narratives together, something stronger will emerge.

But culture does not work like that.

A civilisation is more like a carefully prepared meal than a smoothie. A fine dinner—wine, meat, vegetables, herbs, spices—retains its character because each element has integrity and order. Put the same ingredients into a blender and you do not get something more sophisticated. You get something grey. Indistinct. Unrecognisable.

What makes France *French*? What makes England *English*? What makes Australia *Australia*? These are not racial questions, nor nostalgic ones. They are civilisational questions—about inherited norms, shared stories, moral expectations, and habits of restraint that shape behaviour long before laws are enforced.

When a nation forgets its own narrative, it does not become neutral. It becomes vulnerable.

The vacuum never stays empty.

Give the Devil His Due

It would be dishonest to write about the erosion of faith without acknowledging its most energetic critics. Over many years,

I have known a committed, proselytising atheist—not merely sceptical, but sermonising. He does not simply disbelieve; he preaches disbelief. Faith, in his telling, is not mistaken or incomplete, but dangerous, backward, and morally suspect.

What is striking is not his atheism—that is his right—but his inability to see the mirror.

He rails against religious dogma while displaying it. He condemns proselytising while practising it. He denounces moral absolutism while exhibiting an unyielding moral absolutism of his own.

I noticed another pattern. His animus was directed consistently toward Christians and Jews in public life—those whose faith was visible rather than private. Alongside this ran a reflexive hostility toward certain American presidents—Reagan, the two Bushes, and Donald Trump—who became convenient symbols in the secular imagination. These men were not engaged as fallible leaders operating under constraint. They were portrayed as moral grotesques: stand-ins for everything allegedly dangerous about religion, conservatism, and power.

I do not claim personal knowledge of these men, nor do I defend their records here. What I recognise is the pattern. Public Christianity becomes a trigger. Political figures become proxies. Faith itself becomes the accused.

There is another hypocrisy embedded in this posture. The animus is directed relentlessly toward Christians and Jews, yet conspicuously *not* toward Muslims. That asymmetry is often excused as sensitivity. It is not. It is selective moral blindness.

I cannot recall a moment when hearing "Baruch Hashem" or "in the name of the Father, the Son, and the Holy Ghost" caused me to fear for my life in a public space. By contrast, "Allahu Akbar" shouted in such spaces now carries a very different psychological and historical weight. That is not prejudice. It is pattern recognition shaped by lived experience.

This is not a condemnation of Muslims as people. It is an observation about moral cowardice. Christianity and Judaism are safe targets. Islam is treated as exempt from serious scrutiny—not out of respect, but out of fear, confusion, or paralysis.

That is not moral courage. It is abdication.

Assimilation Requires a Centre

The vacuum is being filled—not only by secularism, but also by the growth of other faiths, most notably Islam. In Australia's 2021 Census, Islam accounted for 3.2 percent of the population. Globally, it is projected to grow significantly in coming decades.

This matters for two reasons.

First, it punctures the comforting Western myth that religion is fading everywhere. It is not.

Second, it forces a serious question: What exactly are we inviting people into? A nation cannot assimilate newcomers into emptiness. Pluralism only works when there is a confident moral centre. If we hollow out our own inheritance, we should not be surprised when more confident belief systems expand—sometimes peacefully, sometimes politically, sometimes with friction.

This is not an argument against Muslims as people. It is an argument for civilisational clarity.

What We Owe the Next Generation

I see this tension in miniature at home. My daughter is, in her own way, more religious than I am. She is not performing piety.

She is searching for the real—for moral seriousness, meaning, and a community that asks something of her.

That may be the most hopeful sign of all.

The West can survive wealth, comfort, and diversity. What it struggles to survive is meaninglessness—and the slow loss of the moral and spiritual traditions that once taught us how to be free without falling apart.

Civilisation is not self-sustaining. It must be renewed, taught, and sometimes defended—or it quietly dissolves, leaving a god-sized hole in the heart that no ideology, appetite, or screen can ever fill.

11

The Pixie Dust Politics and Perspectives of Peter Beinart

Introduction

"Pixie Dust Politics" examines a recurring Western impulse: the belief that good intentions, loudly expressed, are sufficient to overcome human nature, history, and power.

This essay was written not to mock idealism, but to interrogate it—to ask what happens when moral imagination detaches itself from consequence. Through a critical engagement with the work of Peter Beinart, it explores a strain of progressive thought that treats conflict as a misunderstanding, violence as a failure of empathy, and concession as a substitute for strategy.

The danger examined here is not malice, but fantasy—the belief that words alone can disarm those who are animated by ideology, grievance, or faith. When such thinking migrates from private opinion into public policy, it ceases to be benign. It becomes corrosive.

***

A reflection on and review of Peter Beinart's book Being Jewish After the Destruction of Gaza *(published in 2024 by Knopf, an imprint of Penguin Random House).*

Much of my work—raising awareness of the threats posed to Western values and our way of life by sustained assaults on the Jewish state and the global Jewish diaspora—is directed primarily at a non-Jewish audience. It is about building allies: people of goodwill who can empathise with the Jewish experience and understand that its stakes are, in fact, their own. Much of this work happens quietly, beneath the surface, through private conversations rather than public declarations.

One such conversation began when a long-standing friend asked whether I was familiar with Peter Beinart and whether I would read his book. I had certainly heard of him. He is often described by commentators I respect as a "naive idealist," or more sharply as "dangerously misguided," and, within parts of the Jewish community, as a "self-hating Jew"—a term frequently deployed to describe hard-left, uber-progressive, and thoroughly liberal critics of Israel. Out of respect for my friend and our two-decade relationship, I accepted her recommendation and engaged with Beinart's work in good faith.

In a single sentence—and to paraphrase The Beach Boys' "Wouldn't It Be Nice"—it would indeed be lovely if we lived in the world Mr. Beinart imagines.

It is a fantasy world in which Western governments could boycott, sanction, divest from, or publicly criticise Israel into peace, harmony, and collective self-actualisation. A world where laying down weapons, apologising, or making further territorial or moral concessions would be enough to disarm hatred and neutralise violence. It is a worldview animated by good intentions yet untethered from hard realities.

But compromise and concession have already been tried—repeatedly, sincerely, and often at great cost. Israel has sought peace and coexistence since its founding. Its adversaries, more often than not, have sought *Judenrein*—a Nazi term meaning "free of Jews"—and endless conflict. That is not to suggest Israel is perfect. No nation is; no human being is. Perfection does not exist in nature. But the notion that this most scrutinised, litigated, and self-critical of nations has failed to pursue peace is not merely wrong—it is dangerous. It is a fantasy that costs lives. Beinart's work is notably thin on nuance, context, and balance.

As someone who, in a previous career, wore my nation's uniform for decades and served in multiple war zones, I have seen what Joseph Conrad described as the "heart of darkness." I have seen what human beings are capable of when ideology eclipses morality and restraint. That is the world into which we raise our children. If we lack the will to defend what we have built—our institutions, freedoms, and hard-won norms—we risk losing them altogether.

The values at stake are not abstract. Jewish values, Israeli values, Western values, Australian values—they are, in essence, one and the same: the rule of law, free-market economics, the emancipation of women, freedom of conscience, and the protection of minorities. These values are now under sustained assault by ideologies that romanticise grievance and excuse barbarism.

I believe in the forward movement of humankind. Many of my instincts are progressive; they look toward the horizon and seek a better tomorrow. But progress that jeopardises survival is not liberal—it is reckless. The conservative instinct exists for a reason: to temper idealism with reality, to ensure civilisation advances without destroying itself in the process. Mr. Beinart's worldview fails that test. In my assessment, it belongs firmly in the category of "what not to put too much stock in."

When progress becomes a threat to the continued existence of a people who comprise just 0.2 percent of the world's population—and who have contributed immeasurably to human advancement—it ceases to be noble. It becomes naive at best, and destructive at worst.

Late in his otherwise forgettable work, Beinart urges readers to "consider the suffering of Gazans." On this, I agree—though not in the way he intended. In October 2025, on the same day I finished his book, an Australian national newspaper carried a harrowing image of Hamas executing fellow Gazans: Levantine Arabs murdering Levantine Arabs in a desperate effort to cling to power. These terrorists rarely wear uniforms anymore, save for moments of performative theatre—or when the bodies of Shiri Bibas and her two beautiful children, Kfir and Ariel, were returned—murdered—to their family and to the care of the Jewish state earlier this year.

Beinart may not realise it, but his life's work risks undermining the very civilisation that nurtured him, educated him, and granted him the freedom to advance such ideas. His arguments are eagerly seized upon by those who seek Israel's destruction and who would see Jews erased first—and every other culture and faith subjugated or eliminated thereafter. More troubling still, they are believed by kind, tolerant, and decent people like my friend. Beinart has helped confuse a generation and contributed, in part, to an obscene inversion of reality that is, quite frankly, Orwellian.

For my part, I say no.

I will not go gentle into that good night.

From my perspective—which increasingly feels like living inside a Dylan Thomas poem—I will resist the dying of the light. Perhaps the unintended value of Peter Beinart is that he reminds us of a truth as old as civilisation itself: Societies do not die of old age; they commit suicide.

In that sense, Beinart's work is an intoxicant—a dangerous ideological narcotic. One taste was more than enough for me: ninety minutes, an audiobook at triple speed, and I was done.

For those who, like my friend, find themselves disoriented by the "he said, she said" swirl of competing narratives—and who want history, context, and moral clarity—I have poured years of research, experience, and lived insight into my own book, *A Light Still Burns: Israel and the Values Worth Defending.*[3]

I have sought to do some of the heavy lifting. In Appendix C, I include a carefully curated list of recommended resources to help readers navigate one of the defining moral challenges of our age—a challenge that, if ignored, may one day threaten the safety and survival of your own children and grandchildren.

---

[3] *A Light Still Burns: Israel and the Values Worth Defending* (Post Hill Press, Wicked Son imprint, 2025) is available globally on Amazon, Apple Books, Audible, and Kindle.

Gangrenous

Introduction

In medicine, gangrene describes tissue that has lost its blood supply—cut off from the oxygen and nutrients required to survive. It does not announce itself with sudden pain. It spreads quietly, often beneath intact skin, until intervention becomes unavoidable.

Societal decay follows a similar pattern.

What begins as accommodation hardens into habit. What was once exceptional becomes routine. Failures that would once have demanded accountability are reinterpreted as complexities beyond anyone's control.

This chapter examines what happens when institutions charged with safeguarding moral and civic health instead normalise dysfunction—and why delay, in such circumstances, is not neutral but destructive.

***

Australia—the country I love—is no longer meeting my reasonable expectations of itself. That failure carries consequences for all of us and demands considerations we can no longer ignore.

Author's Perspective

This has been a difficult article to write. These are dire and deteriorating times. In an earlier career, I served as an Australian soldier, deploying to East Timor, Bougainville, Iraq, and Afghanistan, and rising to the rank of Colonel. From July 2019 to September 2021, I served in a senior leadership role as an unarmed United Nations peacekeeper, operating across Israel, Lebanon, Syria, Jordan, and Egypt.

I am now the non-Jewish founder of a charity dedicated to combating antisemitism through lived personal experience. In that work, I have grown close to the Australian and global Jewish communities. I have come to understand that an assault on them is an assault on me. It is also an assault on Australia itself, and it must not be left unchecked.

I no longer operate as a participant in an organ of the state or government. But I have spent much of my adult life working at the seam between the lawful, ethical, and moral application of lethal force—consistent with the expectations of a democracy—and the responsibilities of domestic policing and public safety. I do not profess to have all the answers. I seek only to play a small part in beginning the difficult conversations that this country I love—Australia—is failing to have, and in challenging a trajectory that no longer meets my reasonable expectations of it.

The Medical Metaphor

Several years ago, someone I was once close to shared with me an account that has never left me. She was a medical doctor. She described a patient who lost his leg to what should have been a preventable condition: a septic infection originating in the lower limb. When the wound was still modest, the patient sought treatment not from a clinician, but from an herbalist. Honey was applied. The infection progressed—predictably and relentlessly. By the time he finally presented to the emergency department of an Australian hospital—within the last fifteen years and in the penicillin age—what should have been muscle tissue was instead litres of pus. The leg was amputated to save the rest of him.

It is extraordinary that this could occur in modern Australia. But as we are reminded time and again, common sense is anything but common.

Bondi Beach: The Infection Revealed

That vignette returned to me forcefully in December 2025, three days after the massacre of Jews at Bondi Beach. A pogrom. In Australia. In 2025. A friend of mine was murdered. Many more—also friends—were present and are now traumatised. They are managing their own shock while parenting children who are equally traumatised. The full psychological toll will take years to surface.

Beyond the Gun Control Reflex

Much of the public discussion since has focused on gun control.

In my judgment, this is barking up the wrong tree.

In between deployments and command roles earlier in my career, I served in the Directorate of Army Research and Analysis, where the discipline was horizon scanning and meta-trend analysis: looking over the horizon, around corners, and beyond the comfort of short-term assumptions to analyse the future of war.

That experience informs my prima facie view that Australia needs a more sophisticated and honest public conversation—one not driven by the imperatives of the next election cycle, nor by the reflex to reach for familiar but insufficient answers.

What I am attempting here is not to prescribe immediate policy, but to grapple with difficult questions that we may choose—or, if we do not, will be forced—to confront over the coming decade to 2035, as our strategic, social, and security environment continues to harden.

The only thing worse than having difficult conversations about difficult topics is the alternative: the continued murder of innocent Australians by Islamic terrorists. That must be stopped.

Australia already has very strict firearms laws by international standards. The problem at Bondi was not a lack of regulation; it was the presence of violent intent, ideological radicalisation, and prolonged state failure to confront it. I would argue that the opposite course deserves serious consideration: licensing the right people, with appropriate training, vetting, and demonstrated need, to carry.

I was recently at a restaurant in Tel Aviv. My companion, a former Sayeret Matkal commander—Israel's equivalent of our SASR—long retired, carried a pistol on his hip. I found that reassuring, not alarming. Israel understands something we appear determined to forget: Deterrence matters, and capability in responsible hands saves lives.

Australia has tens of thousands of retired military personnel and police officers—individuals already trained, disciplined, and accustomed to the lawful use of force. I would feel significantly safer knowing that such professional people were permitted to carry firearms under a tightly controlled licensing regime. At present, we disarm precisely those most capable of responding while hoping violence politely waits for first responders.

In the same vein, the Jewish Community Security Group should be properly empowered and equipped, consistent with law, training standards, and oversight. I attend many Jewish events. Volunteers already shoulder extraordinary responsibility while threats escalate. Expecting unarmed civilians to deter ideologically motivated violence is not realism; it is wishful thinking.

Policing, Force, and Reality

Policing doctrine also requires candour. When confronted with active terror, police must be trained, resourced, and authorised to stop the threat immediately—put simply, through the lawful application of lethal force. This is not about brutality; it is about saving lives. Hesitation costs lives. This is precisely the kind of serious legislative and legal discussion that a law-abiding Australian community is entitled to expect from its leaders.

National Service and Social Cohesion

We should also speak plainly about national service. I sense a growing appetite—and a growing need—for structure, purpose, and contribution among young Australians leaving school. Again, the Israeli model is instructive not because it is militaristic, but because it is civic. Service includes the military, yes—but also ambulance services, emergency response, aged care, and cultural institutions.

Imagine young Australians serving as guides in the National Museum of Australia or the Australian War Memorial, learning and transmitting the story of the nation they are inheriting. This occurs today in Israel through civil national service pathways.

Borders, Vetting, and Domestic Radicalisation

On deportation and visa cancellation, we have seen how rapidly the state can act when it chooses. The recent case of Matthew Gruter, a South African national whose visa was cancelled and who was removed from Australia after publicly associating with neo-Nazi ideology, demonstrated that decisive action is possible when the will exists. That capability must be matched by consistency: Those who advocate violence, glorify terror, or pledge allegiance to hostile causes should not be indulged with endless procedural delay while the public carries the risk.

This inconsistency becomes more concerning when viewed alongside admissions from extremist or terror-governed environments. A small number of Australian women and children who lived under Islamic State control are understood to have returned to Australia, and civilians departing Gaza do so from territory governed by Hamas. Explicitly, Hamas determines who leaves Gaza. To treat admissions from such environments as routine humanitarian cases—without full transparency about vetting, coercion, and ideological exposure—is not compassion. It is not the careful application of medicine. It is closer to introducing a virulent pathogen into an already compromised patient and hoping the immune system copes.

But borders are only one part of the problem. Radicalisation does not occur solely overseas; it can and does occur at home. Muslim reformers and Arab liberals have warned Western governments for years that Islamist extremism is often incubated in plain sight—sometimes within religious institutions shielded from scrutiny by a misplaced fear of offence. Amjad Taha, a UAE-based analyst and advocate for Muslim reform, has cautioned that Western societies have been dangerously naive in allowing radical ideologies to be preached under the cover of religious freedom, warning that the greatest threat is often not foreign fighters, but domestic radicalisation ignored until it erupts.

To acknowledge this is not to impugn Islam, nor to stigmatise the many peaceful and law-abiding Muslims who are themselves victims of Islamist extremism. It is to recognise an observable pattern: When radical preaching is tolerated, when grievance is sanctified, and when authorities look away for fear of controversy, the result is not harmony—it is escalation. Ignoring home-grown radicalisation is not tolerance. It is neglect.

Institutions, Media, and Education

We cannot afford to monitor thousands of individuals with hate in their hearts indefinitely. Singapore offers a hard but instructive lesson: The needs of the many outweigh the indulgence of the few. Social cohesion is not preserved by endless tolerance of those who reject it.

We must also confront the role of our national broadcasters. The ABC and SBS have been manifestly negligent—and in some respects culpable—in shaping the informational environment that has allowed this infection to spread. For more than two years, footage of so-called "intifada" marches has been visible to anyone willing to look: calls for violence, open celebration of terror, and the normalisation of genocidal slogans. Yet this has too often been sanitised, contextualised away, or presented as legitimate "protest."

A national broadcaster funded by taxpayers carries obligations, not indulgences. When it persistently fails to meet those obligations—when it amplifies grievance while minimising threat—it forfeits its moral claim on public money. Defunding the ABC and SBS, if they cannot be fundamentally reformed, should now be on the table—not as retribution, but as institutional triage.

Equally confronting is the sight of extremist marches featuring banners and placards from organisations such as the NSW Teachers Federation. Those entrusted with educating children carry a heightened duty of care. Individuals who openly align themselves with movements that excuse or celebrate political violence should not be shaping young minds. This is not about suppressing dissent; it is about safeguarding children from ideological poisoning. Where lines have been crossed, professional consequences must follow.

History, Leadership, and the Absence of Illusion

Our nation has changed. The infection is systemic. Penicillin will not work—because we waited too long. The diagnosis was clear. The prognosis was obvious. Honey was applied anyway.

History offers uncomfortable guidance. During the Second World War, between 1939 and 1945, Australia—like other Western democracies—interned nationals of enemy states, including Japanese, German, and Italian residents. These measures were blunt, imperfect, and in some cases unjust. But they were taken in the context of an existential threat, when governments understood that liberal democracy must not be suicidal.

No one argues for crude replication of past policies. But the refusal even to discuss decisive measures today is itself a failure of leadership. Democracies that cannot defend themselves do not remain democracies for long.

Instead, we have witnessed evasion and denial at the highest levels of government. The holders of the offices of prime minister, Foreign Minister, and Home Affairs Minister have each, in different ways, applied honey to a spreading infection—soft language in the face of hard realities; process in place of judgement; hollow reassurance where resolve was required; and decisions, as well as indecision, that will be judged poorly by history. Our nation does not need herbalists. It needs leaders. The prevailing mood of the nation towards its elected officials is one of profound disappointment.

Tough or Terminal

There is also a dangerous assumption taking hold: that we have somehow reached rock bottom. History suggests the opposite. I struggle to find a single precedent in the human record where problems admired, minimised, or ignored have resolved themselves. The pattern, more often than not, is the reverse.

Much of what I have written here sits uneasily with views I have held for most of my adult life—particularly deep reservations about conscription shaped by Australia's experience of Vietnam. But as the boxer Mike Tyson observed, "Everyone has a plan until they get punched in the face." And as John Maynard Keynes reminded us, "When the facts change, I change my mind. What do you do, sir?"

The patient in the opening vignette survived, but only because a tough decision was made in time. By the end, the choice was no longer whether to act, but whether the outcome would be grievous—or fatal. In the end, the limb was lost.

That is where Australia now stands.

Delay and drift have eliminated all good options; Jewish Australians were murdered, among them a ten-year-old girl. What remains is the responsibility to choose between what is tough—and what is terminal.

As John Stuart Mill warned: "Bad men need nothing more to compass their ends, than that good men should look on and do nothing."

A light still burns—but only if we are prepared to act before it is snuffed out.

13

Perverse and Unintended Consequences: The Road to Hell Is Paved with Good Intentions

Introduction

Modern moral failure rarely announces itself as cruelty. More often, it arrives cloaked in compassion.

"Perverse and Unintended Consequences" examines how institutions, policies, and movements that claim humanitarian intent can generate precisely the outcomes they profess to oppose. It traces how moral language becomes a shield—protecting actors from scrutiny while amplifying harm.

Drawing on aid frameworks, protest movements, and international bureaucracies, this essay exposes a pattern of consequence denial where results are subordinated to intention, and accountability is indefinitely deferred.

***

"The most effective way to destroy people is to deny and obliterate their own understanding of their history."—George Orwell

That single sentence explains much of what we are seeing in the world today. A generation untethered from historical truth has been taught to see Israel not as a miracle of national rebirth, but as a colonial project; to view Jews not as survivors of centuries of persecution, but as oppressors; and to treat civilised values—like democracy, law, and pluralism—as negotiable luxuries rather than the foundations of a free society. The consequences of this lie are no longer theoretical. They are playing out in our streets.

Melbourne, Australia's second-largest city by population, has become the latest to fall under the shadow of this perverse moral inversion, marked by the Nakba Day rally of 18 May 2025.[4] A so-called "Free Palestine" march flooded the CBD with chants of "From the river to the sea"—a slogan that plainly calls for the eradication of Israel. Protesters proudly displayed the terrorist emblem of the paragliding Hamas fighter. Jewish Australians, who have long lived peacefully and contributed richly to our nation, were warned to avoid certain neighbourhoods for their own safety. The media's response? Tepid, timid, and telling. Violence, intimidation, and the glorification of terror are no longer even considered newsworthy—so long as they are dressed in the garments of "activism."

Thomas Sowell reminds us: "There are no solutions. There are only trade-offs." Yet for decades, the West has clung to utopian fantasies of peace in the Middle East—fictions maintained at the

---

4 Nakba (Arabic for "catastrophe") refers to the displacement and flight of a significant number of Arab Palestinians during the 1948 Arab–Israeli War following the establishment of the State of Israel. The term is commonly used today within political activism to frame Israel's creation as an inherent injustice rather than the outcome of a war initiated by surrounding Arab states

expense of hard truths. Billions in aid have poured into Gaza, often via UNRWA, under the guise of humanitarian relief. The result? Not peace. Not prosperity. But terror tunnels, rocket arsenals, and the ideological radicalisation of an entire generation. UNRWA schools still teach children to glorify "martyrs" and deny Israel's right to exist.

This is not compassion. It is complicity.

Albert Camus warned: "The welfare of humanity is always the alibi of tyrants." We now see that tyranny cloaked in activism is no less dangerous than that cloaked in uniforms. Hamas, a terrorist organisation with an explicitly antisemitic charter and a proven record of using civilians as human shields, is excused in Western discourse as a "resistance movement." Meanwhile, Israel—a liberal democracy under siege—is vilified for defending itself.

Even the once-vaunted "two-state solution" has become a tragic case study in good intentions gone awry. The Oslo Accords were met not with peace, but with waves of suicide bombings. Israel's withdrawal from Gaza brought not coexistence, but the rise of Hamas and thousands of rockets fired at civilians. And yet, Western diplomats and academics keep repeating the same mantras—mistaking their own inertia for moral clarity.

Milton Friedman observed: "One of the great mistakes is to judge policies and programs by their intentions rather than their results." This is a mistake the West makes again and again. On campuses awash with critical theory and postcolonial grievance, students chant slogans they scarcely understand. Jewish students are harassed, silenced, and threatened. University administrators—so vocal about inclusion when it suits them—are paralysed by cowardice when the targets are Jewish.

The effects are global. Antisemitism is no longer fringe—it is fashionable. It masquerades as solidarity and speaks the language of liberation. But it is hatred, plain and simple. And it is directed not only at Israel, but at the Jewish diaspora—and, by extension, at the very values Jews have long helped uphold.

Golda Meir famously said: "Peace will come when the Arabs love their children more than they hate us." That remains tragically true. But peace will also come only when the West begins to love the truth more than it fears discomfort; when we remember the difference between resistance and terrorism; when we stop rewarding grievance and start rewarding responsibility.

The Jewish people—both in Israel and across the diaspora—have stood for centuries as guardians of civilisation. They have gifted the world unparalleled contributions in ethics, medicine, law, science, and the arts. In return, they have been scapegoated, expelled, and massacred. Today, they face a newer, more insidious threat: a world in which victimhood is currency, truth is disposable, and moral cowardice is fashionable.

This is not just about Israel. The demonisation of Israel is a dress rehearsal for a broader civilisational collapse. A society that cannot distinguish between a democracy defending itself and a death cult hiding behind civilians is not morally serious. And a civilisation that punishes its defenders while lionising its destroyers is writing its own suicide note.

But it is not too late. We can rediscover the clarity of our convictions. We can still speak truth, even when it is unfashionable. We can stand with the Jewish people—not only because they need us, but because we need them. To defend Israel is to defend the West. And to defend the West, we must confront the perverse and unintended consequences of our own indulgent illusions.

Bigoted, Dishonest, & Sinister

Introduction

There is a point at which neutrality becomes evasion.

After patterns have been established, evidence weighed, and consequences observed, continued refusal to name bad faith is no longer restraint—it is complicity.

This chapter does not argue for outrage. It argues for clarity. Because when dishonesty is rewarded with deference and bigotry is excused as grievance, the cost is borne not by abstractions, but by people.

***

The BDS movement masquerades as a human rights campaign, but its true aim is to isolate and delegitimise the world's only Jewish state.

There is nothing noble about the Boycott, Divestment, and Sanctions (BDS) movement. Its language may be dressed in the vocabulary of human rights, but its purpose is far from humanitarian. BDS is not about peace or justice. It is a deliberate campaign to delegitimise the world's only Jewish state and to punish Israel for existing. Its aims are bigoted, its methods dishonest, and its consequences sinister.

The origins of the BDS movement can be traced to the 2001 Durban Conference, a United Nations anti-racism forum hijacked by activists who turned it into an anti-Israel hate fest. In 2005, a coalition of Palestinian organisations launched what we now know as BDS, calling on the world to boycott Israeli goods, divest from Israeli companies, and impose sanctions on the Israeli government. Framed as a grassroots civil rights campaign, BDS claims to be a non-violent means of opposing Israeli policy towards Palestinians. But beneath the surface, its intent is far more radical: to isolate Israel economically, culturally, and academically—until it collapses from within.

This is not conjecture. Its founders have stated it openly. Omar Barghouti, one of BDS's leading ideologues, has declared that the movement opposes a Jewish state "in any part of Palestine." In other words, the issue is not the so-called "occupation"—it is the very existence of Israel. BDS is not about borders or policy; it is about identity. It aims to lock Israelis out of the world community so that lies about them may be more easily believed.

The university sector has become a key battleground. Across the Western world, BDS campaigns have taken hold in student unions, faculty associations, and campus groups. Australia is no exception. What began as fringe rhetoric has spread—like an ideological contagion—through institutions that were once bastions of liberal inquiry. The movement punishes academic collaboration with Israelis, silences pro-Israel voices, and intimidates Jewish students under the guise of political activism.

Those who support BDS—an exclusionary campaign grounded in bias and misinformation—are among the least suited to be entrusted with the education of our youth. Participation in such a movement raises serious questions about judgment, impartiality, and the moral responsibilities we expect of educators.

Like the herpes simplex virus (commonly experienced as cold sores), it is unlikely to ever be fully eradicated. But, like that virus, it can be managed—in this case through vigilance, resilience, and the moral clarity of those willing to stand up.

Two organisations doing remarkable work in this space are the Australian Academic Alliance Against Antisemitism (5A) and StandWithUs Australia. These institutions do more than merely push back against antisemitism; they expose its roots, challenge its champions, and create safe space for truth.

5A a bold and necessary initiative. Launched by a diverse group of scholars from across the academic spectrum, 5A challenges the institutional biases and double standards that give antisemitism cover within higher education. It has exposed the growing trend of scholars who justify or rationalise violence against Jews and Israelis, and those who misuse academic freedom to promote political propaganda. 5A works to restore balance, reason, and intellectual honesty to an academic culture increasingly susceptible to ideological capture.

But what makes 5A truly important is its moral courage. Its members understand that antisemitism is a systemic toxin that, left untreated, corrodes not just Jewish safety but the entire academic enterprise. They are not content to simply condemn antisemitism when it becomes fashionable to do so—they are willing to name it, confront it, and hold their peers to account.

Meanwhile, *StandWithUs Australia* is fighting this battle from the ground up—student by student, campus by campus. Their work with university programs is essential. Through training, education, and advocacy, they equip students with the tools to speak up for Israel and to confront hate when it appears in lecture halls or student politics. They also run leadership programs that help develop the next generation of informed, confident advocates for coexistence and peace.

Importantly, *StandWithUs* focuses on building bridges, not burning them. They work with people of all backgrounds and beliefs, countering propaganda with facts, and fear with human connection. In an era when social media mobs are quick to vilify and shame, *StandWithUs* reminds us that knowledge, compassion, and courage remain our strongest tools.

At its core, BDS is a movement of exclusion. It seeks to deny Israel the right to participate in the global conversation. It punishes the Jewish people for their sovereignty. It cloaks itself in virtue but traffics in lies. But there is good news: it is losing. As more Australians become aware of BDS's true aims, and as organisations like 5A and StandWithUs continue to shine light into dark corners, the movement's credibility continues to erode.

This is a time for moral clarity. We must be prepared to call things by their name. BDS is not progressive. It is not anti-racist. It is bigoted, dishonest, and sinister. And it has no place in a society committed to truth and justice.

Six Hundred: A Horrible Milestone

Introduction

Numbers can obscure as easily as they reveal.

Counted individually, each death, hostage, or casualty carries its own story, its own circle of grief. Aggregated over time, those same lives risk being absorbed into abstraction—milestones rather than moral emergencies.

And yet milestones matter.

They tell us not only what has happened, but what has been allowed to continue. They mark the point at which denial becomes untenable, and where the cost of inaction can no longer be plausibly ignored.

This chapter is about one such milestone—and about what it exposes when patience, process, and restraint are repeatedly rewarded with indifference.

***

On 28 May 2025, the world marked a grim and shameful milestone—six hundred days since the October 7 massacre. And still, fifty-eight hostages remain in the hands of Hamas. Among them are women, elderly civilians, young people abducted from a music festival, and the bodies of the dead. Their continued captivity—and the silence, moral confusion, or outright equivocation of much of the international community—is an indictment not only of failed political leadership, but of the moral direction of the Western world itself.

This is not a Jewish tragedy alone. It is a Western one. Because what we choose to tolerate, we eventually become.

The Geneva Conventions—cornerstones of civilised warfare—are unambiguous: The taking of hostages is strictly prohibited. Article 3, common to all four conventions, forbids "violence to life and person," including murder, torture, and "the taking of hostages." These are not technicalities or cultural preferences. They are universal principles, written in the blood of the twentieth century. That they are now routinely flouted by a terrorist organisation that openly declares its genocidal intent should provoke widespread outrage. Instead, too many Western governments have chosen appeasement, abstraction—or worse, moral relativism masquerading as nuance.

In Judaism, the sanctity of life is paramount—and so too is the dignity of the dead. The refusal to return the bodies of hostages is not a political ploy; it is a deliberate psychological torment, designed to prolong suffering, prevent closure, and weaponize grief. It is cruel. It is calculated. And it works—because we care. Because civilised societies care.

We've seen this script before.

In June 2006, Corporal Gilad Shalit was kidnapped by Hamas in a cross-border raid near the Kerem Shalom crossing—an attack that, for comparison, would be akin to an ADF Reserve soldier being abducted by insurgents while on peacekeeping duties in a Pacific island nation. Shalit was just nineteen years old. He was held in Gaza for over five years, in isolation, without access to the Red Cross or outside communication. In 2011, Israel agreed to a painful exchange: 1,027 Palestinian prisoners in return for Shalit's freedom. Among them was Yahya Sinwar, a founding member of Hamas's military wing—one of the chief architects of the October 7 massacre.

That exchange, driven by humanitarian instinct, should have served as a cautionary tale. Instead, it became a blueprint—a signal to terrorists that Western empathy and Israeli humanity can be weaponised.

The hostage enterprise functions because it is effective. It preys on the very values that underpin democratic civilisation. But when that moral framework is manipulated—and when that manipulation is rewarded by naïve, compromised, or cowardly leaders—we don't just embolden terrorists. We betray our own values.

The Western world must now confront a hard truth: Who benefits when we pressure Israel to show restraint? Who gains when calls for "proportionality" echo louder than the cries of those still buried in tunnels beneath Gaza, denied light, freedom, and hope?

Terrorists understand the West better than many Westerners do. They know exactly which buttons to push—how to prompt a UN resolution, dominate a news cycle, or stir outrage on university campuses. They speak our language—"resistance," "colonialism," "decolonisation"—not because they believe it, but because they know we do. And they have no qualms about holding hostages in children's bedrooms or stockpiling weapons in hospitals.

And yet, under impossible pressure, Israel's democratically elected government has shown moral clarity and resolve. While Israel's enemies use civilians as shields and corpses as currency, Jerusalem has upheld its duty to protect its people and recover its citizens—despite a global chorus of weak-willed, posturing statements from leaders more concerned with social sentiment than security.

To those leaders I say: History will not be kind. Your timidity in the face of barbarism—your moral posturing while families mourn without graves—will not be remembered as diplomacy, but as dereliction.

We are witnessing not merely a war for territory, but a war for truth itself. And the truth is this:

Israel did not start this war. Hamas did.

Israel does not target civilians. Hamas does.

Israel values life. Hamas glorifies death.

To argue otherwise is to invert morality.

As Israeli statesman Abba Eban once remarked, *"History teaches us that men and nations behave wisely once they have exhausted all other alternatives."* Let us pray we do not exhaust our conscience before then.

And as Golda Meir so powerfully observed, *"We will only have peace with the Arabs when they love their children more than they hate us."*

Until that day, let the world mark this horrible milestone:

Six hundred days. Fifty-eight hostages. Countless shattered families.

And a Western world at the crossroads—forced to decide, yet again, whether it still stands for anything at all.

The Genocide Libel

Introduction

Few accusations carry greater moral weight than genocide.

It is therefore unsurprising that the term has been weaponised—stripped of its legal meaning and redeployed as a rhetorical instrument designed to end debate rather than clarify it.

This chapter examines the origins, misuse, and consequences of the genocide allegation against Israel—and explains why its casual invocation is not merely inaccurate, but corrosive to international law itself.

A Response to Omer Bartov's "I'm a Genocide Scholar. I Know It When I See It."[5]

On 15 July 2025, *The New York Times* published a provocative opinion piece by Dr. Omer Bartov titled "I'm a Genocide Scholar. I Know It When I See It." In it, Bartov—a Jewish professor of Holocaust and genocide studies at Brown University—accuses the State of Israel of actions that, in his view, bear the

---

5 Omer Bartov, "I'm a Genocide Scholar. I Know It When I See It," The New York Times, July 15, 2025, https://www.nytimes.com/2025/07/15/opinion/israel-gaza-holocaust-genocide-palestinians.html.

hallmarks of genocide. He contends that Israel's military campaign in Gaza is not only disproportionate but reflects a broader intent to erase Palestinian life and presence.

Bartov is not a fringe activist or conspiracy theorist. He is a credentialed and well-regarded academic—more thoughtful and grounded than many who have rushed to condemn Israel in recent months. Precisely for that reason, the piece is both disappointing and damaging. It diminishes his credibility while muddying the already fraught waters of international legal and moral discourse. The charge of genocide—arguably the gravest crime in human history—is too serious to be diluted by political assertion masquerading as analysis.

Let me begin with the short answer: Israel is not committing genocide.

Israel's three stated war aims in Gaza are clear:

- To return the remaining hostages.
- To dismantle Hamas as a governing and military entity, and
- To ensure that Gaza can never again pose an existential threat to the State of Israel.

These aims are proportionate and lawful. They align with Israel's inherent right to self-defence under Article 51 of the UN Charter. To conflate these objectives with genocidal intent is not merely inaccurate—it is defamatory.

Moreover, any article that leans on the moral authority of Francesca Albanese, Amnesty International, or the current Government of South Africa ought not be cited by a scholar who claims to take legal and evidentiary standards seriously.

The longer answer requires us to clarify what genocide is. The UN Convention on the Prevention and Punishment of the Crime of Genocide (1948) defines it as specific acts committed "with intent to destroy, in whole or in part, a national, ethnical, racial or religious group." Intent is the cornerstone. Destruction alone is not enough.

If anything, the tragedy of modern warfare is that genocide—when pursued—is now easier to execute than ever before. Consider Rwanda. The Uyghurs in China. The Khmer Rouge. The tools of industrial-scale murder have evolved, but the moral clarity remains: Genocide is deliberate, premeditated, and absolute. None of that applies here.

The battlefield reality in Gaza must not be ignored. It is not only densely populated—it is one of the most comprehensively militarised civilian environments in modern history. Hamas has spent more than a decade embedding its fighters, weapons, command posts, and tunnels beneath homes, mosques, schools, hospitals, and even UN facilities. These are not allegations—they are facts.

What is often overlooked is the depth of radicalisation among the civilian population itself. Gaza is not merely a military theatre—it is a society shaped by decades of ideological indoctrination. The scale and saturation of this radicalisation eclipses historical parallels. Not even the Hitler Youth were subjected to the generational, religiously wrapped, genocidal programming faced by Gazan children in UNRWA schools, summer camps, and state-run media. This is not a population merely living under Hamas—it is, in large part, shaped by it.

And yet, in this hostile environment, the IDF consistently takes steps to minimise civilian harm. These include text message alerts, phone calls, loudspeaker warnings, leaflet drops, "knock on the roof" munitions, and designated evacuation corridors. Entire city blocks are gazetted as Areas of Operation. This is not the conduct of an army intent on annihilation. Israel foregoes the tactical advantage of surprise—allowing terrorists time to lay ambushes or flee—in order to reduce civilian casualties. It puts IDF soldiers at greater risk to uphold a higher moral standard.

Israel and its soldiers—save for the rare bad actor or inevitable errors in the fog of war—have not lost their moral compass. For those who fail to see this now, perhaps time will offer clarity. For those ideologically incapable of seeing at all, Golda Meir's words remain apt: "A bad press headline is better than a good eulogy." In my objective assessment, Israel continues to act lawfully, ethically, and morally—even as partisan critics shout from the sidelines.

When I entered Gaza with the IDF in September 2024, I travelled the length of the Philadelphi Corridor—from Kerem Shalom to the Swedish Village. This fourteen-kilometre zone was once the lifeblood of Hamas, a hub of smuggling and external support from Iran, Qatar, and others. I saw some of the two hundred tunnels used to ferry weapons and fighters from Egyptian Rafah into Gaza. One was large enough to drive a truck through—its entrance, predictably, in the grounds of a mosque. Another was so narrow it could barely fit a man. I was briefed on Israel's efforts to drill more than two thousand vertical shafts to map and neutralise this subterranean threat. The IDF believed it had located all Egyptian smuggling tunnels, though no army can ever claim total certainty in war.

My delegation included respected figures such as General Sir John McColl, Colonel Richard Kemp, Major Andrew Fox, Barrister Natasha Hausdorff, and other distinguished journalists and veterans. In Rafah, we reviewed IDF operations that had successfully separated terrorists from civilians. At that point, nearly one thousand Hamas fighters had been eliminated, while reported non-combatant deaths were less than ten. The IDF was operating under intense global scrutiny, and in my professional judgment, doing so with extraordinary restraint and precision.

So let us return to Bartov's claim.

Is every building in Gaza a Hamas site? No. But far too many are booby-trapped, conceal tunnel shafts, or serve as weapons depots. Hamas deliberately uses civilian infrastructure to shield its fighters. Ironically, Israeli soldiers are often killed in these very homes precisely because the IDF refuses to flatten entire neighbourhoods. The destruction critics decry is often the direct result of Israeli restraint. That, too, is proportionality—a term widely misunderstood and frequently misused.

Occam's razor is useful here. The simplest explanation is often the correct one. Bartov, writing from the safety of a US university campus, may be mistaking complexity for conspiracy. He is engaged in a battle over narratives—but in doing so, he lends credibility to those who oppose liberal, pluralistic values.

Attempts to pacify Israel's enemies—through apology, concession, or withdrawal—have not brought peace. They have brought emboldenment. The hostages remain in captivity. The rockets continued to fall. History teaches that clarity, not capitulation, is the only path to deterrence.

And let us be honest: If Israel were to fall, does anyone believe the Church of the Holy Sepulchre would survive under Hamas or the Muslim Brotherhood? Or would it, like the Bamiyan Buddhas under the Taliban, be reduced to rubble? Speculative, yes—but not without precedent.

The better explanation for Israel's current operations is that peace was tried. In 2005, Israel unilaterally withdrew from Gaza.

The result was not peace, but a decade of rockets, tunnels, and trauma inflicted on a people already burdened by history. As Ronen Bergman argued in *Rise and Kill First*, sometimes survival demands pre-emption and perseverance.

What we are witnessing is not genocide—it is the lawful use of force within a defensive framework, confronting the latest front in an ancient hatred made modern. Once, Jews were vilified for being stateless; now, they are vilified for having a state. Zionism, once a lifeline for a persecuted people, is now slandered as colonialism. Today's antisemitism doesn't march in jackboots—it cloaks itself in the language of "intersectionality," "decolonisation," and performative solidarity. It no longer targets the individual Jew, but the collective Jew: the State of Israel.

It cannot be easy being a Jewish academic teaching genocide studies in a modern US university. It must feel like being a vegan in an abattoir. Whether Stockholm syndrome explains Bartov's position is not for me to say. But whatever the motive, the result is discrediting—particularly from someone who should know better.

There is also a broader moral question. If certain political factions among the Arab populations of the Levant—known collectively since Yasser Arafat's 1964 declaration as "Palestinians"—continue to pursue the destruction of the world's only Jewish state, they cannot simultaneously claim the privileges of peaceful coexistence with it. That is not racism. It is the moral logic of national survival.

President Trump once proposed a clean geographic separation. Another idea—rooted not in modern diplomacy but ancient wisdom—is to allow those who reject coexistence to remain stateless, like the Israelites once did, until a new generation arises ready for peace. The biblical precedent of forty years in the wilderness is apt. Reconstruction must never be a reward for genocidal hate.

In my judgment, the answer lies in separating Gaza into smaller, non-contiguous zones. When I served in Iraq (2007) and Afghanistan (2011 and 2013–14), I learned a hard truth: The people who rule a region are those who come to your house at 2 a.m., put a gun to your child's head, and demand obedience. This is what the anti-Israel commentariat fails to understand.

A freely mobile population of 2.2 million is an impossible security proposition—even for Israel. But a smaller, biometrically enrolled group of two hundred thousand, committed to peaceful coexistence, could begin anew. Likely comprising nuclear families—parents, grandparents, and infants/minors—living in traditional tribal structures, with a calibrated mix of carrots and sticks, safely separated from irreconcilables and malevolent actors. Let these families and reconcilable tribes live in a demilitarised "Zone D" in northern Gaza, with IDF-provided security and deradicalisation efforts led by Abraham Accords partners and Israeli Muslims in schools, mosques, and workplaces. The United Arab Emirates's Ministry of Tolerance is a compelling model of what a better tomorrow may look like. But for such a vision to succeed, the irreconcilables must be separated. The terrorists, the jihadists, and the ideologues have no place in a peaceful tomorrow. For now, their place is in tent camps—or perhaps Saudi Arabian prisons.

And another thing: One ought not to lose sight of the opportunity costs of this relentless focus on Gaza. How morally inverted have we become, that nearly thirty-seven million genuine refugees—registered with the UN High Commissioner for Refugees—suffer in camps across the globe, while billions of dollars flow into Gaza to prop up a radicalised population ruled by genocidaires and glorified by activists who've never read the Hamas Charter.

Academics should challenge power—but they must also practise humility, especially when passing judgment on the life-and-death decisions of democratic governments acting under fire. Israel's war is being fought by professional citizen-soldiers—many of whom likely did not vote for the current government and have no desire to take life, even when facing enemies who, given the chance, would repeat October 7 repeatedly. These young lions and lionesses are the best of us. They serve with discipline, restraint, and humanity in a conflict not of their choosing.

Bartov's credentials give his words weight. But in this case, he has confused the moral legacy of the Holocaust with a false equivalence that does not stand. His words will not protect civilians—they will be weaponised by Hamas, Iran, and their sympathisers. For them, genocide is not a slander. It is a strategy.

PART II
Conclusion

Decay is rarely acknowledged while it is underway.

It is easier to describe it as complexity, to attribute outcomes to forces beyond control, or to reassure ourselves that intentions matter more than results. But decay does not require malice to advance. It only requires delay.

By the time consequences are undeniable, societies often discover that the opportunity for clean correction has already passed. What remains is mitigation, containment, and the hope that damage has not yet become irreversible.

The question that follows, then, is not whether failure occurred, but how it came to be tolerated—and by whom.

To answer that, we must look not only at events, but at the stories told about them, the institutions that repeated those stories, and the moral frameworks that allowed fiction to replace judgment.

PART III

THE CAPTURE

How narrative replaced judgment

PART III
Introduction

Decay alone does not explain what followed.

Societies have endured corruption, incompetence, and even violence without losing their moral compass. What distinguishes this moment is not simply failure, but the stories told to excuse it.

When narrative replaces judgment, facts no longer correct error; they are rearranged to preserve belief. Language shifts. Responsibility dissolves. Harm is reframed as context, and restraint is recast as guilt.

This is not accidental. It is the result of capture—of institutions, ideas, and moral frameworks that once existed to clarify reality, now repurposed to obscure it.

What follows examines how that capture occurs, why it spreads so easily, and why its consequences are never confined to theory.

17

Based on Lies

Introduction

Most moral failures do not begin with cruelty.

They begin with a false premise—repeated often enough, and with sufficient confidence, that questioning it comes to feel impolite, even dangerous.

Once a lie is established as the foundation of a moral framework, everything built upon it acquires the appearance of legitimacy. Good intentions are redirected. Language is softened. Accountability is displaced.

This chapter examines how a small number of persistent falsehoods came to dominate public discourse—and why their endurance matters more than their origin.

***

Something has shifted in our public culture, and it is most visible not in extremists, but in ordinary conversations. I share here, without attribution, a message I was sent by an Upstander in late December 2025—a decent, non-Jewish Australian woman working quietly and diligently to correct an inversion that has taken hold in our society as it relates to Israel:

> I don't need you to reply, but I would like to understand something. I have a group of Labor-voting acquaintances, all aged between fifty-five and seventy-five. I would say that many of them now exhibit antisemitic traits—not always overt hostility, but a marked lack of empathy for Jewish people, a readiness to dismiss Jewish concerns, and an instinctive suspicion of Jewish power, influence, or motive. I am not suggesting this out of malice. I am trying to understand how this took root. When did it happen? How did it happen? And what, exactly, is it?

That question sits at the heart of this article.

Antisemitism rarely announces itself with swastikas. More often, it enters quietly—as moral certainty, ideological fashion, or the comforting belief that one is standing on the "right side of history." Historically, this is how it has always begun: not with violence, but with lies that soften conscience and dull compassion.

In my book *A Light Still Burns: Israel and the Values Worth Defending*, I wrote: "Antisemitism does not begin with hatred. It begins with permission—permission to believe things about Jews that we would never tolerate being said about any other people." Once that permission is granted, everything that follows becomes easier.

History is unambiguous. The Kishinev pogrom of 1903 was triggered by a lie—a blood libel accusing Jews of ritual murder. That lie was printed, repeated, and tolerated by respectable society before violence erupted. In Weimar Germany, the "stab-in-the-back" myth blamed Jews for Germany's defeat in the First World War. It did not emerge from the gutter; it was cultivated in universities, newspapers, salons, and political movements that regarded themselves as enlightened.

Violence followed lies—not the other way around.

So what is happening now?

From the late 1960s onward, large parts of the Western left underwent a profound ideological shift. Class struggle gave way to identity politics. Power displaced evidence as the organising principle. Groups were no longer judged by behaviour or values, but by where they sat in an invented hierarchy of victimhood. In this framework, Jews—inconveniently successful, stubbornly non-compliant, and possessing a sovereign state—ceased to qualify as victims and were reclassified as oppressors.

This is not a fringe observation. As the late Christopher Hitchens warned, "Anti-Zionism is the gateway drug to antisemitism." Douglas Murray has put it more starkly: "The world has decided that Jews are no longer allowed to be victims—only perpetrators." Historian Bernard Lewis noted decades ago that antisemitism survives by mutation, adopting the language of each new age while retaining its essential animus.

This reframing was not accidental. It was driven by intellectual movements that fused Marxism with post-colonial theory, recasting Jews as "white," "colonial," or "privileged," while erasing both Jewish indigeneity and Jewish history. The Holocaust became a museum piece—acknowledged, ritualised, then quietly bracketed off as no longer relevant to contemporary moral judgement.

As I observed in *A Light Still Burns*: "When Jews are weak, the world pities them. When Jews are strong, the world resents them." That resentment now routinely masquerades as progressivism.

Australia did not invent this phenomenon, but it imported it wholesale—through universities, activist networks, and, critically, through publicly funded media institutions. Over time, these ideas filtered into mainstream left-leaning voters, many of whom still see themselves as anti-racist, compassionate, and morally serious. The tragedy is that they often do not recognise what they have absorbed.

Compassion is not withdrawn because Jews have done something wrong; it is withdrawn because Jews no longer fit the story.

Here the role of the Australian Broadcasting Corporation warrants scrutiny. As the nation's most influential cultural narrator, the ABC does not merely report events; it frames moral understanding. Through persistent "contextualisation," selective omission, and the normalisation of activist language, it has too often blurred the distinction between explanation and excuse—particularly when it comes to Israel and Jewish self-defence.

This confusion is compounded by a phenomenon unfamiliar to many non-Jews: that a very small minority of Jews actively promote narratives hostile to Jewish self-determination. Their presence is then weaponised to legitimise antisemitism under the guise of "Jewish dissent." That such voices are frequently elevated by the ABC and other media outlets creates a distorted impression of Jewish opinion and provides moral cover for prejudice.

This is not about a single program or journalist. It is institutional drift—negligent at best, deceptive at worst—and it matters because trust in a national broadcaster confers authority. When that authority is misused, lies acquire legitimacy.

There is a bitter historical irony here. During the Second World War, both Britain and Australia enacted strict laws to prevent speech or conduct that might undermine morale or national cohesion. Governments understood that narratives could weaken a society long before an enemy ever fired a shot. Today, we appear to have forgotten that lesson entirely.

We now tolerate claims about Jews and Israel that would be socially—and in some cases legally—unthinkable if directed elsewhere. Assertions of genocide, famine, or apartheid are repeated as fact, despite failing legal, demographic, and evidentiary tests. Meanwhile, the documented radicalisation of parts of Gaza and the West Bank—funded in no small measure by international aid streams, including through UNRWA—is minimised or ignored. Australian taxpayers deserve better scrutiny of where their money has gone and what it has enabled.

This is not accidental drift. It is all based on a lie—the lie that antisemitism has changed its nature; that it is now virtuous; that it can cloak itself in the language of justice while retaining the same ancient animus.

History shows that when antisemitism becomes respectable—when it is explained away rather than confronted—violence eventually follows. In Australia, that warning is no longer theoretical. It is no longer future tense. We have crossed that threshold.

I did not write *A Light Still Burns* to sell books. I wrote it to sound an alarm. As a father, I wrote it as though the safety of my unborn descendants depended on its message—because history suggests that it does.

There is no easy fix for cutting through the lies, artifice, and deception now embedded in our institutions. But there is a starting point. Read *A Light Still Burns* as though your own children's future depends on understanding what is unfolding. Then pass it quietly to five open-minded, non-Jewish friends. Change does not begin with mass movements; it begins with ripples—and ripples, over time, become waves.

And by the time violence becomes undeniable, the lie has already done its work.

18

Losing Ourselves: Has the West Forgotten What Made It Strong?

Introduction

Civilisations do not fail for lack of information.

They fail when confidence in their own moral inheritance erodes—when the values that sustained them are treated as liabilities rather than achievements.

This chapter steps back from events to ask a broader question: What has the West forgotten about itself, and what must be recovered if renewal is to be possible?

***

I grew up in a home where Sunday dinners were sacred. Extended family, a roast in the oven, stories passed across generations, and the comforting sense that you were part of something enduring. That was the Australia I knew as a boy—one with deep roots in tradition, family, and shared values. Today, in our gleaming cities packed with people, it's astonishing how lonely so many feel.

The bonds that once tied us—faith, family, ritual, community—are fraying, and in many places have snapped entirely.

What the Christian West has drifted away from—at great peril—has been preserved for millennia in Judaism. Not just in abstract theology, but in lived ritual: Shabbat dinners that bring families together without screens; holidays that reconnect communities to history and meaning; multi-generational homes that revere wisdom and tradition. These aren't just customs—they are civilisational pillars. Their erosion hasn't made us freer. It has made us rootless.

On a Saturday in May 2025, while visiting a family member in Denver, Colorado, I attended Shabbat services at Aish Shul. I witnessed three or four generations of Jewish families—grandparents, parents, and young children—gathered in worship, song, and warmth amid great turbulence and uncertainty in the wider world. An armed guard stood at the entrance—not to intimidate, but to protect this peaceful, joyful community from the ignorance and barbarism that still lurks outside. Inside, children played without a care in the world. The adults prayed, reflected, and laughed. As an outsider—a non-Jewish Australian Army veteran—I was made to feel completely welcome. The Rabbis spoke with wisdom, humour, and charisma. I left humbled, inspired, and strengthened by the beauty of what I had witnessed.

Even Richard Dawkins—perhaps the world's most famous atheist—has had cause to reconsider. In a striking public shift, he recently declared himself a "Cultural Christian," acknowledging that the stories, music, and moral framework of Christianity form the bedrock of Western civilisation. Dawkins, who once dismissed religion as mere superstition, now warns that abandoning Christianity wholesale risks ushering in something far worse. "I prefer the sound of church bells to the call of the muezzin," he said—not to disparage others, but to defend the civilisational culture we've inherited. If even Dawkins sees the danger in losing our moral foundations, should we not ask what else we're carelessly letting slip?

Since October 7, 2023, when Hamas launched its barbaric assault on Israel, I have watched the West's reaction with a mixture of despair, disbelief, and—ironically—renewed inspiration. Despair, at the moral confusion displayed by so many in our universities, newsrooms, and streets. Disbelief, at how easily otherwise educated people swallowed Hamas propaganda. But also, inspiration—in the quiet strength, moral clarity, and communal cohesion of Jewish communities around the world.

From July 2019 to September 2021, I lived in Jerusalem while seconded to the United Nations as a senior unarmed peacekeeper. For twenty-seven months, my wife and I had the extraordinary privilege of seeing Israel not as a headline but as a home. We were welcomed into the lives of Jewish, Druze, Christian Arab, and Muslim Arab citizens. I saw what most Western commentators never bother to explore: the complexity, coexistence, and resilience that define the real Israel.

That experience forged bonds that have only deepened since October 7. I count many Jews among my closest friends—some of the most intelligent, hard-working, and decent people I have ever met. I know their values because they are, or once were, ours too: the courage to defend life, the sanctity of truth, the strength of tradition, the love of learning, and the willingness to sacrifice for others.

And yet now we see masked agitators parading through our cities chanting "From the river to the sea"—a genocidal slogan calling for the eradication of the world's only Jewish state. These aren't just misguided chants; they are vile, juvenile slogans embraced by cowards and useful idiots. And too many in the West lack the courage—or clarity—to call them out. This is not compassion. It is complicity.

Let me be clear: The attack on Israel was not just an attack on Jews. It was an assault on civilisation itself—on the right to live in peace, the dignity of women, the safety of children, and the fundamental truths that underpin Western liberal democracy. Israel is not perfect, but it is our ally, our mirror, and our warning.

Our warning, because what has made Israel strong is precisely what the West has forgotten. Israel still believes in nationhood. In family. In responsibility. In faith—whether religious or civil. In the truth that freedom comes with duties, not just rights. Meanwhile, too much of the West has sunk into narcissism, nihilism, and performative outrage.

We are being led to the brink by fools—many cloaked in fashionable ideologies and keffiyehs, shouting slogans they barely understand. Their sense of justice is a mile wide and an inch deep. And we—especially our elites—have grown too timid to speak plainly: Hamas are terrorists. Antisemitism is a moral cancer. And the West is still worth defending.

If you want to know what strength looks like, look to the Jewish people. Look at a community that has buried its dead, mourned its murdered children, and still finds time to gather for Shabbat, to sing, to teach, to build. That is not weakness. That is civilisational power.

The West still has time. But not much. We must return to our roots—not in a reactionary or exclusionary way, but with the courage to reclaim the virtues that once sustained us. Traditions matter. Family matters. Truth matters. And unless we are willing to defend them, we will lose them.

We don't need to become Jews. But we must learn from them.

And if you are a person of goodwill—regardless of faith or background—I encourage you: Introduce yourself to the local Jewish community where you live. Get to know the Rabbis. Across my military service, I found that chaplains—our 'padres'—whether Catholic, Anglican, Jewish or otherwise, were among the kindest, wisest, and most compassionate people in any formation. Their mission was never about proselytising. It was always about service, decency, and care for their fellow man. In an age where so many feel lost, perhaps the answers are simpler, and closer to home, than we care to admit.

19

Lies Have Consequences

Introduction

Words are often treated as harmless—as expressions rather than actions.

But language does not merely describe reality. It shapes it. Repeated often enough, certain narratives do more than mislead; they authorise.

When violence is contextualised, responsibility blurred, and intent inverted, the result is not neutrality, but permission.

This chapter traces the path from rhetorical distortion to physical consequence—and explains why the distance between the two is far shorter than many assume.

***

On the night of May 21, 2025, a young couple—Yaron Lischinsky and Sarah Lynn Milgrim—were murdered outside the Capital Jewish Museum in Washington, DC. Both worked at the Israeli Embassy and had just attended an event hosted by the American Jewish Committee. According to eyewitness reports, their alleged killer shouted "Free, free Palestine" as he was arrested. The motive appears disturbingly clear: They were targeted not for anything they had done, but for who they were—young Jews, visibly affiliated with the Israeli state.

Their deaths are not isolated tragedies. They are the latest and most visible warning of a deeper moral rot spreading throughout the West—a rot legitimised by lies, fuelled by ignorance, and tolerated, even enabled, by far too many. We are now reaping the harvest of ideological indulgence and cowardice. And no one should be surprised.

I woke up to this horrible news. Overnight, a non-Jewish friend messaged me: *"Mate, I hope you're not in DC."* That simple sentence gave me pause. How has it come to this? Is my life now at risk too? For what, exactly? For the crime of serving my country honourably for over thirty-one years in the Australian Army, a defence force? For having served as an unarmed military peacekeeper in Israel, Lebanon, Syria, Jordan, and Egypt? For forming close friendships with Israeli Jews, Druze, Christian Arabs, and Muslim Arabs—alongside Lebanese and Syrian nationals—based on mutual respect and shared humanity?

Having lived in the Levant for over two years, I can say categorically that the way Israel is portrayed in much of the Western media is utter nonsense. The crude distortions, the double standards, the erasure of context and history—it's as if truth itself has become the enemy.

Is my life now at risk because I have founded a nascent global charity to combat antisemitism—modelled on the visionary work of Senator J. William Fulbright after the Second World War—to allow reasonable, open-minded non-Jews to safely experience Israel for themselves? Does that make me guilty of some modern "thought crime"? It certainly feels that way.

Since October 7, 2023—the day Hamas launched its monstrous assault on southern Israel, murdering, raping, and abducting civilians in acts of medieval savagery—I have found myself repeatedly shocked not just by the depravity of terrorists, but by the reactions of those I once thought reasonable. I have seen it up close, among people I've known for most of my adult life.

A former schoolmate from Brisbane Grammar—someone I shared classrooms and rugby fields with in the early 1990s—now parrots slogans that would make Hamas propagandists blush. "From the River to the Sea," he declares online, apparently unaware—or unwilling to admit—that such a slogan calls for the eradication of the world's only Jewish state.

Another example: A Sri Lankan-born defence contractor working in Canberra's Department of Defence, who once impressed me with his intellect and professionalism, now floods social media with vitriol. Sharing memes and propaganda indistinguishable from that of open antisemites, he packages his hatred as "human rights advocacy." It is anything but.

Even an Australian Army veteran of Iraq and Afghanistan—someone who wore the same uniform I have proudly served in for over three decades—has embraced this descent. Now involved in the Australian union movement, his public posts cast Israel as a colonial oppressor, while studiously ignoring the atrocities of those who slaughtered children in their beds and burned families alive.

I am no longer surprised. But I remain outraged.

Because the truth matters. And lies—repeated often enough, broadcast widely enough, left unchallenged long enough—have consequences.

We are not talking about policy disagreements or differences of opinion. We are talking about a complete moral inversion. By endlessly pontificating about what they *think* is happening in

Gaza—while refusing to confront what *has* happened in Israel—far too many have become useful idiots in a propaganda war waged by terrorists.

We are living in Orwellian times. Truth is no longer a defence; it is an inconvenience. Every instinct and historical precedent suggests that things may get worse before they get better—if, indeed, they improve at all. The times amidst which we live are deeply troubling. Perhaps we in the West are closer to midnight than many may perceive.

But there is still time—if we act. I call on people of good will to help end this madness. To call out the terrorists and terrorist sympathisers in our midst and ensure they face consequences befitting their behaviour. A helpful tip: They are the ones concealing their identities in keffiyehs, not those quietly wearing a kippah on their way to and from synagogue.

Silence is complicity. And appeasement is betrayal.

Lies have consequences. We see them now—in broken lives, in bloodstained sidewalks, in the haunted eyes of a community once again forced to bury its young. It is not too late to speak, to stand, to act. But time is short. And the stakes could not be higher.

20

When the Watchdog Becomes the Arsonist

Introduction

Institutions earn trust slowly.

They are granted authority on the assumption that they will correct excess, challenge falsehood, and apply standards evenly—especially when public emotion runs high.

When those same institutions abandon that role, the damage is compounded. The problem is no longer error, but amplification.

This chapter examines what happens when bodies entrusted with restraint instead legitimise distortion—and why institutional failure is uniquely corrosive to public judgment.

***

There are many brave and professional men and women working within the United Nations system. I've had the privilege of meeting some of them—officers, analysts, translators, peacekeepers, humanitarian workers—many of whom serve with courage, competence, and deep moral conviction in some of the world's most dangerous and complex environments.

But when a noble institution is captured by activists, even the best among its ranks are undermined. The United Nations, founded on the ashes of world war to uphold peace and human dignity, is being steadily hollowed out by a creeping ideological bias that is not just unhelpful—it is dangerous.

Nowhere is this more apparent than in the case of Francesca Albanese, the UN Special Rapporteur on the Palestinian Territories.

Let us be clear: The problem here is not merely ineptitude. It is bias. And that bias is fuelling conflict, not resolving it.

Albanese was appointed to an important and sensitive role—reporting on the human rights situation in geography the United Nations refers to as "the Palestinian territories occupied since 1967." But rather than discharge that mandate with balance and rigour, she has become a partisan crusader. Worse still, her record reveals repeated expressions of deeply troubling prejudice and open hostility to Israel—not just its government, but its very legitimacy as a state.

A misconduct review published by Israel's Ministry of Foreign Affairs on 20 June 2024, titled *United Nations Agencies Bias Uncovered*, provides extensive evidence of Albanese's disqualifying conduct.[6] The report is worth reading in full. Yes, it comes from an official Israeli source. Some may see that as partisan. But the facts speak for themselves—and the quotes are drawn directly from her own speeches, articles, and public remarks. In them, Albanese accuses Israel of genocide. She suggests the "Jewish lobby" controls the United States. She downplays the Holocaust and openly defends terrorist acts as "resistance." These are not isolated lapses of judgment. They form a consistent

6 Francesca Albanese: A Comprehensive Review of Misconduct as a UN Special Rapporteur, Israel Ministry of Foreign Affairs, June 20, 2024, https://govextra.gov.il/mda/francescaalbanese/un-misconduct-review.

pattern—one that renders her unfit to serve as a UN Special Rapporteur.

A case could reasonably be made that Francesca Albanese is the most odious employee currently on the UN payroll.

The tragedy is not only that she has failed Israelis—whose legitimate concerns for security and sovereignty she dismisses with contempt. She has also failed the very people she claims to advocate for: Palestinians, and more broadly, Arabs across the Levant.

In Lebanon, Syria, Jordan, and the West Bank, generations of young people are growing up with grievance, not opportunity; with incitement, not hope. What they need are peacemakers, bridge-builders, and truth-tellers. What they get instead is a UN official who stokes division and radicalism—undermining the very cause of peace she purports to advance.

When the UN grants such a platform to someone like Albanese, it forfeits its role as an honest broker. Worse, it emboldens extremists on all sides. Moderate Arabs and Israelis alike are pushed to the margins, while international discourse descends into tribalism, slogans, and selective outrage.

This is not a failure of detail. It is a failure of principle.

Albanese's defenders argue she is simply "telling hard truths." But telling half-truths soaked in animus is not bravery—it is propaganda. She does not offer a path to peace; she is a demolition crew masquerading as a diplomat.

Of course, the UN's problems do not begin or end with Francesca Albanese. Agencies such as UNRWA—which receive hundreds of millions in Western funding—have long been plagued by credible allegations of corruption, incitement, and direct ties to terrorism. Some of its employees actively participated in the atrocities of October 7. Its school textbooks have glorified violence for decades. And yet, year after year, the funding has flowed.

This is not mere dysfunction. It is moral abdication.

When an institution fails this comprehensively, the instinct of many good people is to walk away in disgust. But we cannot afford that luxury. The UN still matters. Its mission still matters. But for it to mean anything, we must demand far higher standards of conduct, transparency, and integrity.

The first step is accountability. Francesca Albanese should be removed from her role immediately. The credibility of the United Nations depends on it. But even that is not enough.

Western democracies must stop writing blank cheques to the UN while its bodies behave like ideological echo chambers instead of neutral guardians of peace.

The world's leading economies and financial contributors to the United Nations—already burdened by mounting debt—can no longer afford to throw good money after bad. In mid 2025, the United States, for instance, carries a national debt exceeding $36 trillion, amounting to approximately 124 percent of its GDP. Japan's debt stands at over 234 percent of GDP—the highest among developed nations. France and Italy also grapple with debt-to-GDP ratios above 115 percent and 138 percent, respectively. These are not theoretical concerns. They demand discipline.

Continued financial support for the UN as a whole—and for entities within it that betray their mandates—is not just fiscally irresponsible. It corrodes the very values those institutions were created to defend. In an era of competing priorities and shrinking trust, accountability must be the price of admission.

To those who care about fairness, decency, and the moral foundations of our civilisation—regardless of faith or background—don't take my word for it. Read the report. Examine Albanese's own words. Ask yourself whether someone who traffics in conspiracy, grievance, and contempt for an entire people should speak for the international community.

The answer is self-evident.

The United Nations must choose reform or irrelevance. Because in its current state, it is not advancing peace—it is obstructing it. And with every day that Francesca Albanese remains in office, the institution drifts further from the ideals on which it was founded.

The time for polite silence is over. When the watchdog becomes the arsonist, our only responsible course is to sound the alarm—and act decisively to extinguish the flames before the house is reduced to ash. That begins by removing the accelerants. Starting with Francesca Albanese.

Public Funds, Private Agendas: The Decline of the ABC

Introduction

Public broadcasters occupy a privileged position.

Funded by citizens and insulated from commercial pressure, they are meant to provide ballast—to slow narratives rather than accelerate them.

When that role is compromised, the effects ripple outward. Trust erodes. Polarisation deepens. And citizens are left unsure not only of what to believe, but whom.

This chapter examines how one such institution lost its way—and why the consequences extend far beyond any single network.

***

The Australian Broadcasting Corporation (ABC), once a trusted pillar of public life, is increasingly drawing criticism for editorial conduct many now view as deeply partisan and corrosive to informed democratic debate. Its handling of antisemitism—one of the most urgent and sensitive issues in contemporary Australian society—is becoming indefensible.

This was again laid bare during the 10 July 2025 edition of 7.30, hosted by Sarah Ferguson, in which Jillian Segal—Australia's special envoy to combat antisemitism—was given anything but a fair hearing. Segal, a respected lawyer and business leader, was appointed in 2024 to address the unprecedented rise in antisemitism across the country. Her proposals are measured, serious, and long overdue, including tougher penalties for hate crimes and oversight mechanisms to ensure public institutions fulfil their obligations.

Yet Ferguson, rather than allowing Segal to present her case and inform the public, adopted a confrontational posture more befitting a political adversary than a public servant appointed to address a national crisis. Would another eminent Australian—Sir Peter Cosgrove, for instance—have been treated in such a manner while assisting Queensland's recovery after Cyclone Larry in 2006?

Ferguson's conduct was not only unprofessional; it was also a missed opportunity. Viewers—many of whom are grappling with growing unease about antisemitism—would have benefitted from hearing directly from Segal. Appointed by our elected government, her role carries national weight. Her perspective, grounded in broad consultation and policy development, deserved to be heard respectfully. I suspect many Australians tuned in hoping to learn more. What they received instead was an exercise in editorial disdain.

A dear friend of mine—an interfaith leader and descendant of Holocaust survivors—was so disturbed by Ferguson's 7.30 interview that she penned an open letter. She wrote:

"Rather than allowing Jillian to inform the listeners of her proposal, you went into attack mode immediately.... You are not serving the public by your biased attitudes dominating a discussion that could have informed your listeners."

This is not a new problem. In 2015, an internal ABC review found that Ferguson's interview with then–Treasurer Joe Hockey breached the organisation's impartiality standards. These are not isolated lapses; they reveal a pattern—and a cultural drift that is now endemic.

To demonstrate that the ABC's problems are systemic—not limited to one presenter—Segal was subjected to further mistreatment the following morning on Radio National Breakfast, 11 July 2025. The first question she faced wasn't about her proposals, but a hostile challenge apparently sourced from the so-called "Jewish Council of Australia."

For those unfamiliar with the internal politics of the Australian Jewish community, let me clarify: This is not the respected Jewish Communal Appeal (JCA) of New South Wales. The so-called "Jewish Council of Australia" is a fringe outfit that speaks for virtually no one. Its posture is little different from a handful of anarchists calling themselves the "Council for Western Civilisation." That such a group was chosen to frame the first public question to Australia's Special Envoy is telling. It suggests not a desire to inform or clarify, but to undermine and provoke.

This is not public broadcasting. It is editorial activism masquerading as journalism.

Antisemitism in Australia is surging. Since October 7, we've witnessed graffiti, bomb threats, violent protests, the desecration of Jewish schools and childcare centres, and physical attacks. The Jewish community is not crying wolf—it is crying out for help. Yet the ABC, whose taxpayer-funded charter obliges it to reflect the diversity of Australian life, increasingly gives voice to those who deny, distort, or downplay that reality.

How can reasonable, open-minded Australians better understand antisemitism when even basic efforts to explain it are shouted down or sideswiped?

As a taxpayer, I can no longer support public money being used to fund this kind of bias. If the ABC cannot uphold its own charter—if it cannot treat Jewish Australians and their concerns with the same respect it demands for others—then its role as a national broadcaster must be re-evaluated.

This is not a call to silence voices. It is a call to restore fairness, professionalism, and decency. The ABC need not agree with Jillian Segal. But it must afford her—and all Australians concerned about hatred and bigotry—the right to be heard without hostility.

22

Balcony over Jerusalem: Five Failings of John Lyons's Worldview

Introduction

Narrative capture rarely announces itself.

It does not arrive as censorship or conspiracy, but as professional consensus—a shared moral language, reinforced by institutions, rewarded by peers, and rarely examined from within. Over time, the role of journalism subtly shifts from interrogating power to enforcing a frame; from informing the public to instructing it how to feel.

This chapter examines one prominent case within that broader pattern.

John Lyons is not a marginal voice. He is a senior journalist writing from the centre of Australia's most influential public broadcaster, carrying institutional authority into a conflict most Australians will never experience firsthand. His work matters not because it is uniquely hostile or malicious, but because it exemplifies a mode of reporting that feels humane while quietly narrowing understanding.

This essay does not argue that Israel should be beyond criticism. Democracies require scrutiny. What it examines instead is how criticism becomes distorted when it is guided by unexamined assumptions, reinforced by professional echo chambers, and insulated from strategic consequence.

Balcony over Jerusalem is treated here not as an isolated memoir, but as a case study in how moral certainty can coexist with analytical blindness—and how journalism, once captured by a worldview, can obscure reality even as it claims to illuminate it.

A View from a Balcony Is Still a View from Above

Few Australian journalists have exercised as much influence over domestic perceptions of Israel as John Lyons, the long-serving Middle East correspondent and Global Affairs Editor for the Australian Broadcasting Corporation. Over a career spanning more than three decades, Lyons has reported from major conflict zones and political flashpoints, building a public reputation as a hard-nosed correspondent with a strong human-interest instinct—and a pronounced tendency to frame power as suspect and the powerless as morally central.

That stature matters because it confers authority—particularly among Australian audiences who will never live in the Levant, never serve in uniform, never sit in a shelter during rocket sirens, and never have to make real-world decisions under existential threat. Lyons is not writing from the margins. He is writing from the centre of Australia's most influential public broadcaster, with all the institutional legitimacy that implies.

Balcony over Jerusalem: A Middle East Memoir – Israel, Palestine and Beyond was first published by HarperCollins Publishers Australia in July 2017. The edition examined here is the updated version—now including a foreword by Stan Grant and a new author's note—explicitly framed in the shadow of the post–October 7 Gaza war. A widely distributed release of this updated edition, including the HarperCollins digital audiobook, is dated April 2024. It is this retrospective framing—this attempt to "give context" to the current war—that makes Lyons's worldview more consequential, not less.

In *Balcony over Jerusalem*, Lyons invites readers to see Israel—and the conflict surrounding it—through his eyes: those of a foreign correspondent positioned, as he presents it, at a privileged vantage point over one of the world's most contested cities. The metaphor is revealing. A balcony offers elevation, distance, and comfort. It allows one to observe without being immersed; to comment without bearing responsibility; and to feel informed without being implicated. Lyons's book is fluent, morally certain, and notably insulated from the strategic, cultural, and civilisational realities that shape Israel's behaviour and its enemies' intentions.

This critique does not argue that Lyons should not criticise Israel. Criticism is legitimate—and necessary—in any democracy. It argues instead that *Balcony over Jerusalem* fails as serious analysis because it rests on a narrow worldview—reinforced by professional consensus and ideological habit—rather than rigorous engagement with the region as it actually is.

Five major failings stand out, addressed in turn below. Before doing so, it is worth briefly situating the man and his professional formation.

Who Is John Lyons—and How Does He See the World?

To understand *Balcony over Jerusalem*, it is necessary to understand its author.

John Lyons was born in 1961 and has spent most of his adult life in journalism. He has worked in senior editorial roles at *The Australian* and *The Sydney Morning Herald*, served as a foreign correspondent in the Middle East, and later became Global Affairs Editor at the ABC. Over the course of his career, he has won multiple Walkley Awards and has been named Australian Journalist of the Year—honours that reflect both longevity and institutional esteem.

Lyons spent six years based in Jerusalem earlier in his career, reporting on Israel and the Palestinian territories during a period of sustained violence and political upheaval. That experience forms the narrative backbone of *Balcony over Jerusalem*. More recently, he served as the ABC's North America correspondent, based in Washington, DC, covering US politics, global affairs, and international security.

He is not a marginal commentator or a fleeting visitor. He is a senior journalist operating within a recognisable Western foreign-correspondent tradition: sceptical of state power, emotionally attentive to suffering, and inclined to treat military force as presumptively suspect. Those instincts can produce valuable journalism. But when they harden into a default template—when they become the lens through which all facts are filtered—they produce something else: a predictable morality play.

Lyons's worldview, as it appears in this book, places Israel in the role of dominant moral actor: a strong Western-aligned state whose legitimacy is perpetually conditional, whose security claims are routinely questioned, and whose use of force is treated less as tragic necessity than as evidence of moral failure. Palestinian society, by contrast, is typically framed through grievance and constraint, with violence contextualised rather than confronted and internal dysfunction treated as peripheral. Lyons rarely needs to state these priors explicitly; they sit beneath the prose like foundations.

And when foundations go unexamined, the structure built upon them is rarely stable.

The Trump Exchange: What Happened, When, and Why It Matters

For international readers unfamiliar with Lyons, one moment in September 2025 brought his profile sharply into global view.

On Tuesday, 16 September 2025, at a White House press event in Washington, DC, Lyons—then serving as the ABC's North America correspondent—asked Donald Trump whether it was appropriate for a sitting president to be engaged in extensive private business activity while in office. The question was framed directly and publicly.

Trump responded combatively. After asking Lyons where he was from and hearing "the Australian Broadcasting Corporation," he replied that Lyons was "hurting Australia," accused him of setting "a very bad tone," and instructed him to be quiet when Lyons attempted to follow up. Two days later, the ABC was excluded from a subsequent Trump–Keir Starmer press conference during Trump's UK visit—officially described as a logistical decision, but widely understood as connected to the earlier exchange.

Whether one admires Lyons for asking the question or dislikes him for it, the episode illustrates his professional brand:

adversarial, morally charged, and confident that the journalist's role is to prosecute the powerful. The deeper question is what happens when that same posture is applied habitually, predictably, and asymmetrically to a small democracy fighting adversaries who openly articulate annihilationist aims.

Voices Favourable to Lyons—and What They're Really Praising

It is worth acknowledging the strongest case made in Lyons's favour, because it explains the book's appeal.

Lyons is frequently praised—particularly within ABC and aligned media circles—for his empathy and focus on civilian suffering. The updated edition of *Balcony over Jerusalem* is endorsed in its promotional framing by figures such as Stan Grant and Sarah Ferguson, who characterise the work as humane and morally serious.

Many readers experience this as corrective: a counterweight to propaganda, a reminder that strategy has victims, and that narratives can desensitise. There is a genuine moral impulse here, and it deserves respect.

But empathy is not analysis. And "standing with the suffering" can become a substitute for holding the architects of suffering accountable—particularly when suffering is strategically cultivated, prolonged, and weaponised for political ends.

Voices Critical of Lyons—and What They're Actually Saying

Criticism of Lyons does not come only from partisan defenders of Israel or ideological opponents of the ABC. Some of the most substantive critiques focus on method rather than motive—on how the story is constructed, what is foregrounded, and what is persistently marginalised.

One such critique comes from the Australia/Israel & Jewish Affairs Council (AIJAC), which has examined *Balcony over Jerusalem* as emblematic of a broader pattern in Western reporting. AIJAC argues that Lyons' memoir relies heavily on narrative selection: foregrounding Israeli actions while treating Palestinian political culture, leadership failure, and ideological drivers as contextual background rather than causal forces. The criticism is not that Lyons invents facts, but that he assigns weight asymmetrically—guiding readers toward moral conclusions without fully engaging the strategic realities that explain Israeli behaviour or the internal dynamics that perpetuate the conflict.

A second, related critique has been articulated by analysts associated with CAMERA (Committee for Accuracy in Middle East Reporting and Analysis). CAMERA's concern is not Lyons's empathy, but what that empathy consistently displaces. Their analysis notes that Palestinian violence is frequently contextualised as reactive or inevitable, while Israeli decision-making is treated as discretionary and ideological. Islamist ideology, incitement, and the strategic use of civilian suffering are acknowledged, but rarely examined as central explanatory variables. The result, they argue, is journalism that feels morally serious while leaving audiences strategically ill-informed.

Taken together, these critiques converge on a single point. The charge is not always malice. It is narrowing.

When a moral frame is selected early and reinforced through emphasis, selection, and narrative tone, reporting can appear balanced while quietly steering readers away from uncomfortable causes and toward familiar conclusions. Over time, a style of journalism emerges that feels humane and sophisticated but leaves its audience less capable of understanding why the conflict persists, why concessions repeatedly fail, and why Israel behaves as it does under conditions most Western societies have never faced.

The ABC and the Echo-Chamber Problem

Any serious critique of Lyons must also address the institutional ecosystem that rewards his style of reporting.

The ABC prides itself on independence, but like most Western public broadcasters it is vulnerable to a particular form of groupthink: not conspiracy, but cultural homogeneity. In foreign coverage, this often manifests as reflexive suspicion of Western-aligned states and near-automatic sympathy for actors framed as weaker or marginalised.

That dynamic is intensified in Jerusalem, where a recognisable professional-social circuit exists among foreign correspondents, NGO staff, diplomats, and activists—often intersecting in the same venues, reinforcing shared assumptions, and treating dissenting frames as morally suspect. In such an environment, a journalist can feel embattled while being continuously affirmed.

This is how an echo chamber forms: not through censorship, but through reward. Certain storylines travel further. Certain emphases are applauded. Certain complexities become inconvenient.

Balcony over Jerusalem reads less like an interrogation of that ecosystem than a product of it.

Failing One: An Ideological Frame That Precedes the Evidence

The most fundamental weakness of *Balcony over Jerusalem* is that its conclusions are evident before its arguments begin.

Lyons writes from within a settled ideological framework in which Israel is cast as the dominant moral actor, Palestinian society as primarily reactive, and Western liberal norms as universally portable regardless of context. Evidence is then selected, arranged, and interpreted to reinforce that frame.

This is not investigative journalism; it is confirmatory narration.

What complicates moral asymmetry—rejectionism, internal repression, eliminationist ideology, and the strategic use of civilian suffering—appears, but rarely as a driver. Israeli actions, by contrast, are treated as primary causes: discretionary, ideological, and morally freighted.

The effect is not balance. It is moral choreography.

Failing Two: The Erasure of Palestinian Agency

A persistent distortion in Lyons's work is the minimisation of Palestinian agency.

Violence emerges as response rather than choice. Radicalisation appears as outcome rather than strategy. Leadership failure is framed as consequence rather than cause of political stagnation and perpetual conflict.

This is not only analytically weak; it is quietly patronising.

Palestinian society is not a passive object acted upon by Israel. It is a political culture with its own factions, incentives, ideologies, and responsibilities. Treating it as morally non-autonomous—forever "driven" rather than deciding—keeps readers emotionally engaged but strategically illiterate.

In *Balcony over Jerusalem*, Palestinians are rarely wrong in ways that matter.

Failing Three: The East Jerusalem Correspondent Circuit

Lyons's worldview is not unique. It is representative of a closed professional ecosystem that dominates Western reporting from Israel.

Foreign correspondents, NGO personnel, diplomats, and activists circulate through the same social-professional spaces, where assumptions are reinforced and dissent quietly filtered out. Scepticism toward Israeli security claims becomes a badge of sophistication. Engagement with Israeli strategic thinking is dismissed as advocacy. Palestinian voices critical of Islamist ideology or internal repression rarely rise to prominence.

Balcony over Jerusalem reads less like a challenge to this environment than a dispatch from within it.

Failing Four: Strategic Blindness in a Civilisational Conflict

Perhaps the most consequential failure of Lyons's book is its inability—or refusal—to situate Israel's struggle within a broader strategic and civilisational context.

Israel is not merely managing a dispute. It is confronting ideological movements—Islamist, theocratic, eliminationist—that reject not only Israel's existence, but the foundations of pluralism, secular law, and liberal democracy itself. These forces are not confined to the Levant; they echo through Western cities, campuses, and institutions.

To treat Israeli security measures as mere overreach without grappling seriously with the nature of the adversary is not moral clarity. It is strategic naivety.

Western observers readily accept that journalists openly hostile to the Kremlin face severe restrictions inside Russia. Israel, uniquely, is expected to tolerate sustained hostility from journalists operating within its borders—often under Israeli protection—while confronting enemies who state plainly that they seek its destruction.

Lyons treats this asymmetry as hypocrisy. It is more accurately restraint.

Failing Five: Moral Certainty Without Consequence

There is a recurring tone in *Balcony over Jerusalem*: confidence derived from proximity without consequence.

Lyons observes, critiques, and judges from a position of safety guaranteed by the very state he holds responsible for instability. He does not face conscription. His family is not targeted. His children were not living under rocket threat, as Israeli families in Ashdod and Ashkelon were for years.

This does not invalidate his right to speak. But it does place limits on the authority of his moral certainty—especially when that certainty is packaged for comfortable Western consumption.

A Policy Question Israel Will Eventually Face

If Israel continues to be treated as the one state in the region obliged to host and credential foreign journalists who operate not as critics but as campaigners—flattening strategic reality into moral indictment—it is reasonable to ask whether such access should remain automatic.

No democracy is obliged to facilitate its own delegitimisation during a protracted war for survival.

Journalists who insist Israel is the core problem can still report—from Ramallah, entering via Amman and the Allenby Crossing—without the privileges conferred by operating inside the society they routinely malign.

On Reading Widely—and Why It Matters

I encourage people to read widely, including voices with whom they profoundly disagree. I have benefited from reading across the ideological spectrum—from Gore Vidal and Noam Chomsky to Dick Cheney and Alan Dershowitz; from Peter Beinart to Douglas Murray.

Exposure to competing frameworks sharpens judgement. It reveals assumptions. It forces intellectual humility.

The problem with *Balcony over Jerusalem* is not that it is critical of Israel. It is that it is insulated—from challenge, from strategic realism, and from the downstream consequences of the worldview it normalises.

A Harder Interpretation: When "Analysis" Becomes Advocacy

Up to this point, Lyons's approach can be understood as professional instinct hardened into habit: empathy elevated into governing lens; suspicion of state power made reflexive; the underdog position granted moral primacy by default.

But a compelling case can also be made that, over time, this posture shifts from tendency to intent—from framing to advocacy—and that the line between reporting and activism becomes unacceptably thin.

One respected leader in the Australian Jewish community has argued that Lyons and the ABC have, at critical moments, inserted Lyons's personal opinions into ABC television news bulletins under the label "Analysis," immediately following highly emotive reports from Gaza—reports that, by the nature of the environment, are vulnerable to censorship and narrative management by Hamas. The effect is not merely to "add context," but to steer audiences toward a preferred conclusion, as though Lyons's interpretation carries the status of fact rather than contestable judgement.

That same critic points to Lyons's response when his book was publicly challenged. After AIJAC critiqued *Balcony over Jerusalem*, Lyons reportedly denounced AIJAC as a sinister lobby acting at the direction of the State of Israel to Australia's detriment—language that, whatever one's politics, trades on insinuations of Jewish power and divided loyalty. The argument here is not that criticism of Israel should be taboo. It is that shifting from substantive disagreement to insinuation suggests something more than professional imbalance.

To be clear: I am not asserting that Lyons set out in 2017 to write a malicious book. My judgement is that he wrote from conviction—conviction formed and reinforced within a closed professional culture that rewards moral certainty over intellectual humility. Yet when those convictions are reiterated over time, reinforced through editorialising presented as "analysis," and delivered within news environments the public reasonably assumes to be neutral, motive becomes beside the point. What matters is conduct and effect. Read in that light, *Balcony over Jerusalem* functions less as memoir than as an exhibit in how institutional prestige can be used to launder advocacy into the public square under the protective cover of journalism itself—a pattern that raises serious questions not merely of bias, but of mala fides.

Conclusion: When the Balcony Becomes the Problem

Lyons's *Balcony over Jerusalem* is an unbalanced polemic. I do not assess it to be the work of malice, though a reasonable case could be made for a conclusion other than my own. Rather, it is shaped by ideology, intellectual closure, and the reinforcing dynamics of a closed professional milieu. In such environments, assumptions go unchallenged, dissenting evidence is filtered out, and narrative symmetry yields to moral certainty. Books written under these conditions rarely endure. This one is unlikely to age well.

Lyons writes with confidence, empathy, and conviction. He believes he is standing with the vulnerable and speaking truth to power. But conviction is not understanding, and empathy is not a substitute for judgement. When journalism becomes trapped in a single moral frame—when it mistakes proximity for insight and suffering for explanation—it ceases to illuminate reality and begins to distort it.

Over time, distortion hardens into consequence. Worldviews normalised in classrooms, newsrooms, and public broadcasters do not remain abstract. They shape what audiences see, excuse, fear, and dismiss. They shape the moral reflexes of societies—especially societies geographically and psychologically distant from the fight.

The deeper problem, therefore, is not Lyons alone. It is the ecosystem that affirms his worldview, amplifies it, and treats deviation as moral failure rather than intellectual disagreement. Within that ecosystem, journalists come to believe they are dissenters when they are, in fact, reinforcing an orthodoxy. They believe they are challenging power while consistently challenging only one side of a profoundly asymmetric conflict.

Israel does not ask to be beyond criticism. No democracy should. But Israel is uniquely expected to defend itself, explain itself, restrain itself, and accommodate those who narrate its actions through a lens that systematically discounts the nature of its enemies and the reality of its predicament. That expectation is not neutrality. It is exceptionalism of another kind.

Narratives shape policy. Policy shapes outcomes. And outcomes shape lives.

In an age where ideological movements openly committed to violence and elimination are no longer confined to the Levant—but echo through Western streets, campuses, and institutions—the cost of misunderstanding Israel is not borne by Israel alone. It is borne by societies that discover too late that moral posture is not a defence strategy.

A balcony may offer a view.

But history is not made from balconies.

It is made on the ground—where decisions have consequences, enemies have names, and mistakes are paid for in blood rather than column inches.

Journalism that forgets this does not merely mislead.

It leaves its audience unprepared for the world as it is.

23

The Winds of Change

Introduction

Cultural shifts rarely announce themselves with fanfare. They arrive as pressure changes.

"The Winds of Change" documents early signs that institutional indulgence of antisemitism—long disguised as advocacy—is encountering resistance. Through sanctions, resignations, and policy reversals, it traces a quiet reassertion of moral boundaries that many had assumed were gone for good.

This chapter examines how moments of accountability begin—not when outrage peaks, but when tolerance for indulgence finally runs out—and why what happens next will shape the credibility of our institutions for a generation.

***

A powerful gust of transformation is sweeping through institutions that once cloaked bias in legitimacy. And while it may have begun abroad, the winds of change are fast approaching Australia.

Just days ago, on 9 July 2025, the United States imposed financial sanctions, and travel bans on Francesca Albanese, the

UN's Special Rapporteur for the Palestinian Territories. This unprecedented move—authorised under Executive Order 14203 and signed by Secretary of State Marco Rubio—cited Albanese's antisemitic rhetoric and her abuse of legal mechanisms to target American and Israeli nationals through the International Criminal Court. The designation is serious: It freezes any US-based assets and restricts her access to the United States. It marks the first time a UN special rapporteur has faced such penalties from a Western democracy. But beyond its legal force, the decision signals something deeper: a growing intolerance for bigotry disguised as human rights advocacy.

Albanese is no outlier. She is simply the most extreme face of a system that, for years, has misused its moral authority to demonise the world's only Jewish state. But this month, that system began to fracture. On 14 July 2025, three central figures in the UN's so-called Commission of Inquiry into Israel—Navi Pillay, Miloon Kothari, and Chris Sidoti—resigned en masse.

These are not marginal characters. Pillay is a former UN High Commissioner for Human Rights. Kothari previously invoked antisemitic tropes about Jewish control of the media and questioned Israel's very legitimacy. Sidoti, an Australian, gave intellectual cover to a process so brazenly biased that its conclusions were often dismissed before the ink had dried.

The inquiry itself was always a farce—a permanent, open-ended investigation against a single state, launched by a Human Rights Council that includes some of the world's worst human rights abusers. The resignations are welcome. But they do not mark the end of the rot. They are merely the first visible cracks in a façade that has long shielded hatred behind the veneer of international respectability.

And here's where the story turns sharply toward home.

Australia now faces its own reckoning with the same moral hypocrisy. Our Special Envoy to Combat Antisemitism, Jillian Segal AO, recently released a national strategy aimed at tackling antisemitism with urgency and clarity. Among her key recommendations: that public funding be reviewed—or withheld—from institutions such as broadcasters, universities, and cultural bodies that tolerate or enable antisemitism.

The response from the ABC was nothing short of disgraceful. Rather than engage with the strategy on its merits, the national broadcaster leaned into insinuation—the kind that would never be tolerated were the target any other minority group. It platformed critics who framed the strategy as a threat to free speech, while barely acknowledging the reality of rising antisemitism—particularly in spaces funded by the taxpayer.

The parallel with the United States is impossible to ignore. Washington is now making clear that public funds and diplomatic legitimacy should not be granted to individuals or organisations that weaponize human rights frameworks to promote hatred. That is precisely what Segal's strategy proposes here. Her message is clear: Institutions that permit bigotry should not be subsidised by a society that claims to stand for decency and justice.

On any given weekend in Australia, it's now common to see protestors marching through our cities chanting "Death to the IDF"—not just fringe agitators, but sometimes individuals from professional sectors, including healthcare staff, educators, and others who otherwise present respectably during the week. These contradictions should disturb every fair-minded Australian. They expose a society at risk of forgetting that freedom of expression is not freedom from consequence.

We must ask ourselves: What are we willing to tolerate in the name of tolerance? If Albanese's conduct was enough to warrant US sanctions, how can we justify continued funding to Australian institutions that excuse or enable the same sentiments—under the veil of academic freedom or journalistic neutrality?

We must not allow a double standard to take hold—one that punishes every other form of hate, but makes excuses for antisemitism. And we must not allow our public institutions to remain complicit.

The resignations in Geneva and the sanctions from Washington are not isolated events. They are signals. The world is beginning to wake up to the institutional decay that has allowed antisemitism to flourish under the guise of advocacy. Now is the time for Australia to do the same.

The winds of change are here. They've blown through Turtle Bay and Geneva. And just as the *Scorpions* once sang of freedom sweeping through Eastern Europe, today's winds demand a reckoning of our own—across Canberra, Ultimo, and every institution that has looked the other way.

24

Taken for a Ride

Introduction

Manipulation is most effective when it flatters.

Those who are "taken for a ride" are rarely coerced. More often, they are reassured—told they are on the right side of history, aligned with justice, and exempt from the hard work of verification.

Over time, moral certainty replaces curiosity, and alignment replaces judgment. Narratives are absorbed not because they are true, but because they feel virtuous.

This chapter examines how Western audiences, institutions, and good-faith actors were not merely misinformed, but strategically indulged—and why the cost of that indulgence is now unavoidable.

***

I write this as a father and a humanist, not as a polemicist. I do not believe most people are born cruel, and I do not believe compassion is a weakness. But after decades of military service, time in the Middle East, and watching events unfold in Australia and across the West, I have come to believe that misplaced sympathy can become an accelerant for violence, not a remedy for it.

Nowhere is this more evident than in the way the West has been emotionally and intellectually taken for a ride by the Palestinian cause.

In Australian slang, being taken for a ride means being deliberately misled—manipulated into believing a story that serves someone else's interests, often at your own expense. In this case, it describes how decent, well-intentioned Western societies have been emotionally and morally steered into excusing behaviours that prolong conflict, reward extremism, and ultimately harm the very people they claim to defend.

Sympathy Detached from Truth

Australians are instinctively generous. We want to believe that every conflict is a misunderstanding, every grievance a plea for justice, every slogan a cry for peace. That instinct usually serves us well.

But sympathy detached from truth does not remain benign. It becomes a tool—wielded by those who have learned that failure, violence, and rejection can be monetised if framed correctly.

The shock many Australians felt watching brutality unfold at Bondi was not merely horror at an act of violence. It was the dawning realisation that fanaticism is not a distant problem, nor one that confines itself to battlefields and failed states. What Israelis experienced routinely during the Second Intifada—mass-casualty attacks on buses, cafés, markets, and family celebrations—has brushed far closer to our own lives than we once imagined.

This is not to equate contexts or statistics. It is to recognise a pattern of behaviour that has been normalised elsewhere—and long excused by those who prefer comforting narratives to hard truths.

Barbarism, Then and Now

History is not short of cruelty. The Mongols razed cities. The Huns terrorised Europe. The Vandals sacked Rome. The Tartars ruled through fear. These were brutal societies by any modern standard.

Yet there is a critical distinction worth making.

Those historical barbarisms were not sustained by moral inversion. They were not endlessly excused, subsidised, or sanctified by a global information ecosystem that rewarded perpetrators with sympathy, status, and material support. When they attacked their neighbours, they invited retaliation. When they lost wars, they lost territory, legitimacy, and often their leaders. Violence carried consequences.

What distinguishes the contemporary Levant is not brutality alone—history has seen worse—but the fusion of fanaticism with permanent victimhood as a political strategy, supercharged by the information age.

This is new.

The Broken Feedback Loop

In most of history, political failure imposed costs. Leaders who led their people into disaster were overthrown. Societies that chose endless war paid a price until behaviour changed.

In the modern Palestinian political ecosystem, that feedback loop is broken.

Lose wars? International recognition increases.

Target civilians? Headlines multiply.

Reject peace offers? Aid continues.

Glorify martyrdom? NGOs issue statements.

Indoctrinate children? "Context" is provided.

This is not conjecture. It is an observable incentive structure reinforced for decades.

No other group on earth has retained hereditary refugee status across generations, received billions in aid without meaningful institutional reform, and faced so little accountability for political decisions made in its name. Victimhood has become not a tragedy to be escaped, but an asset to be curated.

That is not compassion. It is corrosion.

What is at stake here is not simply a foreign conflict misread from afar, but the corrosion of Western judgment itself. Being taken for a ride does not merely waste money or distort sympathy; it degrades the habits of mind on which free societies depend. When moral clarity is replaced by narrative conformity, when institutions learn that accusation is safer than truth, and when leaders prefer applause to responsibility, civilisation does not collapse—it erodes. The danger is not sudden catastrophe, but quiet habituation: to intimidation, to inversion, and to the idea that defending life, law, and democratic norms is somehow suspect. This is how societies lose confidence in themselves long before they lose their freedom.

A Century of Missed Exits

The claim that Palestinians have never been offered a viable future alongside a Jewish state is simply untrue.

Over roughly a century, there have been repeated opportunities—each one imperfect, each one painful, but each one real. They were not offers to displace an "indigenous" Arab or Muslim people in favour of foreign interlopers, but attempts—often clumsy, sometimes rushed—to reconcile two national movements on a land to which the Jewish people are ancient and indigenous. Jews did not arrive in the Levant as a colonial imposition; they returned to the cradle of their civilisation, a land woven into their religion, language, and identity for more than three thousand years.

In 1937, the British Peel Commission acknowledged that competing nationalisms had made the Mandate unworkable and proposed partitioning the territory into separate Jewish and Arab states. It was the first serious international recognition that the conflict could not be resolved by denying Jewish self-determination. The proposal offered both communities sovereignty, but Arab leadership rejected it outright—objecting not merely to borders, but to the very existence of a Jewish state in any form.

A decade later, in 1947, the United Nations General Assembly adopted Resolution 181, recommending the creation of two independent states—one Jewish, one Arab—with economic cooperation and a special international regime for Jerusalem. The Jewish leadership accepted the plan, despite its severe territorial compromises and strategic vulnerabilities. The Palestinian Arab leadership, joined by surrounding Arab states, rejected it and chose war instead. That decision—and its consequences—still echo today.

Decades later, the most consequential diplomatic opening came at Camp David in 2000. After intensive negotiations, US President Bill Clinton articulated what became known as the Clinton Parameters: a framework for a Palestinian state encompassing all of Gaza and the vast majority of the West Bank, with land swaps, shared arrangements in Jerusalem, and an agreed mechanism for refugees. The parameters were not perfect, but they were serious—and they marked the closest the Palestinians had ever come to statehood.

No final agreement was reached. Clinton later described Yasser Arafat's refusal as a "colossal mistake," expressing deep frustration that a once-in-a-generation opportunity had been squandered.

This pattern matters. It speaks not to a single failed negotiation or an isolated miscalculation, but to a political culture that treats rejection as virtue and acceptance as betrayal—one that prefers permanent grievance to permanent settlement, and ambiguity to responsibility.

Arafat and the Politics of Avoidance

Yasser Arafat was not a misunderstood statesman undone by bad luck. He was a seasoned revolutionary entrepreneur—corrupt, duplicitous, and adept at surviving by balancing factions and violence.

He also understood something grimly realistic: Making peace would likely get him killed—not by the Jews, who welcome peace, but by his own people.

Leadership built on perpetual struggle rarely survives its end. To accept Israel's permanence, to renounce armed "resistance," and to pivot toward state-building would have stripped Arafat of the very mythology that sustained him.

This does not absolve him. It condemns the system that elevated him—and that continues to elevate successors who promise everything, deliver nothing, and blame everyone else.

Ideology Matters

It is fashionable to insist that ideology is a distraction, that "material conditions" explain everything. This is comforting—and wrong.

Within Islamist movements that dominate Palestinian political life in Gaza and exert immense influence elsewhere, death is sacralised. Martyrdom is not an unfortunate by-product; it is celebrated. Killing civilians is not a moral failure; it is reframed as righteousness.

This is not a claim about all Muslims. It is a claim about specific ideological currents that have proved catastrophically influential.

By contrast, Jewish ethical tradition places extraordinary weight on the sanctity of life—often expressed in the principle that saving one life is like saving an entire world. I believe deeply in that sentiment. But it does not extend to indulging those who actively seek to murder children, nor does it require civilisational suicide.

There is another ancient maxim, far less sentimental and far more realistic, drawn from Jewish law and moral reasoning. It appears in the Talmud, most commonly cited from Sanhedrin 72a: "If someone comes to kill you, rise and kill him first."

This is not a call to vengeance, nor a glorification of violence. It is a doctrine of preemptive self-defence, grounded in the recognition that moral systems which refuse to confront lethal intent do not preserve life—they endanger it. Jewish law treats the would-be murderer as having already forfeited the moral protections afforded to peaceful civilians, precisely because inaction would mean the death of the innocent.

In a modern democracy, this principle is not exercised through vigilantism. It is discharged through lawful self-defence, intelligence operations, policing, and—when unavoidable—lethal force, constrained by law and ethical restraint. The purpose is not punishment or revenge, but the protection of life.

Not vengeance. Responsibility.

Why This Is Not Hard-Hearted

To say this plainly is not to deny Palestinian suffering. It is to explain it.

Most people, everywhere, want safety for their children, dignity in work, and hope for the future. Yet the empirical record shows that this aspiration has not translated into dominant Palestinian political preferences. Repeated public opinion polling by the Palestinian Center for Policy and Survey Research (PCPSR)—an independent Palestinian research organisation founded in the mid-1990s—has consistently found that a majority of Palestinians, often in the mid-50 percent range and at times higher, identify armed struggle as the preferred means of achieving national goals, while support for negotiated compromise lags well behind. During periods of escalation, approval for violence against Israeli civilians has likewise registered at majority levels. These figures do not describe a marginal fringe; they reflect the prevailing political mood across both Gaza and the West Bank over time.

When suffering is treated as detached from culture, ideology, and repeated political choice, it cannot be meaningfully understood or addressed. A political culture that elevates grievance over growth, martyrdom over life, and rejection over coexistence will inevitably immiserate its own people first.

I also suspect that most Australians would be genuinely horrified to learn that their hard-earned taxpayer dollars have, in effect, helped sustain a war without end against Jews and Israel. Few Australians would tolerate the idea that their taxes were indirectly funding Vladimir Putin's illegal war of aggression against Ukraine—yet many would be astonished to discover that aid intended for humanitarian relief has too often been diverted, directly or indirectly, to entrench a political culture committed not to peace or state-building, but to perpetual conflict. Australians are generous, but they are not naïve. When presented plainly with the facts, most would insist that their compassion not be weaponised against the very values they work, pay tax, and vote to defend.

This is not theory. It is documented reality.

In Gaza and parts of Judea and Samaria (the West Bank), martyrdom is openly praised, taught, and ritualised. Hamas-run media has for years glorified "resistance" and lionised those who kill civilians as heroes. Public spaces and institutions have been named after perpetrators of mass-casualty attacks. Children are socialised—explicitly and repeatedly—into a moral inversion in which the highest honour is not building a life, but ending one for a cause.

Public opinion polling has repeatedly shown majority support for attacks on Israeli civilians during periods of heightened violence, including the suicide bombings of the Second Intifada and the mass atrocities of recent years. In parts of the ecosystem that surrounds Hamas, grief is often reframed as pride; death is not merely endured, but dignified as achievement; and compromise is treated as treason.

Hamas does not deny this worldview. It articulates it plainly. Its leaders have long described jihad and martyrdom not as tragic necessities but as virtues, and Israel's destruction not as a bargaining position but as an obligation.

This is not resistance warped by desperation. It is an ideology organised around death.

To acknowledge this is not dehumanising. It is refusing to lie.

As a father, I cannot romanticise a culture that teaches children that dying young is a form of success.

As a humanist, I cannot excuse the moral inversion that sanctifies murder while demanding endless sympathy.

And as a realist, I cannot pretend this will resolve itself if the West simply offers more empathy, more money, and fewer expectations.

Empathy without accountability is not kindness. It is abandonment.

It abandons Palestinian children to an ideology that consumes them.

It abandons Israeli children to those taught that killing them is holy.

And it abandons Western societies to the fantasy that compassion alone can tame fanaticism.

That is not mercy. It is moral negligence.

Tikkun Olam and the West's Fantasy Causes

The Jewish idea of tikkun olam—repairing the world—is profound and demanding. It requires moral seriousness, courage, and a willingness to confront evil rather than aestheticize it.

In recent decades, the West has replaced this ethic with something far thinner: fantasy causes that flatter the self while avoiding risk. It is easier to posture about abstract apocalypse, or to lionise simplistic activism, than to confront the reality that monsters exist—and that some ideologies are irreconcilable with peaceful coexistence.

We have ceded the language of "healing the world" to movements that confuse moral vanity with virtue, and in doing so we have lost sight of a harder truth: The world is not healed by indulging those who burn it.

What Must Change

If we are serious—about peace, about safety, about dignity—then several things must change.

First, Australia must stop incentivising bad behaviour. Throwing money at this problem has not produced peace, moderation, or dignity. It has rewarded violence, entrenched corruption, and removed incentives for reform. Unconditional aid teaches one lesson only: Rejection pays, extremism is subsidised, and consequences will be absorbed by someone else.

Between 2015 and 2023, Australian governments of both political persuasions committed well over A$400 million in development and humanitarian assistance to Palestinians in Gaza and the West Bank, much of it through multilateral agencies such as UNRWA. Since 7 October 2023 alone, a further A$130 million has been committed. Measured against outcomes, this has not been money well spent. It has not produced institutional reform, moderation, or a credible pathway to peace.

Australia should therefore cease payments into this ecosystem and redirect its aid to causes where lives are saved and stability reinforced rather than conflict prolonged.

Claims that Gaza is deliberately deprived also require honesty. Israel, through the Coordinator of Government Activities in the Territories, coordinates and publicly reports on humanitarian flows into Gaza, even while under sustained attack. Standing by Israel—insisting on security first, accountability always, and aid that is conditional rather than indulgent—is the only position consistent with reality. Aid without conditions is not compassion. It is incentive.

Second, the West must acknowledge that premature recognition of a Palestinian state was a serious error—and must now reverse course, regardless of political embarrassment. Considerations of face-saving cannot outweigh the obligation to do what is right. Statehood is not a therapeutic gesture. It is the culmination of responsibility, not a substitute for it.

Australia's 2025 recognition—alongside similar moves by the United Kingdom, Canada, and France—did not advance peace. It rewarded rejectionism and signalled that violence carries no lasting penalty. This failure is not accidental. It reflects a political class across the West that has been led by the nose—by activist bureaucracies, captured media, and ideologically uniform academic institutions—rather than exercising moral and strategic leadership.

The current US Administration warned explicitly against this logic. The forty-seventh President and senior US officials, including Secretary Rubio, argued that unilateral recognition would reward terrorism, harden positions, and undermine any prospect of peace grounded in accountability and reform. That judgment was correct.

"Palestinianism" has become a cause célèbre—a fashionable moral posture detached from outcomes, accountability, or truth. Governments have preferred applause to judgment, symbolism to substance, and activism to statesmanship. That is how the West has been taken for a ride.

And the ride is not meandering. It is heading straight toward a cliff.

Recognition divorced from reform does not advance peace; it locks in failure.

Third, incitement must end and accountability must begin. End the glorification of murder. End the naming of streets and schools after mass killers. End the indoctrination of children into a cult of death. Build transparent institutions. Meet clear benchmarks in governance, education, and the rule of law. Permanent indulgence produces permanent failure.

Fourth, Western societies must enforce clear boundaries at home. Counter-radicalisation is not racism. Enforcing laws against the glorification of terrorism is not Islamophobia. Assimilation is about shared civic values—respect for life, equality before the law, and loyalty to democratic norms—not ancestry or faith.

This is not about vengeance. It is about protection. It is about responsibility.

Compassion with Backbone

The tragedy of the Palestinians is not that they have been insufficiently indulged by the world, but that they have been indulged into catastrophe—shielded from consequences that have historically forced political cultures to change.

The West is not required to hate anyone. But it is required to stop lying—to itself, to its children, and to those it claims to help.

Mercy without judgment is not compassion. It is abdication. And abdication is how civilisations fail—quietly at first, then all at once.

PART III
Conclusion

Narrative capture is seductive because it offers moral comfort.

It allows people to feel compassionate without being accurate, righteous without being responsible, and engaged without being accountable. It replaces judgment with alignment, and complexity with certainty.

But narratives do not remain confined to discourse. Once institutionalised, they shape policy, legitimise behaviour, and determine whose suffering counts.

By the time consequences become visible, the story has already been told—and retold—often enough to resist correction.

To understand what follows, then, we must confront not only what was said, but what those stories were designed to make permissible.

PART IV
THE RECORD

War, truth, and the moral alibi

PART IV
Introduction

By the time war enters the conversation, judgment has often already been compromised.

Narratives formed in peacetime struggle to survive contact with reality. Complexity is reduced. Moral asymmetry is flattened. The demands placed on soldiers and states bear little resemblance to those imposed on any other actor in history.

This part does not argue that war is clean, simple, or virtuous. It argues something narrower—and more necessary: that war must be understood as it is, not as it is wished to be.

Israel's wars have been fought under conditions unlike those faced by any other modern democracy—against enemies who embed themselves within civilian populations, reject the laws of war outright, and wage conflict not only on the battlefield but in the cognitive and moral domains.

To assess Israel's conduct honestly, one must first discard the moral alibis that have flourished in the absence of evidence—and replace them with record, restraint, and reality.

Khartoum: Looking Back on the Three Nos of September 1967

Introduction

History often supplies clear answers long before they become acceptable.

In September 1967, in the aftermath of a war Israel did not seek but decisively won, the Arab League met in Khartoum and issued a declaration that would shape the conflict for decades: no peace, no recognition, no negotiations.

That moment is frequently treated as an embarrassment to be smoothed over by later optimism. Yet it remains one of the clearest statements of intent ever made in the conflict.

This chapter revisits Khartoum not as provocation, but as record—and asks why clarity offered so plainly was so quickly set aside in favour of comforting illusion.

***

In September 1967, only weeks after Israel's decisive victory in the Six-Day War, representatives of the Arab League gathered in Khartoum, Sudan. The military shock they were responding to was profound. In six days, Israel had shattered the combined forces of Egypt, Jordan, and Syria, seized control of the Sinai Peninsula, the Gaza Strip, the West Bank (including East Jerusalem), and the Golan Heights, and overturned assumptions that had governed the Middle East since 1948. The war did not merely redraw maps; it upended certainties. For the Arab world, Khartoum was intended to be a moment of regrouping, unity, and resolve. What it produced instead was a declaration that would harden the conflict for decades: the Three Nos.

To understand Khartoum, one must first understand the intellectual and political climate that preceded it. The Arab world of the 1950s and 1960s was animated by pan-Arab nationalism, infused with revolutionary zeal, and increasingly dominated by the rhetoric of Egypt's Gamal Abdel Nasser. Israel was not treated as a neighbour with whom disputes might one day be resolved, but as an illegitimate colonial implant whose removal was both inevitable and just. The language of compromise had little currency. The language of eradication did. In this environment, Israel's survival itself was seen as provisional—a historical error awaiting correction.

The months leading up to June 1967 intensified these assumptions. Egyptian forces moved into the Sinai. The United Nations Emergency Force was expelled. The Straits of Tiran were closed to Israeli shipping, an act Israel had long declared a casus belli. Arab leaders spoke openly of impending war and promised annihilation. Regional radio broadcasts were saturated with martial bravado. The expectation was not merely victory, but finality. That expectation collapsed with astonishing speed.

The Six-Day War was not just a military defeat for the Arab states; it was a psychological and ideological rupture. Israel, a small state with limited strategic depth and no great-power patron willing to fight on its behalf, had demonstrated overwhelming superiority in planning, execution, and adaptability. The scale of the defeat left Arab leaders humiliated and exposed. In its aftermath, the Arab League faced a dilemma: whether to absorb reality and adjust course, or to deny it and entrench refusal.

Khartoum chose the latter. The outcome of the summit was formalised in the Khartoum Resolution, whose most enduring legacy was its uncompromising formulation: no peace with Israel, no recognition of Israel, and no negotiations with Israel. These Three Nos were presented as a unified Arab position, intended to restore dignity after defeat and to signal resolve. In practice, they froze the conflict into a posture of permanent rejection.

It is important to be clear about what the Three Nos were—and what they were not. They were not a bargaining position designed to extract concessions. They were not a pause for reflection. They were an explicit refusal to accept Israel's existence as a legitimate fact. By ruling out peace, recognition, and negotiation simultaneously, the Arab League closed every pathway through which conflict might have been transformed into coexistence. Israel was denied not merely territory, but standing.

For Israel, Khartoum clarified something essential. The territories captured in 1967 were not seized as part of a grand expansionist vision. Israel suddenly found itself administering populations it had neither sought nor wished to govern. The prevailing assumption within Israeli leadership circles at the time was that these territories could form the basis of future land-for-peace arrangements. Khartoum extinguished that assumption. The response from the Arab world was not an offer to talk, but a declaration that there would be nothing to talk about.

From that moment, Israeli strategy evolved along pragmatic rather than rhetorical lines. Security became paramount.

Deterrence replaced trust. Peace remained a goal, but only with those prepared to abandon absolutism. This posture would later be vindicated in Israel's peace treaty with Egypt, which followed President Sadat's historic decision to break the Arab consensus, recognise Israel, and negotiate directly. But Sadat's move was revolutionary precisely because Khartoum had made it taboo.

Over time, however, the rigidity of the Three Nos proved unsustainable. The Arab world itself changed. Pan-Arabism waned. National interests reasserted themselves. Regime survival, economic development, and internal stability gradually displaced ideological hostility to Israel as primary concerns. The Palestinian cause, once the unifying banner of Arab politics, began to lose its centrality—particularly among Gulf states with little direct stake in the conflict.

This shift did not happen loudly. It happened quietly, pragmatically, and often in private. Intelligence cooperation between Israel and several Arab states deepened, particularly in response to shared concerns about Iranian expansionism, Islamist militancy, and regional instability. Trade relationships developed discreetly. Channels of communication multiplied. Public rhetoric remained hostile long after private behaviour had changed.

The Abraham Accords did not create this reality; they formalised it. When the United Arab Emirates, Bahrain, Morocco, and Sudan normalised relations with Israel, they did so not out of sentimentality, but self-interest. They recognised Israel as a permanent, capable, and valuable regional actor. They also signalled, implicitly, that the Palestinian issue would no longer hold veto power over their foreign policy.

This moment marked the effective collapse of the Khartoum consensus. The Three Nos were not repudiated in a single speech or resolution. They were simply abandoned. What replaced them was not universal peace, but strategic realism. Arab governments increasingly distinguished between rhetorical support for Palestinians and concrete willingness to sacrifice national interests on their behalf. The gap between the two has widened steadily.

At the same time, it has become increasingly clear that Arab states have little appetite for absorbing Palestinian populations permanently. This reluctance is often framed in the language of solidarity—preserving Palestinian identity, resisting "resettlement." In reality, it reflects a sober assessment of political risk, social cohesion, and internal stability. The Palestinians have become a cause without patrons within the Arab world: invoked frequently, supported selectively, and contained carefully.

What has surprised many—including me—is that as this cause has quietly lost priority in much of the Arab world, it has been taken up with extraordinary intensity by activists in the West. Universities, NGOs, and social movements far removed from the region have adopted deeply emotional and absolutist positions on a conflict they often know only in fragments. It is a reminder that it is entirely possible—indeed increasingly common—for people to hold fierce moral convictions about causes and contexts they understand only superficially, or through ideological mediation rather than lived experience.

Where does this leave us now? The Arab street and Arab regimes are no longer aligned. Governments act with calculation; publics often respond with emotion. Israel is no longer universally rejected, but it is not universally accepted either. The Three Nos have lost their force, but their shadow remains. Rejectionism has not disappeared; it has been regionalised, radicalised, and increasingly outsourced to non-state actors.

Looking back on Khartoum from the vantage point of 2025, one conclusion is unavoidable. The Three Nos were not a moral stance. They were a strategic error. They delayed peace, entrenched conflict, and condemned generations to war without offering a path to victory. Israel adapted. The Arab world moved on—slowly, unevenly, and often reluctantly. The Palestinians were left behind.

History has rendered its verdict. Absolute refusal could not survive reality. The question now is not whether Khartoum was wrong, but how much damage its legacy continues to inflict—and how much longer the region, and those who claim to speak for it from afar, can afford to pretend otherwise.

Jerusalem Day: A Celebration of Truth in the City of Peace

Introduction

Jerusalem is more argued over than understood.

"Jerusalem Day" is written from residence, not rhetoric. It reflects on what the city is—rather than what distant observers insist it must be—and examines the reality of religious freedom, coexistence, and continuity under Israeli sovereignty.

Against a backdrop of manufactured outrage and selective reporting, this essay offers a grounded account of daily life in Jerusalem, where access, worship, and civic order are extended to faiths that are often denied the same protections elsewhere in the region.

This chapter examines how truth is displaced by narrative in one of the world's most contested cities—and why the gap between lived reality and distant accusation matters far beyond Jerusalem itself.

***

For twenty-seven unforgettable months—from July 2019 to September 2021—my wife and I called Jerusalem home. Eight months before COVID-19 changed the world, and the rest during it. To live in Jerusalem during that extraordinary period was to be immersed in the complexity, resilience, and profound beauty of one of the most remarkable cities on earth.

Each year, Jerusalem Day (*Yom Yerushalayim*) is celebrated on the twenty-eighth of Iyar in the Hebrew calendar—this year falling on 27 May 2025. It marks the reunification of the city in 1967, when Israeli forces gained control of East Jerusalem and, for the first time in millennia, ensured full access to the Old City for people of all faiths. While much of the world obsesses over narratives of division, those of us who have lived in Jerusalem know it is, in fact, a model of religious coexistence—however imperfect—unequalled in the region.

One of the most powerful realities that struck me during my time in Israel was the *freedom of worship* in Jerusalem. Unlike Mecca and Medina—Islam's two holiest cities—where non-Muslims are strictly forbidden to enter, Jerusalem welcomes Christians, Muslims, Jews, Bahá'ís, and many others. The city is administered by the State of Israel, and under Israeli governance, adherents of all three Abrahamic faiths are free to practise their religion openly and without fear. The *status quo* on holy sites is maintained with great care. Churches operate freely. The Muslim Waqf manages the Al-Aqsa Mosque. And the Jewish people, after centuries of exile, can again return to the Western Wall.

It goes further. Israel also protects the rights of *minorities often forgotten elsewhere in the Middle East*: the Bahá'í—whose global centre is in Haifa—and the Circassians, Sunni Muslims originally from the Caucasus, who live peacefully as Israeli citizens with full rights. In a region too often torn apart by sectarianism, Jerusalem under Israeli governance stands as a living rebuke to those who claim religious harmony is impossible.

And yet, the world does not see it that way.

When I lived in Jerusalem, I became increasingly aware of what can only be described as *confected outrage* directed at the city from afar. I recall reading with incredulity an Australian news article decrying the supposed horrors unfolding in Sheikh Jarrah—a suburb in East Jerusalem. That very night, I had been in the area, farewelling a dear colleague: a remarkable Armenian woman from Jordan who had worked alongside me in a sensitive and high-stakes international mission. The quiet civility of that evening bore no resemblance to the sensationalised accounts peddled by so-called correspondents, many of whom rarely ventured beyond the confines of their ideological echo chambers at the American Colony Hotel.

The same applied to reports about violence at the Damascus Gate or on the Temple Mount. What I witnessed on the ground was usually starkly at odds with the headlines I would later read in Western newspapers. It was as though certain journalists—whether from the BBC, Al Jazeera, or Australian outlets that once had credibility—were actively invested in distorting the truth. Their narratives served not their readers, but their prejudices.

It was during this time that I began to understand the wisdom of the old saying, *"You can fool some of the people all of the time."* And many of those being fooled are sitting in newsrooms, universities, and political chambers across the West. This realisation helped spark what is now *The 2023 Foundation*, a non-Jewish-led initiative I founded to counter antisemitism through lived experience, not lazy dogma. Our model is simple: introduce reasonable, open-minded people to the reality of Israel—its complexity, its challenges, its humanity. We don't preach. We immerse.

To those seeking a dispassionate and apolitical account of the city's past, I can't recommend highly enough *Jerusalem: The Biography* by Simon Sebag Montefiore. His masterful chronicle of this ancient city's tumultuous history makes clear that Jerusalem has always been at the crossroads of faith, identity, and empire. Its contemporary status is not a historical aberration, but the latest chapter in an unbroken—and often violent—saga spanning more than three thousand years.

And yet, Jerusalem endures. The ancient stones of the Old City bear witness to tragedy and triumph alike. On Jerusalem Day, Israelis of all backgrounds—religious and secular, Jewish and Arab—walk its streets, waving flags, singing songs, and affirming a commitment to unity. Yes, there are tensions. Yes, there are flashpoints. But walk the length of Jaffa Road, through the Mahane Yehuda Market, or past the churches of the Holy Sepulchre, and you will see what too few Western pundits ever bother to witness: *a city that works.*

For my wife and me, Jerusalem was never merely a place of work. It was our happy home. And though we have since returned to Australia, a part of us will always remain there. As the sun sets behind the golden Dome of the Rock, casting its glow over Mount Zion and the Mount of Olives, it becomes clear that Jerusalem is not just a city. It is a living story. And like all great stories, it deserves to be told with honesty.

This Jerusalem Day may more of the world learn to see it not as the caricature drawn by ideologues, but as it truly is: a city of faith, freedom, and fierce resilience.

Unmatched Restraint: The Israeli Government, the IDF, and the Moral Burden of War

Introduction

Israel is often judged by standards no other nation is asked to meet.

Its enemies violate the laws of war openly and strategically. Israel, by contrast, is condemned not for brutality, but for restraint—restraint that slows operations, increases risk to its own soldiers, and prolongs conflict.

This chapter examines what restraint actually looks like in modern war, why it carries real cost, and why moral seriousness demands that it be acknowledged rather than inverted.

***

In the theatre of modern warfare, there are few examples of military restraint as profound as that demonstrated by the Israel Defense Forces (IDF) and the Israeli Government since the atrocities of October 7, 2023. As the world watches, often through a distorting lens of misinformation and moral relativism, it is imperative to state plainly what too many refuse to admit: No Western military has ever been held to the impossible standard that Israel now meets, every single day.

The scale of the October 7 attack was grotesque in both intent and execution. Civilians were butchered, babies burned alive, women raped, families slaughtered, and hostages taken—including young Kfir Bibas and his brother Ariel, along with their mother Shiri. The recent return of their bodies to Israel in February 2025, alongside the still-grieving Eli Sharabi—whose wife and daughters were also murdered by Hamas—should sear the conscience of any who claim to care about justice or humanity. These families weren't "collateral damage." They were the *targets*.

Yet even in the face of such horror, Israel has exercised extraordinary discipline in the conduct of its military operations. The IDF issues advance warnings before strikes. It allows humanitarian corridors. It pauses offensives to permit aid and evacuations. What other nation on Earth would drop leaflets, make phone calls, and send text messages to enemy civilians, urging them to seek shelter—knowing full well that doing so may cost the element of surprise and risk the lives of its own soldiers?

Compare this with the open declarations of genocidal intent from Hamas and even the Palestinian Authority. Consider Ghazi Hamad, a senior Hamas official, who publicly vowed that "October 7 was just the first time," and that it will be "repeated again and again." Or the chilling statement by Mahmoud al-Zahar, another senior Hamas leader: "Israel must be erased." These are not the words of misunderstood militants. They are the language of extermination. They make no distinction between soldier and civilian, Jew and gentile, adult and child.

Meanwhile, voices from the Palestinian Authority offer little in the way of moderation. PA President Mahmoud Abbas has a long and troubling record of Holocaust minimisation, having claimed in a 1983 dissertation that Zionists collaborated with Nazis. More recently, PA representatives have refused to condemn the October 7 massacre, instead continuing to glorify "martyrs" and incentivise terror through the notorious "pay-for-slay" program.

It is within this environment—a culture that venerates death, dehumanises Jews, and distorts truth—that Israel is fighting for its survival. And yet, Israel fights not as its enemies do. The restraint is not only tactical, but moral.

Critics, often sitting comfortably in the safety of Western capitals, cry "disproportionate response" from behind keyboards. But they forget history—or ignore it. After 9/11, the United States launched a global war on terror that included airstrikes, drone campaigns, and the decapitation of entire terrorist networks. The NATO-led invasion of Afghanistan toppled a regime within weeks. The British, in the nineteenth century, waged a campaign of retribution after the First Anglo-Afghan War that saw Kabul burned and retribution meted out with ruthless precision.

And during World War II, Allied forces firebombed Dresden and Tokyo, reducing entire cities to rubble. Civilians died in the tens of thousands. These were not war crimes—they were wartime decisions made under the moral calculus of defeating evil. Victory sometimes demands ferocity. Yet Israel, even when justified by any historical standard, chooses restraint.

This restraint is not a sign of weakness. It reflects the values Israel was built upon. The IDF is not only a fighting force—it is the moral spine of a democratic nation. Its commanders make impossible decisions in impossible circumstances. And they do so with one hand tied behind their back by the international community, while the other shields their civilians from slaughter and their soldiers from moral corruption.

The double standard is deafening. No other army is expected to win a war against terrorists embedded within civilian populations while facing global condemnation for defending its own people. No other democracy would tolerate thousands of rockets raining down upon its cities before acting. And no other people, having endured a pogrom on live television, would be scolded for daring to defend themselves.

Yet Israel does. With courage, clarity, and a conscience.

Golda Meir once said, *"A bad headline is better than a good eulogy."* In today's media climate, Israel has endured plenty of bad headlines. But thanks to the restraint and resolve of its leaders and soldiers, far fewer eulogies than its enemies intended.

28

Swords of Iron, Hearts of Flesh: The Post-Traumatic Growth of Today's IDF Warriors

Introduction

Written after entering Gaza as part of a senior veteran delegation, this essay documents something largely absent from Western commentary: the moral interior of Israeli soldiers fighting an existential war under conditions designed to erase moral distinction.

What follows is not romanticism, nor denial of trauma. It is an examination of post-traumatic growth—of how meaning, restraint, and responsibility can survive even amid destruction. Drawing on lived military experience across multiple theatres, this chapter challenges the caricature of Israeli soldiers as instruments of cruelty and replaces it with something far more unsettling to critics: humanity under pressure.

This chapter examines what ethical soldiering looks like when restraint carries real cost—and why that reality is so often ignored by those most eager to pass judgment from a distance.

***

In September 2024, I entered Gaza as part of a senior veteran delegation hosted by the Military Expert Panel and the European Leadership Network. We met with senior Israeli commanders and walked the shattered corridors of war. Yet what struck me most was not the debris or destruction—it was the quiet resolve of the soldiers. Young and old, they carried rifles, yes—but also something far heavier. They carried the burden of moral clarity in a world that too often mistakes it for cruelty.

The IDF has been fighting an existential war since the atrocities of October 7, 2023. And yet, in my judgment, the men and women of this "Swords of Iron" generation will not merely survive—they will grow. These warriors will not be defined by trauma. They will be refined by it.

Theirs is the most ethical, lawful, and moral fighting force in recorded history, operating under diabolical circumstances against an enemy that hides behind civilians, stores weapons in hospitals, launches rockets from schools and mosques, and caches war material in children's bedrooms. I have seen this with my own eyes. In Gaza, I met soldiers who had every reason to hate—but chose instead to serve with dignity and restraint. Some had buried their friends. Others had rescued hostages. All were committed to something greater than themselves. This is the fertile ground from which post-traumatic growth springs.

The Austrian psychiatrist Viktor Frankl, a Holocaust survivor, wrote in *Man's Search for Meaning*, "When we are no longer able to change a situation, we are challenged to change ourselves." Frankl understood that suffering, while inevitable, can be transformed into purpose. The IDF soldiers I encountered have made that transformation. The experience of war has not hollowed them—it has given them depth.

In my military career spanning over thirty years, I have commanded troops in Afghanistan, Lebanon, Syria, and East Timor, and served in Iraq, Bougainville, and beyond. I've seen courage in many forms—on the battlefield, in peacekeeping missions, and in the quiet moments of leadership under pressure. I have witnessed moral courage in places as varied as the villages of Timor-Leste and the Qal'ah compounds and towering cornfields of southern Afghanistan. But what I saw in Gaza was something distinct: a purity of purpose that stood out. These are not just warriors. They are human beings who have chosen to remain human in the face of barbarity.

I recall a conversation with a young Special Forces reservist, Etay. He had responded to the south on October 7. He killed many terrorists, saw a close mate lose his life in front of him, and was himself shot multiple times. "We don't want to be here," he told me. "But if we're not, who will protect our families?" His eyes—older than his years, tired, but unbroken—told a deeper story. He had seen evil and decided to fight it without becoming it. As Carl Jung once wrote, "No tree can grow to heaven unless its roots reach down to hell." This young man had descended into darkness and emerged with his values intact.

My belief in the capacity for post-traumatic growth is not theoretical. In 2017, while serving at the Warrant Officer and Non-Commissioned Officer Academy in Australia, I met Dion Jensen—a former New Zealand Defence Force soldier and police officer who reframed PTSD not as a diagnosis but as a passage. His book, *The Good News About PTSD*, offered hope and purpose where others saw only pathology. It helped one of my former corporals recover from the brink of suicide and build a new life as a husband, father, and firefighter. That journey—from darkness into meaning—mirrors what I now see in the IDF.

Israel's struggle is unique, but its lessons are universal. Today's young IDF veterans will emerge stronger, not despite their trauma, but because of how they confront it. As Sir Winston Churchill observed during the darkest days of World War II, "To each, there comes in their lifetime a special moment when they are figuratively tapped on the shoulder and offered the chance to do something special. What a tragedy if that moment finds them unprepared." The soldiers of the IDF were prepared. They rose.

Their healing will require care, community, and continued purpose. I've seen firsthand the power of peer-led recovery programs, purpose-driven mental health models, and the quiet strength of shared service. What these men and women need is not pity, but opportunity. Not platitudes, but purpose.

We in the West must be their allies—not only in war, but in peace. Their story is one of resilience, morality, and meaning in the face of savagery. Their wounds, both visible and invisible, are not the end of the story. They mark the beginning of a new chapter.

As General James Mattis, former US Secretary of Defense, once said: "The most important six inches on the battlefield is between your ears." These Israeli warriors, forged in fire, will return home and build lives of depth and dignity—because they understand what it means to fight for civilisation itself.

When Will Israel Be Allowed to Win? The West's Dangerous Double Standards

Introduction

Wars end when one side is permitted to prevail.

In Israel's case, victory is often framed as immoral by definition, while defeat is treated as a prerequisite for peace.

This chapter explores the double standards that underpin this paradox—and why denying Israel the right to win prolongs conflict, empowers extremists, and destabilises the very international order the West claims to defend.

***

In May 2025, the governments of the United Kingdom, France, and Canada intensified diplomatic pressure on Israel, demanding an immediate cessation of military operations in Gaza. The then UK Foreign Secretary David Lammy condemned Israel's actions as "monstrous" and announced a suspension of trade talks, citing alleged breaches of international law. France and Canada joined the chorus, threatening "concrete actions" unless Israel halted its campaign and allowed increased humanitarian aid into Gaza.

It is difficult to overstate how misguided—and dangerous—this position is. By rushing to condemn Israel at a critical moment in the war, these Western nations risk undermining the very people they claim to support: Palestinian civilians who seek a future free from tyranny. Instead of helping, such interventions shield Hamas from the consequences of its actions and prolong suffering on both sides.

Consider the brutal reality Israelis face. On 14 May 2025, Tzeela Gez, a thirty-year-old pregnant mother of three, was shot and killed by a Palestinian terrorist while travelling with her husband to hospital near the settlement of Bruchin in the West Bank. Her husband was wounded, and their baby was delivered via emergency caesarean section. This was not an isolated anomaly—it was part of a sustained campaign of terror targeting civilians and sabotaging any hope for peace.

Colonel Richard Kemp, former commander of British forces in Afghanistan and a seasoned analyst of asymmetric warfare, recently addressed these contradictions in *The Telegraph*. "Hamas's most powerful tool is aid distribution," he warned. "We cannot allow these terrorists to weaponise it." His critique exposes a deeper failure in Western policy: the inability to recognise that humanitarian aid, when misappropriated by terrorists, can fuel conflict rather than alleviate it.

Amid escalating violence and distorted international pressure, the Chief of Staff of the Israel Defense Forces, Lieutenant

General Eyal Zamir, issued a clarifying statement directed at the residents of Gaza:

> We are not the ones who brought this destruction upon you. We are not the ones who started this war. We are not the ones who have deprived you of food, shelter, and money. We do not hide in hospitals or schools. We do not live in luxury hotels while you live in hardship. This is your leadership—the ones holding our hostages. Hamas is responsible for starting the war. It is responsible for the difficult situation of the civilian population—it brought destruction, and it will not be the one to rebuild. Hamas has one option—to release our hostages. If an agreement is reached, the IDF will know how to adjust its operations accordingly.

This is not a call for vengeance—it is a plea for clarity and a reminder that peace cannot emerge while Hamas remains entrenched and unaccountable. It is the voice of moral clarity, not aggression. And it is a voice Western governments should be amplifying, not undermining.

Yet instead of empowering peace-seeking Palestinians—those who might imagine a future living side-by-side with their Jewish neighbours—the UK, France, and Canada continue to reward failure. Their posture effectively sustains the very forces that have entrenched misery in Gaza. Hamas survives because the world keeps paying the bill.

Western aid continues to flow generously to the Palestinian Authority and UNRWA—organisations whose business model too often perpetuates grievance rather than resolving it. Year after year, money pours in with few conditions, while textbooks teach hatred and terrorists are rewarded with stipends. The well-meaning generosity of liberal democracies has, however inadvertently, become a subsidy for stalemate.

So we must ask the obvious question: Why is Israel never allowed to win its wars?

Since its rebirth in 1948, Israel has faced repeated existential threats. And in every war of survival, international intervention arrives not to restrain the aggressors—but to clip the wings of the Jewish state just as it gains the upper hand. This twisted cycle ensures the aggressors never face real consequences, and the defenders are never permitted peace through victory.

This is not merely counterproductive—it is immoral.

Israel is a liberal democracy governed by the rule of law, with a free press and an independent judiciary. Its military operates under greater scrutiny than any other. It does not seek conquest. It seeks peace. But peace requires the defeat of those who preach annihilation and act with savagery.

What is unfolding in Gaza is not a battle between equals. It is a confrontation between civilisation and barbarism. If Hamas is defeated, Gazans may finally have a chance at a different future—a future no longer held hostage by theocratic fascists, but open to coexistence, reconstruction, and dignity.

For that to happen, Western governments must stop throwing good money after bad. They must stop demanding "restraint" from the only party acting within the laws of armed conflict. They must stop indulging narratives that blame the consequences of Hamas's terror on those forced to respond.

Instead, they must summon the moral courage to say what should be obvious: Hamas must lose. And for the sake of all decent people—Jew and Arab alike—Israel must be allowed to win.

30

Echoes of Vietnam: The Demonisation of Soldiers Then and Now

Introduction

History has seen this pattern before.

In Vietnam, soldiers were burdened with the moral failures of political leaders and the distortions of media narratives. Decades later, many of those judgments have been reassessed—but only after irreparable damage was done.

This chapter draws the parallel deliberately, not to excuse war, but to warn against the cost of moral amnesia.

***

It is hard to think of a more shameful moment in Australian history—perhaps save the one we are living through today—than the vile reception afforded to many of our Vietnam veterans. Australia deployed nearly sixty thousand servicemen and women to Vietnam between 1962 and 1975. They served with courage, honour, and professionalism. But on their return home, they were met not with gratitude, but with disgrace.

They did not start that war. They did not choose their deployment. They went because their government sent them—because duty called. And yet, on their return to Australia, many were spat on, jeered at, and labelled "baby killers." These scenes were repeated in other Western capitals then, as we see again today—to our great societal shame.

One Australian Vietnam veteran, Denny Whitmeyer, recalled: "I changed my military clothes on an airplane into civilian clothes because there was [sic] problems in the airports." Another remembered protesters hurling abuse and animal blood. These weren't fringe outbursts. They were part of a broader cultural sickness—a readiness to scapegoat those who bore the burden of service.

Today, a new generation of soldier faces an eerily similar campaign of vilification.

This time, it's the young men and women of the Israel Defense Forces (IDF). They too did not choose this war. They too were called to serve. Many were roused from their beds on October 7 as Hamas terrorists launched the worst massacre of Jews since the Holocaust. Entire families were butchered. Babies burned. Holocaust survivors abducted.

As Rudyard Kipling observed in his poem *Tommy*, written more than a century ago: "It's Tommy this, an' Tommy that, an' 'Chuck him out, the brute!' But it's 'Saviour of 'is country' when the guns begin to shoot."

And yet, in the days and weeks that followed, it was not the perpetrators who faced condemnation, but those who defended their people. The blood libel has returned—repackaged for the digital age.

Across the West, IDF soldiers have been branded "genocidal," "monsters," "war criminals." At Columbia University, Professor

Joseph Massad referred to the October 7 attack as "awesome" and a "stunning victory of the Palestinian resistance." Social media teems with invective. Posters of kidnapped children are ripped down. On July 4, 2025, masked protesters stormed Miznon, an Israeli-owned restaurant in Melbourne, chanting "Death to the IDF" and damaging property. That same night, a man set fire to the front door of the East Melbourne Hebrew Congregation while twenty worshippers were gathered for Shabbat. It was a deliberate act of arson—domestic terrorism. Thankfully, no lives were lost. The alleged perpetrator was arrested and charged the following evening. These were not isolated acts of vandalism. They were premeditated attacks on Jewish life. Just days earlier, the stage at Glastonbury in the United Kingdom had hosted an abominable rapper whose lyrics trafficked in rage, not reason. This is not protest. It is hate.

Let the law respond with appropriate weight. Not just for justice, but for deterrence. Sentencing principles exist not only to punish but to uphold societal standards. That matters here.

Because there is a troubling passivity to modern antisemitism. It rarely marches in black boots anymore. It hides behind "human rights" slogans. It chants "ceasefire" with one hand and posts glorification of Hamas with the other. It dehumanises Israelis and then feigns surprise when Jews are attacked on city streets.

Let us be clear: Mistakes happen in war. They happen in every war. And wherever there is a collective of humans, some will fail to uphold the high standard expected of them. That is true in every army. It was true in Vietnam and in Afghanistan. But these instances are the exception, not the rule.

It is my professional judgment that the IDF is the most lawful, ethical, and restrained fighting force in human history. I say this with the experience of commanding Australian combat soldiers on operations in East Timor (1999) and Afghanistan (2011)—being well-versed in the application of rules of engagement, orders for opening fire, and the laws of war. I was also briefed in detail by Israel's Military Advocate General's Corps (MAG Corps) in September 2024, when I returned to Israel as part of a senior veteran delegation named the Military Expert Panel.

General Sir John McColl (Ret'd), former Deputy Supreme Allied Commander at NATO, who was on my trip, remarked to the press after returning: "The operational procedures the IDF have, in terms of the law of armed conflict, are as strong as ours [UK Armed Forces]." He added, "I went there sceptical," but concluded that the IDF are doing "their absolute level best" to minimise casualties.

What the IDF is doing exceeds the standards other Western militaries achieved in the past two decades—in Iraq and Afghanistan—by a factor. There is a stark contrast between the ethical conduct of the IDF in Gaza and the barbarism of Russian forces in Ukraine, or the brutality of the Syrian regimes—past and current—which goes largely unreported by our partisan and manipulative media.

The IDF conducts internal investigations. It cancels missions to avoid civilian harm. It telegraphs operations in ways no other military on Earth does. No other democracy has ever faced the genocidal threat Israel does—with terrorists hiding behind human shields—and responded with such moral restraint.

To the mothers and fathers of IDF soldiers in Israel and across the Diaspora, I say this: Be incredibly proud. Your sons and daughters have not lost their morality. They are guardians. They have stood, lion-hearted, when not only Israel, but the entire civilised world needed them. In time, they will grow to be the best of us.

War is not something any civilised society wishes upon its children. The Vietnamese novelist and veteran Bảo Ninh, in *The Sorrow of War* (1993, Secker & Warburg), wrote a haunting line:

"My life seems little different from that of a sampan pushed upstream towards the past. The future lied to us, there long ago in the past. There is no new life, no new era, nor is it hope for a beautiful future that now drives me on, but rather the opposite. The hope is contained in the beautiful pre-war past."

Elsewhere, he observes:

"The sorrow of war inside a soldier's heart is in a strange way similar to the sorrow of love. It is a kind of nostalgia, a deep, endless sadness."

That is the soldier's burden. The sights. The sounds. The smells. The memories. The silent grief that will accompany them long after the shooting stops. But the burden of narrative—of explanation and oratory and moral defence—is not theirs to bear. That burden falls to the rest of us: the citizens of decent society.

We cannot leave them alone on the battlefield of ideas. It is for those of us who live in safety, who enjoy the freedoms they protect, to confront the radicals in our midst—those who delude themselves that their protestations are noble while glorifying Hamas, denying Jewish pain, and pretending that antisemitism is just another form of political discourse.

For the rest of us who do not bear the burden of the soldier nor carry a gun, I will leave you with the insightful words of

Israeli influencer Yon Gruber—someone I do not know personally, but who has captured the mood of many of my friends in Israel and across the world. On 16 June 2025, he posted:

> This is an important reminder to the world. I am speaking on behalf of 100% of Israelis, from the far left to the extreme right. Our goal is to live in our country and chill. No worries. We have no problem with the existence of Iran, Syria, Lebanon. We don't even have a problem with the Palestinians in Gaza. No. The problem only starts when someone wants to wipe us out. Because it clashes with our desire to live. Sure, we have a land dispute with the Palestinians. But we are great at resolving disputes. We are a nation of lawyers. We know how to settle sh*t. No problem. But when you want to kill us and you say it out loud like a total lunatic, it's a bit difficult to have a conversation. And I won't lie to you guys. All these wars, it's exhausting and depressing. We hate it. I just want to watch the NBA Finals. That's it. But we have no choice. Have a nice, missile-free day. And bring our hostages back, please.

His words encapsulate the truth that too many in the West refuse to see. Israel is not fighting to conquer. It is fighting to survive.

To pretend otherwise is not just morally wrong—it is dangerous. It emboldens terrorists. It betrays our values. And it demoralises those who risk everything for us.

In 2024 and 2025, we face a moment not unlike the 1970s. A clash between truth and propaganda. Between courage and cowardice. Between duty and derision. This time, let us not repeat the same shameful mistakes. Let us not abandon those who stand on the wall.

Israel is a frontier democracy. That reality seems to have flown blissfully over the heads of many in Australian society. But make no mistake—the IDF is not only defending Israel. In confronting Hamas in Gaza and the genocidal ayatollahs in Tehran, they are defending the values, freedoms, and way of life that underpin all liberal democracies, including our own.

As German Chancellor Friedrich Merz recently put it: "Israel is doing the dirty work for all of us."

If we do not speak out, who will?

If we do not act now, when?

To the men and women of the IDF—and to all those who serve with moral clarity in the fog of war—thank you. You carry more than a rifle. You carry the burden of civilisation.

Am Yisrael Chai.

Only the Dead Have Seen an End to War

Introduction

War is not a moral abstraction.

It is endured by individuals who operate under uncertainty, fear, and constraints imposed not only by enemies, but by the expectations of distant observers.

This chapter returns the discussion to first principles—to the limits of idealism, the reality of violence, and the danger of judging war through lenses that refuse to acknowledge its nature.

***

"Only the dead have seen the end of war." These haunting words—frequently misattributed to Plato—were more likely penned by the Spanish-American philosopher George Santayana. Regardless of origin, the sentiment endures: War is not an historical anomaly, but a recurring feature of the human condition. It stalks every era, every civilisation, reminding us that peace is not the natural state of mankind, but a fragile achievement to be defended and preserved.

In the United States, Memorial Day is a solemn occasion set aside to honour those who gave their lives in defence of the nation. It emerged after the American Civil War, formally established in the 1860s, and is now observed on the last Monday of May. Much like Australia's ANZAC Day, it is a time not for celebration, but for remembrance—marked by wreaths, lowered flags, and quiet acts of reverence.

The men and women we honour did not seek out war. They answered a call—to protect, to serve, and ultimately to sacrifice. It is often said, and rightly so, that no one abhors war more than the soldier. Those of us who have witnessed its horrors understand its cost. And yet we also know that peace is never guaranteed, never permanent, and never secured by good intentions or wishful thinking alone.

We live in a world defined by relentless competition—economic, technological, ideological, and military. This competition does not always escalate into conflict, but history has shown time and again that it often does. Crises can erupt with little warning, and the illusion of enduring peace can disappear in an instant. It is a dangerous delusion to believe that peace can be achieved simply by desiring it. Peace, when real, is defended—and never defined by the goodwill of our adversaries.

Our obligation is to protect our families, our values, our freedoms, and our way of life. This duty demands more than military might—it requires vigilance, moral clarity, and civic resolve. Yet across much of the West, a troubling complacency has taken hold. Our societies, enriched and secure for generations, now seem unsure of themselves. Strategic foresight has faded. Military readiness has been allowed to erode. The virtues of sacrifice and service are too often met with cynicism or ridicule.

While we debate pronouns and police microaggressions, our adversaries prepare for war.

Consider China. For decades, the Chinese Communist Party has pursued a methodical, strategic campaign to reshape the global order in its image. In *The Long Game: China's Grand Strategy to Displace American Order* (2021, Oxford University Press), Rush Doshi outlines how Beijing has sought to undermine US influence and assert Chinese dominance across military, economic, technological, and diplomatic spheres. China's military modernisation is not accidental—it is coherent, disciplined, and driven by a worldview that sees the West as a declining rival.

Russia, for its part, has transformed its economy into a war engine. According to multiple Western intelligence assessments, Moscow has been mobilising its industrial base for armed conflict for over two years. The invasion of Ukraine was not a miscalculation—it was an expression of a long-standing ambition to reassert Russian power and dismantle the post–Cold War European security order. Vladimir Putin has actively cultivated alliances with other authoritarian regimes, effectively forging a new axis of autocracy.

Russia, China, Iran, and North Korea are now operating in increasing alignment. Through arms transfers, intelligence sharing, technological cooperation, and coordinated diplomacy, these regimes act with mutual purpose. Iran supplies drones to Russia. North Korea provides munitions and manpower. China offers diplomatic protection. Together, their apparent aim is to erode Western power and dismantle the liberal international order.

This is the world as it exists—not as we wish it to be. We may not want war. We may not feel ready for it. But that does not matter. As American historian Robert Kagan once warned,

"You may not be interested in war, but war is interested in you." That interest may come through cyberattacks, supply chain sabotage, border provocations, or acts of terrorism. It may come gradually—or all at once. Either way, we must be prepared.

At times it feels as though many in the West are blind to this truth. There is a growing chorus of negativity directed at the United States, Israel, and other democracies—as if our own imperfections justify the malevolence of those who seek our downfall. Hostile regimes seem content to watch the postmodern West eat itself from within, fanning the flames of cultural self-loathing through misinformation and manipulation.

This Memorial Day, I reflect on the great operational fear that haunted me during my years commanding Australian soldiers in war: that complacency—and the shortcuts it breeds—can be our greatest threat. War punishes the unready. And too often, the cost is paid in the lives of the best among us.

Have we become complacent? Have we reduced Memorial Day to a day off work, rather than a solemn occasion to pause, reflect, and remember those who died to secure the freedoms we now take for granted?

Human history tends to move in waves—sinusoidal cycles of strength and decline, sacrifice and indulgence. In Australia, there was a time when the commemoration of ANZAC Day waned. But in recent decades, we've seen a resurgence—led, inspiringly, by young Australians who understand the power of remembrance. We must ensure Memorial Day follows a similar path.

Because remembrance is not enough.

On Memorial Day, we honour the dead. But we must also prepare the living. The freedoms we cherish—freedom to speak, to worship, to dissent—are not historical guarantees. They are victories, won by generations past and preserved only through vigilance and resolve.

Let us remember them not only with gratitude, but with action. For only the dead have seen the end of war—and the living must carry the burden of preventing its return.

32

Settler Violence: A Fringe Crime Exploited as a Narrative

Introduction

Moral alibis require examples.

When a conflict resists simple explanation, attention gravitates toward isolated incidents that can be inflated into systemic indictment.

This chapter examines how settler violence—real, criminal, and condemnable—has been repurposed as a narrative device to explain away a far older, deeper, and more persistent conflict.

The record, examined honestly, tells a very different story.

***

The murders at Bondi Beach on 15 December 2025 were not an aberration. They were a manifestation—local, intimate, and horrifying—of a hatred that has travelled well, embedded itself deeply, and now operates with a moral confidence that defies reason. That hatred cannot be reasoned with. It cannot be condoned. And it cannot endlessly be explained away as the fault of

Jews—whether in Sydney, Jerusalem, or the hills of Judea and Samaria.

Yet that is precisely what much of the Western conversation has been programmed to do for decades.

Whenever Jews are attacked—in Israel or in the diaspora—a familiar ritual follows. Context is summoned. Explanations are constructed. Provocations are alleged. Responsibility is diluted. And somewhere in the background, a quiet implication lingers: If only the Jews behaved differently, this would not be happening.

Bondi should have shattered that illusion for every reasonable Australian—and for consumers of news and current affairs across the Western world.

There was no settlement to blame on Bondi Beach. No checkpoint. No occupation. No cycle of violence. There was only murderous intent, fuelled by ideology, hatred, and moral permission. The same hatred that animates attacks on Jews in Europe, the Middle East, and now Australia. The same hatred that insists on rationalising itself as grievance, while expressing itself as slaughter.

It is in this context—not an abstract academic one—that claims about "settler violence" must be re-examined.

From Distance to Proximity

Before I lived in Israel between July 2019 and September 2021, I held views not unlike many in the Western world. I once consumed ABC News uncritically, before learning to recognise its gradual descent into activism and opinion masquerading as journalism. The Second Intifada, I was encouraged to believe, was largely Ariel Sharon's fault. His visit to the Temple Mount was a provocation. How dare he?

But that was only the most convenient of several explanations routinely offered by Western commentators and apologists. In the early months of the Second Intifada, the late Robert Fisk described the violence as the understandable eruption of a humiliated people, repeatedly framing suicide bombings as the tragic but predictable consequence of occupation rather than as ideologically driven mass murder. Edward Said, writing in leading Western outlets, portrayed the uprising as an expression of Palestinian despair and resistance, downplaying the role of organised terrorist groups and dismissing Israeli security concerns as pretexts for repression. Even senior figures at the BBC and other public broadcasters routinely characterised the violence as a "cycle" triggered by Israeli actions, treating the deliberate targeting of civilians as reactive rather than intentional.

Others insisted the violence was an inevitable response to "despair," "humiliation," or "occupation fatigue"—as though suicide bombings of buses, cafés, weddings, and Passover seders were the natural emotional language of the oppressed. Some framed the uprising as a spontaneous grassroots revolt, ignoring the documented role of organised terrorist groups, external funding, clerical incitement, and explicit calls for martyrdom. Others spoke earnestly of cycles of violence, a morally flattening phrase that equated deliberate attacks on civilians with defensive countermeasures, and in doing so dissolved responsibility altogether. Still others pointed to stalled peace talks, economic hardship, or unmet political aspirations—as if failed negotiations somehow licensed the mass murder of civilians.

What united these explanations was not evidence, but moral choreography. Violence was contextualised until it was no longer violence at all, but symptom. Agency was reassigned. Intent was blurred. And the most important fact—that civilians were being deliberately hunted and murdered—became secondary to a narrative in which responsibility was endlessly redistributed but never allowed to rest where it belonged. Hovering over all of it was a deeper, rarely examined assumption: that Jewish sovereignty itself was the original provocation, and that violence was therefore not only understandable, but in some warped moral calculus, inevitable.

What none of these explanations could account for—then or now—was the nature of the violence itself: its ritualistic cruelty, its celebration, its theological framing, and its deliberate targeting of non-combatants. During the Second Intifada (2000–2005), more than one thousand Israelis were killed, the majority civilians, in suicide bombings, shootings, and stabbings deliberately aimed at buses, cafés, markets, and religious celebrations. Sharon's visit did not create that hatred. At most, it provided a pretext—eagerly seized upon—for violence that had long been waiting for an excuse.

What followed bore the hallmarks of preparation rather than provocation. The violence was neither proportionate nor spontaneous; it was medieval in its savagery and ideological in its intent. Yet Western media largely treated it as reactive—even understandable.

That framing did not survive proximity.

While my first-hand exposure to Judea and Samaria (the West Bank) was limited, my wife and I visited Bethlehem (Beit Lahm) several times. We entered the Church of the Nativity, ate falafel and hummus in local cafés, and wandered through the markets, bargaining in Arabic—often under the amused and expert guidance of my former employer, a Norwegian major general who knew exactly which shops to frequent and how to talk prices down to the shekel.

These were not hostile encounters. They were human ones. And they sat uneasily alongside the Western narrative that insisted on flattening the region into a cartoon of Jewish aggressors and Palestinian victims.

What proximity also reveals—uncomfortably, but unmistakably—is why a security barrier exists between Israeli families and those in Judea and Samaria who are prepared to murder civilians without remorse. The same pathology that produced the killers at Bondi Beach exists in far greater concentration there. The barrier is not an ideological statement; it is a defensive one, born of bitter experience. Now that this hatred has breached one of Australia's most intimate and familiar public spaces, one can reasonably hope an awakening is underway among Western publics: that security measures are not symbols of oppression, but often the last line between ordinary families and those who believe slaughter is a form of justice.

Hatred That Does Not Seek Explanation—Only Justification

None of this is to deny that settler violence exists. It does. There are documented cases of assaults, vandalism, intimidation, and arson carried out by Jewish extremists in the West Bank. These acts are morally wrong. They harm Palestinians, undermine Israel's rule of law, and corrode Israel from within. Israel's courts and security services have repeatedly investigated, arrested, and imprisoned Jewish extremists—a distinction rarely acknowledged in Western coverage, but essential to understanding the difference between a democracy confronting its radicals and a culture that celebrates them.

But the critical error—the one Bondi exposes with brutal clarity—is the belief that such fringe violence explains antisemitism.

It does not.

Hatred that murders Jews on a beach in Sydney is not reacting to olive trees in Samaria. Hatred that celebrates the killing of Jewish civilians does not require grievances—it recruits them. It selects facts that suit it, discards those that do not, and then wraps itself in the language of justice.

This ideological environment has been sustained for decades by official incitement—in media, education, and religious institutions—that glorifies "martyrdom" and frames Jewish civilians not as neighbours, but as legitimate targets.

This is the same hatred that drove the Second Intifada long before settlements expanded to their current footprint. The same hatred that emptied ancient Christian communities across the Middle East. The same hatred that now stalks Jewish Australians.

Bad Actors, Bad Faith, and Bad Statistics

Every collective of humanity contains outliers. Bell curves apply everywhere—in religions, nations, ideologies, and political movements. Israel is no exception.

But the scale matters.

Israeli settlers constitute less than 5 percent of Israel's Jewish population. Violent settlers represent a tiny fraction of that already small subset. Yet Western media coverage routinely presents settler violence as systemic, ubiquitous, and defining—a framing that does not survive statistical scrutiny.

As the old saying goes, often attributed to Mark Twain: "There are three kinds of lies: lies, damned lies, and statistics."

In this case, statistics are not being falsified so much as selectively amplified—stripped of context and weaponised to sustain a predetermined moral narrative.

The result is not clarity, but distortion.

The Disappearing Christians—An Inconvenient Reality

Consider Bethlehem itself.

Historically, Bethlehem was overwhelmingly Christian. In the final years of the British Mandate and into the early post-1948 period, Christians comprised approximately 85–86 percent of the town's population. By the 1967 census, Christians still accounted for roughly 45–46 percent of residents—a decline already well underway.

By around 1970, Bethlehem remained one of the last Christian-majority centres in the West Bank, but the trajectory was unmistakable. Over the decades that followed, the collapse accelerated. In the early 1990s, Christians comprised an estimated 60–65 percent of the population. Today, they account for well under 15 percent, with some estimates placing the figure closer to 10 percent or lower.

This decline did not occur under Israeli municipal control. Bethlehem has been under Palestinian Authority governance since the Oslo Accords.

To describe this simply as "economic migration" is to avoid a harder truth: Christian minorities across the region have been squeezed—culturally, politically, and at times violently—out of their ancestral homes—not by Jews, but overwhelmingly by Islamist social pressure and insecurity. This reality sits uncomfortably with a Western narrative that insists all coercion flows in one direction.

If we are willing to use the language of "ethnic cleansing," we should at least be honest about where demographic erasure is actually occurring.

Settler Violence, War, and the Absence of a Peace Partner

Settler violence is confronting to Western eyes, and it should be. Israel is a democracy, and democracies must hold themselves to higher standards. Acts of intimidation, vandalism, or assault committed by Jewish extremists should be denounced—clearly, proportionately, and honestly.

But Israel is also a nation at war. It has been so since the late 1940s.

When the United Nations endorsed the partition plan in 1947—a two-state solution—the Jewish leadership accepted it and celebrated. The Arab leadership rejected it outright. What followed was not coexistence, but invasion: a war launched by neighbouring Arab states bent on the destruction of the Jewish state at birth. That was not resistance to occupation. It was an attempted genocide of a people who had just emerged from one.

That pattern has repeated across Israel's modern history. Peace offers have been made, concessions proposed, territory exchanged—and yet time and again they have been met with rejection, violence, or both. For all the complexity of the conflict, one moral asymmetry remains intact: Only one side has consistently articulated a willingness to coexist. The other has too often pursued Judenrein—land free of Jews—through war, terror, and endless litigation of grievance.

Settler violence must not be weaponised as a moral alibi for antisemitism, nor repurposed as an explanatory framework for atrocities committed thousands of kilometres away. Nor should it obscure the asymmetry in how violence is reported. Western media outlets broadcast alleged or perceived settler violence relentlessly—often stripped of scale and context—while showing far less urgency when Islamist movements brutalise their own people.

In October 2025, after Israeli combat operations in Gaza had largely ceased under a ceasefire arrangement, Hamas publicly executed Palestinians accused of dissent or collaboration—Levantine Muslim Arabs killed not by Israel, but by their own rulers. These extrajudicial killings, ideological and deliberate, received only fleeting international attention. They did not fit the preferred narrative.

This selective outrage matters. It conditions Western audiences to believe that Jewish violence is explanatory, while Islamist violence is invisible or inevitable. It also obscures a central reality: the primary victims of Islamist movements are very often Muslims themselves.

In such an environment, calls for Israel to assume unilateral moral risk in pursuit of peace become detached from reality. Peace requires a partner. Where no viable peace partner exists—where leadership is fragmented, corrupt, violent, or ideologically committed to Israel's eradication—the rational course for a democracy is not retreat, but resilience.

From afar, this is often mischaracterised as intransigence. From proximity, it is strategic coherence: a state incrementally strengthening its security, deepening its defensive depth, and attending first to the safety of its people until such time as the other side demonstrates both the will and the capacity to be part of a genuine solution.

The hatred that came hunting Jews—and non-Jewish Australians—at Bondi Beach exists in far greater numbers in Gaza and across Judea and Samaria. Bondi was not an anomaly. It was a warning.

I have reconsidered my own position on settlements in this light. I do not arrive at this view lightly or callously. I arrive at it as a non-Jewish father, deeply troubled by what I see unfolding not only in Israel, but across a failing Western world increasingly unwilling to defend itself, its values, or its people.

In the absence of a credible peace partner, strengthening Israel's position is not an obstacle to peace. It is the precondition for it.

We need a strong Israel more than many yet appreciate—not despite the lessons of Bondi, but because of them.

33

Long Overdue Accountability

Introduction

For decades, moral asymmetry was tolerated in the name of peace.

"Long Overdue Accountability" assesses a decisive legal turning point: the restoration of consequence to systems that incentivise violence while evading responsibility. It traces how financial, legal, and institutional mechanisms sustained terror—and how that insulation is now beginning to fracture.

This chapter examines what changes when accountability is no longer optional—and why justice delayed has costs not only for victims, but for the credibility of the institutions that once looked away.

***

In a landmark and unanimous ruling on 20 June 2025, the United States Supreme Court upheld federal legislation granting American victims of Palestinian terrorism—and their families—the right to sue the Palestinian Authority (PA) and the Palestine Liberation Organization (PLO) in US courts. This precedent-setting decision marks a long-overdue turning point in the pursuit of justice and accountability after decades of impunity and moral evasion.

At the centre of the case lies the Palestinian Authority's grotesque "Pay-for-Slay" program—a policy that provides monthly stipends to convicted terrorists and the families of deceased attackers. This is no fringe phenomenon. It is institutionalised, enshrined in Palestinian law, and publicly defended by PA leaders. While the PA claims these payments are a form of social support, they are widely viewed as incentives for violence. And for far too long, the broader Palestinian aid system has been underwritten—albeit indirectly—by Western donor nations, including at times Australia.

The Business of Murder

The Pay-for-Slay scheme allocates payments far exceeding average wages in the West Bank. For example:

A terrorist sentenced to over thirty years in an Israeli prison receives approximately US$3,500 per month, more than four times the average local salary.

In 2023, Israel's Ministry of Defence reported that over US$300 million was earmarked by the PA for prisoner and "martyr" payments—roughly 7 percent of its annual budget.

This is not welfare. It is incentive. It is blood money—and it has deadly consequences.

Between 2000 and 2020, hundreds of Israeli civilians were murdered in terrorist attacks carried out by individuals or groups later glorified and financially rewarded by the PA. From the 2001 Sbarro pizzeria massacre to the 2016 murder of thirteen-year-old Hallel Yaffa Ariel in her bed, victims have ranged from Holocaust survivors to toddlers. These atrocities were not condemned by the PA—but celebrated.

Yet Western governments continued to send financial assistance—despite overwhelming evidence that such aid enables the very forces that glorify and reward terrorism. Australia, for example, allocated more than AUD $20 million in 2023–24 to the Occupied Palestinian Territories. A significant portion of this funding was channelled through multilateral intermediaries such as the United Nations Relief and Works Agency (UNRWA)—an organisation that, in my judgment, ought to be relegated to history. For years, UNRWA has operated with impunity, presiding over a system that fosters antisemitism in schools, employs individuals linked to terrorist groups, and perpetuates the fiction of eternal victimhood.

Legal, Moral, and Strategic Repercussions

The Supreme Court's decision delivers three crucial outcomes:

First, it restores dignity to victims. Survivors and families of those killed in cold blood now have a legal pathway to seek redress—not from vague ideologies, but from institutions directly complicit in incentivising these crimes.

Second, it imposes consequence. If the PA and PLO are subjected to damages, asset discovery, and the reputational toll of open court proceedings, they may finally be pressured to end these abhorrent policies. The days of unchecked impunity may be nearing an end.

Third, it shifts the strategic calculus. The ruling invites renewed scrutiny of how foreign aid is used—and whether donor nations like Australia are inadvertently enabling violence through poor oversight or political timidity.

A Doctrine for a Different Fight

This ruling aligns with a broader strategic and moral framework. In a 2009 article with the tongue-in-cheek title "When a Cup of Coffee Becomes a Soy Decaf Mint Mocha Chip Frappuccino," Australian Brigadier Justin Kelly and strategist Ben Fitzgerald critiqued the proliferation of fashionable but ineffective military doctrines in the West.

In their wider body of work, they distilled warfare down to two enduring defeat mechanisms: annihilation and exhaustion. The former—completely destroying an enemy—is often unachievable and incompatible with liberal democratic values. The latter—denying an enemy the legitimacy, resources, and support required to continue fighting—is both feasible and morally sound.

The Supreme Court's ruling does not annihilate Palestinian terrorism. But it contributes to its exhaustion. By choking the financial lifelines of those who glorify murder and exposing them to international legal scrutiny, it represents a principled step toward lasting peace.

What Took So Long?

The moral asymmetry of the Israeli–Palestinian conflict has never been clearer. On one side: a liberal democracy committed to rule of law, pluralism, and restraint in the face of existential threats. On the other: a leadership that glorifies violence, names schools after suicide bombers, and uses public funds to honour perpetrators of terrorism.

Yet for years, parts of the Western world inverted this reality. Terrorists were romanticised as "resistance fighters." Israeli victims were written off as mere "occupiers." The murder of Jews was excused—or worse, lionised.

This grotesque double standard has seeped into academia, media, and political discourse. Antisemitism has not only resurfaced—it has become fashionable, repackaged as activism while repeating the world's oldest hatred.

This ruling strikes at that hypocrisy. It affirms a basic truth: that terror is terror, no matter the flag under which it hides.

The Road Ahead

Expect the PA and its defenders to denounce the ruling as "political." Expect attempts to hide assets, delay judgments, and reframe themselves as victims. But also expect momentum. Legal teams in Canada, the UK, and perhaps Australia may begin exploring similar avenues. The Overton window is shifting—from appeasement to accountability.

It is now up to lawmakers and diplomats to match legal clarity with policy resolve. Aid to the Palestinian Authority must no longer be unconditional. Any future funds must be strictly contingent on the complete dismantling of the Pay-for-Slay system, and a verifiable end to incitement in schools, media, and public discourse.

Western democracies must no longer tolerate the moral incoherence of funding both the victims and the perpetrators of terror.

Conclusion

Justice is not merely about the courts. It is about the values we choose to uphold.

This Supreme Court decision is a long-overdue affirmation of principle. It tells the world that there will be consequences for those who glorify terrorism. It tells the victims and their families that their pain has not been forgotten. And it reminds the free world that its values—when defended—can still prevail.

In the contest between civilisation and barbarism, between justice and bloodlust, let us be clear about where we stand.

PART IV
Conclusion

The record does not offer comfort.

It reveals a conflict shaped by asymmetry, exploitation, and moral complexity—not the cartoon morality demanded by modern discourse. It shows restraint punished, defence reframed as aggression, and legal standards selectively applied.

But the record also offers clarity.

It exposes how far contemporary judgment has drifted from historical precedent, legal definition, and lived military reality. And it makes plain that the moral alibis used to excuse violence do not withstand serious scrutiny.

If truth is to matter, it must survive contact with war.

What follows is what happens when that truth returns home—and when the consequences of distortion are no longer theoretical.

PART V

DANGER: WHEN HATE COMES HOME

The lie returns inward

PART V
Introduction

Hatred rarely announces its arrival with certainty.

It is more often tolerated before it is confronted, excused before it is condemned, and contextualised before it is understood. By the time it becomes undeniable, it has already crossed multiple thresholds without resistance.

For much of the Western world, antisemitism was long treated as a historical inheritance—something remembered, regretted, and presumed contained. When it resurfaced, it was framed as symbolic, rhetorical, or marginal.

But hatred does not remain theoretical.

When narratives are allowed to distort reality, and institutions fail to correct them, the consequences do not remain overseas. They move inward—into synagogues, neighbourhoods, schools, workplaces, and public spaces once assumed to be safe.

This part examines what happens when the lie returns home—and when the cost of indulgence is paid not in words, but in fear.

History is Watching: Israel, Antisemitism, and the Choice Before Us

Introduction

Antisemitism rarely believes it will be judged by history.

"History Is Watching" confronts a generation intoxicated by slogans and shielded from consequence, reminding the reader that ideas are not cost-free—and that moral indulgence is always temporary.

This chapter examines how moments of moral failure are recorded long after slogans fade—and why the choices made now will be judged not by intention, but by outcome.

***

It is no longer shocking to see university students chanting "intifada revolution" or masked agitators tearing down posters of kidnapped Israeli children. What is shocking is how quickly this ugliness has become socially acceptable in polite company. On city streets and social media, young Westerners shout slogans they don't understand for causes they don't comprehend—fuelled not by lived experience, but by ideology. In 2024–2025, antisemitism doesn't always wear a swastika. Sometimes it cloaks itself in 'decolonisation' and speaks the language of human rights.

To the reasonable, open-minded people who find themselves swayed—whether loudly or subtly—by those cheering on Hamas: You are being deceived. You are being manipulated and triggered by monsters who know exactly which strings to pull. This isn't just about the destruction of Israel—it's about dismantling the civilised world, including the one you live in. As Robespierre learned, revolutions always consume the dimwits who ignite the fuse. The same fate awaits today's kaffiyah-clad keyboard warriors and their naïve enablers.

Those waving the Hamas flag are not demanding Palestinian freedom—they are cheering for theocratic fascism, gender apartheid, and the elimination of the Jewish people. These are not values confined to Gaza. Hamas's ideology is exported, adapted, and echoed in the West—in classrooms, on TikTok, and even in parliament. If civilisation does not stand firm now, we are complicit in its slow undoing. Today's appeasement will not buy peace; it will embolden violence. The Islamists marching for blood in Gaza do not stop at Tel Aviv. London, Paris, Sydney, and New York are next.

As Elie Wiesel warned, "We must take sides. Neutrality helps the oppressor, never the victim. Silence encourages the tormentor, never the tormented." This is one of those moments. The siren song of antisemitic propaganda—whether broadcast in the streets or whispered through academic respectability—is a moral test.

And as Dietrich Bonhoeffer reminded the world in even darker times, "The ultimate test of a moral society is the kind of world that it leaves to its children." That test is here again, and it will be judged not by hashtags, but by courage and clarity.

When people ask me who the IDF are, I say this: On an individual level, picture your own children or grandchildren—idealistic, decent, and determined. When asked about the IDF collectively, I remind people it is exactly what its name declares—a Defence Force. It protects Israeli homes and families with innovation, restraint, and conviction like few have seen in military history.

And when asked about Israel, I speak of my Druze, Jewish, Christian Arab, and Muslim Arab mates—citizens who live, serve, and hope together. Israel is more Western, more pluralistic, and more decent than most of its critics ever care to acknowledge. In my years of service, and later during my time in Israel with the United Nations, I saw it with my own eyes.

On a visit to Israel in September 2024, I sat with Jewish and Druze reservists who are as close to me as kin. On a Friday morning, I went mountain biking with a Jewish friend in the Ben Shemen Forest, nestled between Tel Aviv and Jerusalem. Only in Israel will you see five observant Muslim women, riding in hijabs under MTB helmets, with long sleeves and full-length trousers—exercising their freedom, their joy, and their right to belong. Because they are Israeli.

Yes, 20 percent of Israel's population are Arab. Of that 20 percent, roughly 19 percent are Muslim and 1 percent Christian. Do they all support the Jewish State? Of course not. Just as in Australia, where a small number of citizens support terrorist organisations that have been proscribed by our government, Israel too has its fringe elements. But like Australia, those voices are a noisy minority—and no more representative of the average Israeli Arab than extremists in Australia are of mainstream Australians.

Also like in Australia, these minority voices are the ones repeatedly sought out by failing legacy media organisations—among them the ABC, *The Sydney Morning Herald*, the BBC, and Al Jazeera. We live in an Orwellian age, where compromised zealots and activist-journalists insist that two plus two equals five.

Talk about resilience, unity, and purpose. The people I met weren't asking for pity or praise. They spoke of duty, of family, of fear. They spoke of living with the unbearable contradiction of being both demonised and expected to show restraint in the face of barbarism. Their courage reminded me that Israel is not perfect—but it is good. And that matters.

Too many people of influence know the truth yet say nothing. Editors bury the hostage story by paragraph five. Academics twist themselves into knots to justify the unjustifiable. Political leaders mumble about "both sides." But there are not two sides to terrorism. There is only courage—or cowardice. There is standing up—or standing by.

This is not a time for moral ambivalence. It is a time for clarity, courage, and commitment.

The 2023 Foundation exists to engage, educate, and empower the reasonable majority—the good people who, once exposed to truth, may choose to become fierce defenders of it. Together, we are building a new generation of non-Jewish allies for Israel. Because the West cannot survive if it betrays the Jews again.

Not this time.

Not on our watch.

When Hate Comes Knocking: A Shabbat Attack in Melbourne

Introduction

Antisemitism does not require mass movements to be effective.

It requires only permission—the sense that hostility will be tolerated, minimised, or explained away.

When that permission exists, it eventually expresses itself not as slogan or chant, but as action.

This chapter recounts a moment when hatred crossed the threshold from rhetoric into lived reality—not in a distant conflict zone, but in a quiet domestic setting, on a day set aside for rest and worship.

***

On the evening of Friday 4 July 2025, as candles were lit and songs of peace rose in prayer, a domestic terrorist tried to burn down a synagogue in the heart of Melbourne. The target: the historic East Melbourne Synagogue—a cherished centre of Jewish life for more than a century. Rabbi Dovid and Rebbetzin Rachel

Gutnick are its spiritual custodians, offering warmth, leadership, and continuity to a community they have long served with deep devotion.

Founded in 1857, the East Melbourne Hebrew Congregation is the oldest synagogue in continuous use on the Australian mainland. Its heritage-listed architecture has borne witness to generations of Jewish life—bris, bar and bat mitzvahs, weddings and funerals, holy days and ordinary ones. General Sir John Monash, Australia's greatest military leader and one of our finest citizens in any field, celebrated his bar mitzvah within those very walls.

That should still mean something.

Every Friday evening, Jewish families across Australia and around the world gather for Shabbat—the traditional Sabbath meal marking the end of the workweek and the beginning of sacred rest. It is a night of joy, warmth, and welcome. Synagogue services usher in the Sabbath with prayer, reflection, and community. At East Melbourne Synagogue—under the Gutnicks' care—Shabbat unfolds with reverence and belonging. Children often race to the door, eager to greet arriving friends and congregants.

If that sounds much like your family home or mine, then we begin to grasp the gravity of what occurred. This was not just an attack on a Jewish institution—it was an attack on all of us.

But on that Friday night, as kind and tolerant Jewish Australians gathered for dinner in their synagogue, the doorbell rang—and something was terribly wrong.

Inside, children ran to the door, excited to see who had arrived. But this time, they didn't open it. Thank Hashem. What unfolded was a domestic terrorist attack—right here, in Australia, in 2025. Again!

On 22 July 2025, I heard firsthand testimony from inside the shule that terrifying night, as Rebbetzin Rachel Gutnick addressed a Zoom gathering of community Upstanders convened by the Southern Cross Alliance for Israel. Her calm, dignified recounting—children racing to the door, confusion turning to alarm, smoke seeping beneath the threshold—was deeply moving.

Outside, a thirty-four-year-old man had doused the front doors with accelerant and set them alight. It was a deliberate act of hate. Smoke began to stream inside. Panic took hold.

Thankfully, the fire did not. The carpet didn't ignite. The beautiful Australian families gathered for Shabbat escaped physical harm. But the emotional and psychological scars will linger for a long time.

There is a reason that a democratically elected government in the Middle East—subjected to relentless rocket and missile attacks over the past two years, including ballistic missiles launched from Yemen and Iran—has publicly admonished Australian leaders and urged them to do better.

There is a reason that many Jewish friends are now openly considering relocation to Israel, as life in Australia grows increasingly intolerable for our Jewish community.

There were no fatalities. The building was not gutted. But we must not minimise what occurred.

In earlier centuries, Jews trapped inside their houses of worship were burned alive by baying mobs. In 1190, the Jews of York were massacred inside Clifford's Tower. In 1349, during the Black Death hysteria, Jews in Strasbourg were locked in a synagogue and set ablaze.

History is a brutal teacher: When mobs chant and justice sleeps, evil finds its courage.

So how did we come to this—in Melbourne, Australia, in 2025?

The answer is as simple as it is damning: a lack of consequences.

Antisemitism is sweeping across our country. Jewish schools, synagogues, and community centres are secured like fortresses. And not without reason. For decades, Jews in Australia have lived under a level of targeted hate that would be considered intolerable for any other minority.

I recently wrote about the mob that descended on Sydney's Great Synagogue during the Technion Anniversary Event. It was frightening to be inside. Before that piece even reached publication, another synagogue—Adass Israel in Melbourne—was attacked.

These are not aberrations. They are signs of a society failing a fundamental test.

Jewish Australians are not crying wolf. They are crying out for help.

The 2023 Foundation—a grassroots social movement I founded—is responding. We combat antisemitism through lived personal experience. Our mission is to expose non-Jews to the truth about Israel and the Jewish people, to challenge ignorance with empathy, and to grow a new generation of non-Jewish Upstanders—not bystanders.

Having lived in Israel for twenty-seven months—from July 2019 to September 2021—I've seen firsthand the humanity, diversity, and complexity of Israeli society. I returned in September 2024 as part of a senior international delegation with extraordinary access, including into Gaza alongside the IDF. I know the slurs and smears spread in our media and universities are lies. Scurrilous lies.

This is not just about protecting Jewish Australians. It's about preserving the moral fabric of our nation. Because if the oldest hatred is allowed to thrive, all other hatreds follow.

So to my fellow non-Jewish Australians, and to good citizens across the faltering West, I ask you to pause and imagine the conversation you might one day have with your seven-year-old child. The doorbell rings. You say: "Please don't run to the door. Don't open it. We don't know who it is. It might be a friend. But it might be someone who wants to hurt us—just because of who we are."

Now imagine the follow-up question: "But why, Mummy?"

That is what we are asking our Jewish neighbours to explain to their children—in this country, in our time.

This is not a Jewish problem. It is an Australian problem. A Western problem. A moral problem.

Because when hate comes knocking, it's not just Jewish doors that burn.

It is our shared future that is on fire.

36

Unrequited Love, Unpaid Loyalty

Introduction

Australian Jews did not arrive as guests.

They arrived as contributors—to commerce, culture, defence, medicine, law, and public life—investing in the promise of a country that prided itself on fairness, pluralism, and mutual obligation.

For decades, that loyalty was assumed to be reciprocal.

This chapter examines what happens when that assumption fractures—when appeals for protection are met with equivocation, and when a community that has given deeply to the national project is left to wonder whether its trust has been misplaced.

***

"Unrequited love" is love given sincerely but not returned. It is affection, loyalty, and commitment offered into a void—met with indifference, dismissal, or contempt. In 2025, that phrase has become an ugly metaphor for what many Jewish Australians describe as their relationship with the country they love: a deep, longstanding loyalty to Australia—to its institutions, its social compact, its promise of fair play—met, in their hour of need, with minimisation, procedural delay, moral equivocation, and, too often, outright gaslighting.

Australia has never been perfect. But it has long been unusually good: a place where minorities could build and belong, where civic identity was meant to outrank bloodline and tribe. Jews did not arrive yesterday. They were present from the very beginning of the modern Australian story—with Jewish convicts transported with the First Fleet and in the earliest decades of the colony. That origin story matters, because it punctures the lazy contemporary slur that Jews are a "foreign" presence, a recent import, or somehow not part of the Australian "we." Jewish Australians have been here since 1788. The only honest argument is about how we treat one another now.

And now—the period beginning 7 October 2023—has been a national stress test that Australia has failed in ways that should shame any serious multicultural society.

The Warning Flares We Chose to Explain Away

Two days after the Hamas atrocities of 7 October 2023, Sydney saw a pro-Palestinian rally at the Opera House. What was chanted there is not a matter of internet rumour; it has been litigated in public, including by police review and media analysis. What was chanted there is not a matter of internet rumour; it has been examined publicly, including by police and media. NSW Police later said expert analysis did not confirm the specific chant "gas the Jews," concluding the audio captured "where's the Jews." That finding sits in tension with the unequivocal testimony of numerous eyewitnesses present on the steps that night, who insist that "gas the Jews" was indeed chanted, alongside other chants such as "f*** the Jews."

The distinction may matter legally. It does not matter morally. The difference between "gas the Jews" and "where's the Jews" is not the difference between civil discourse and peaceful protest. Either way, a line was crossed—a line any functioning society should have treated as a five-alarm fire.

Many Jewish leaders and organisations said so at the time, publicly and repeatedly, warning that what was being tolerated in the streets would not stay in the streets. Those warnings were not abstract. They were grounded in history, and in a simple operational truth: When incitement is normalised, violence becomes imaginable; when violence becomes imaginable, it becomes executable.

From that point onward, for more than two years, Australia's Jewish communities described a grinding lived reality: armed security at schools and synagogues; cancelled events; shuttered businesses; doxxing and harassment; fear in public spaces; hostility in workplaces and the arts; and an increasingly confident activist subculture that treated Jews as fair game—unless they performed the required political denunciations.

The Executive Council of Australian Jewry documented this pattern meticulously, warning that anti-Jewish racism had moved from the fringes into mainstream spaces, aided by institutional timidity and cultural indulgence.

"Take Our Fear Seriously"

A community can live with risk. What it cannot live with is the feeling that the nation's leadership is not taking that risk seriously—or worse, that its fear is being managed, minimised, or bureaucratised away.

That is why Jewish Australian commentary since October 2023 has been marked first by trauma and alarm—and, following the murders at Bondi Beach, by anger and contempt. Trauma and alarm, because the threats are real, personal, and persistent. Anger, because so much of what followed was foreseeable and yet left unaddressed. And contempt, because repeated warnings were met not with resolve, but with delay, equivocation, and excuse.

This is not a partisan claim. It is a civic one. When Jewish Australians spoke about intimidation at weekly marches, hostility on campuses, and ideological capture in parts of the cultural sector, they were not seeking special treatment. They were asking for the baseline protections any state owes its citizens: equal safety, equal dignity, and equal concern.

The Honourable Julian Leeser MP has repeatedly framed antisemitism as a direct threat to Australia's multicultural fabric, pointing to studied indifference within institutions charged with protecting students and staff. The ECAJ has argued that existing complaint-based mechanisms have proven inadequate, particularly on university campuses. Jeremy Leibler has spoken bluntly about what has been unmasked since October 7 and what has been tolerated. Colin Rubenstein, AM has warned that a permissive climate of incitement makes antisemitic violence more likely.

After Bondi, The Honourable Josh Frydenberg called for far-reaching action against extremist preaching and incitement, arguing plainly that the hate produced this. Different voices. One consistent message: this is real, it is escalating, and it requires leadership—not platitudes.

When Words Became Blood

On 14 December 2025, Jews celebrating Chanukah at Bondi Beach were deliberately targeted in a terrorist attack. Fifteen people were murdered, including a ten-year-old girl. Court documents later indicated that homemade bombs were thrown but failed to detonate, and that extremist material formed part of the evidence.

The point is not to litigate every operational detail while investigations continue. The point is the arc: from tolerated chants and intimidation to mass-casualty violence against Jews in public.

In the aftermath, debate surged over the phrase "globalise the intifada." For Jewish Australians, this was never a semantic exercise. "Intifada" is not poetry; it is historically associated with waves of violence against civilians, including suicide bombings. Whatever activists claim to mean by it, the enduring question has been simpler: Why were Jews expected to interpret threatening slogans generously, while everyone else refused to interpret Jewish fear seriously?

Fire at the Doors

Bondi was not the only marker of escalation. Jewish places of worship were attacked.

In December 2024, the Adass Israel Synagogue in Ripponlea was targeted in a suspected arson attack and burned to the ground. In July 2025, an arson attack struck the East Melbourne Hebrew Congregation while around twenty people were inside. These were not symbolic acts. They were attempts to burn Jews alive in their places of prayer.

These are not "community tensions." They are attacks—the kind that force a minority community to think like a besieged outpost inside a country that insists it remains a safe, settled liberal democracy.

The Institutional Layer—and the Double Standard

A recurring theme in Jewish Australian commentary since October 2023 is that the problem is not only extremists. It is the ambient permission structure created by institutions that should know better: parts of the media, academia, the cultural sector, regulatory bodies, and commissioners whose processes are slow, procedural, and easily weaponised.

From this permissive environment has flowed something more corrosive still: an inversion of moral responsibility that has spread beyond activist circles and into otherwise decent, educated, and well-intentioned Australians. People who would recoil instantly from overt racism against any other minority have been conditioned to rationalise, contextualise, or excuse it when Jews are the target—not because they are malicious, but because they have been misled. Taught that Jews are powerful and resilient, and therefore less deserving of protection; that Jewish fear is political rather than human; that antisemitism is only real if it arrives in its most grotesque historical costume.

This is not accidental. It is the cumulative effect of years of indulgence, equivocation, and narrative capture—a failure of institutional courage that has allowed antisemitism to be reframed as opinion, intimidation as activism, and incitement as "context."

And this is where I part company with growing calls for ever more legislation.

Call me old-fashioned, but my unease does not stem from complacency. It stems from the simple fact that Australia already possesses ample legal tools. The problem is not a vacuum of law. It is a vacuum of will.

The Law Already Exists—It Is Simply Not Being Applied

Across New South Wales, Victoria, and at the federal level, much of the conduct Jewish Australians have endured since October 2023 is already unlawful.

In New South Wales, criminal law prohibits serious vilification, threats, intimidation, and incitement to violence. Public Order offences, anti-terror legislation, and conspiracy provisions already capture conduct that encourages harm or creates reasonable fear. NSW's Anti-Discrimination Act also provides civil remedies—though these are slow, burdensome, and place the onus on victims rather than the state.

In Victoria, the Racial and Religious Tolerance Act prohibits conduct that incites hatred, serious contempt, revulsion, or violence on the basis of religion. The threshold is not abstract genocide slogans; it is whether reasonable members of the targeted group would feel threatened or vilified. Arson attacks on synagogues, intimidation outside Jewish institutions, and repeated exhortations to violence are not legal grey zones. They are criminal matters.

At the Commonwealth level, the Criminal Code already criminalises urging violence against groups, advocating terrorism, providing support to extremist causes, and engaging in conduct intended to intimidate sections of the public. The AFP does not lack statutory authority. What it often lacks is political backing to act early, decisively, and unapologetically.

Apply the rules that already exist. Substitute "gay female Afghan asylum seeker" for "Jewish Australian" in many of these cases—chants, threats, exclusion, intimidation—and the response would be immediate, unequivocal, and enforced. That it is not when the target is Jewish is not incidental or accidental. It is antisemitism—not the cartoon version of the past, but the modern form: procedural, euphemistic, socially respectable, and lethal in its consequences.

Calling for the enforcement of existing law is not authoritarian. It is the bare minimum a state owes its citizens.

Unpaid Loyalty

Jewish Australians have loved Australia. They have defended Australia. They have been loyal to its institutions even when those institutions were imperfect. Since October 2023, many feel that loyalty has gone unpaid—not in money, but in the currency citizenship demands: protection, solidarity, and the presumption of equal belonging.

The anger is not only about fear. It is about betrayal: being told Jewish safety is negotiable; that Jewish pain is "complicated"; that the right to live free from harassment is contingent on adopting the correct political posture; that hate is only hate if expressed in approved language.

This is why the reaction after Bondi—boos at vigils, calls for political leaders to resign, demands for inquiries, calls for tougher action—cannot be dismissed as political theatre. It is a community saying: We tried polite. We tried process. We tried pleading. We tried being reasonable. And then we buried our dead.

The Country We Choose to Be

The First Fleet detail is not trivia. It is a reminder that Jewish Australians have been part of this story from the start—as convicts, builders, citizens, soldiers, voters, donors, neighbours, and friends. That long belonging makes the last two years feel like a rupture, as if the social contract has been quietly revised without consent.

Unrequited love is painful in private life. In national life, it is dangerous. A minority that no longer trusts the state to protect it retreats inward, prepares contingencies, leaves—or stops believing in the shared project altogether.

Australia can still choose differently. But not while insisting the problem is exaggerated, treating Jewish fear as inconvenient, or allowing hatred to dress itself up as fashionable morality.

The debt of unpaid loyalty is now due. The question is whether Australia will pay it—in truth, courage, and action—or continue to ask Jewish Australians to love a country that refuses to love them back.

When Hate Goes Unchallenged

Introduction

Silence is often mistaken for restraint.

But in the presence of intimidation, silence communicates something else entirely: acceptance.

When hateful behaviour is met with equivocation, procedural delay, or misplaced calls for balance, the message received is not caution, but licence.

This chapter examines the cost of that silence—and why failing to confront hatred early makes confrontation later far more dangerous.

***

On Sunday 20 July 2025, I stood in my thirteenth-floor hotel room in central Melbourne and listened—through double-glazed windows—as a crowd on Swanston Street chanted, "Death! Death to the IOF!"

For the uninitiated, "IOF" is a deliberate slur: a bastardisation of IDF—Israel Defense Forces—twisted by anti-Israel activists to mean "Israeli Occupation Forces." It's not a critique of policy. It's a denial of legitimacy—of Israel's very right to exist.

The hate was relentless, venomous, and unmistakable. Around four hundred people screaming for death—in the heart of Australia's second-largest city.

Later that day, I posted on social media:

> Quite confronting and very dispiriting to be in Melbourne today and hear a gathering of ratbags screaming 'Death, death to the IOF.' Watermelon symbols, Palestinian flags, and kaffiyehs aplenty. Loud enough to be heard from the 13th floor of a hotel—behind double-glazed glass. If any of my Australian Jewish friends are feeling like strangers in your own nation, you're not Robinson Crusoe.

One reply cut to the heart of it: this wasn't a one-off. It's been happening every week—for 18 consecutive months. Publicly. Audibly. Brazenly.

Menace has been normalised—and normalised menace becomes mainstream.

And the response from too many in our society? Silence. Or worse, excuse-making.

You don't need to be Jewish to feel the chill of this climate. But to be Jewish in Australia today—especially in Melbourne—is to feel under siege.

I recently spoke with a family who moved here from Birmingham, UK, seeking safety for their children. The father is a doctor. The mother, a barrister. Now they're contemplating

Aliyah to Israel—not despite the threat from Iran, but because life there feels safer than what they're enduring here.

Let that sink in: A patriotic Australian family feels their children may be freer in a war zone than in a city where hate marches unopposed each week.

Had someone predicted this in 2020, they'd have been dismissed as hysterical. Yet here we are—watching the Overton window shift so far that "Death to the IOF" is treated as just another chant.

This is what happens when hate goes unchallenged.

Freedom of speech is essential. But it's not freedom from consequence. As Judge Learned Hand warned in 1944:

"Liberty lies in the hearts of men and women; when it dies there, no constitution, no law, no court can save it."

Laws alone cannot uphold decency if society walks away from it.

Some say these are fringe voices. Perhaps. But fringes tolerated long enough become the new normal.

Ask yourself: if a group shouted "Death to Gays" or "Death to Aboriginals" in the same spot for eighteen months straight—would they still be marching? Would they even reach the third minute?

I suspect not—and rightly so.

So why the double standard when the target is Jews?

I served over three decades in my first career as an officer in the Australian Army—loyally, apolitically, and with pride. I've deployed to war zones and sworn to uphold the law. But the values we defend abroad must also be defended at home.

Tolerance of passivity is endorsement of decay.

So what can we do? We can vote. We can write. We can demand better from our leaders.

But most of all—we can shine a light.

Justice Louis Brandeis said it best:

"Sunlight is the best disinfectant."

If someone is screaming hate on a Sunday and teaching in a classroom on Monday—or sitting on a public board—they shouldn't be shielded by anonymity.

Take a photo. Record it. Share it with their employer, their principal, their governing body.

That's not doxxing. It's accountability.

Veterans know this instinctively. When someone wears unearned medals on ANZAC Day, it dishonours all who serve. We rightly call it out.

If someone incites hate, they should be prepared to own it—not hide behind a mob.

This is the ethic we need now: visibility, consequence, and moral courage.

Eighteen months of hate on our streets is eighteen months too many.

We must do better, Australia—for our children, our democracy, and the values we once held dear.

Because this is what happens when hate goes unchallenged.

She Deserves to Be Heard

Introduction

Moral courage is frequently praised in retrospect.

In the moment, it is more often isolated, questioned, or quietly discouraged—especially when it disrupts comfortable narratives.

This chapter centres a voice that should have been amplified, protected, and defended—and asks what it says about a society when speaking plainly becomes a liability rather than a virtue.

***

An Iranian Christian PhD student's quiet courage—and her academic supervisor's deafness—reveal deeper truths about bias, belief, and the power of lived experience.

On Sunday 6 July 2025, I had the privilege of addressing a multifaith Rally Against Terrorism in Western Sydney. Held in Parramatta and attended by around 130 people, the event brought together members of the Jewish, Hindu, Coptic Christian, and Iranian Australian communities in unity against extremism. It was a powerful reminder that solidarity among decent people—regardless of background—can be both healing and hopeful.

I spoke about the work of *The 2023 Foundation*, a grassroots charity I founded to combat antisemitism through lived experience. But in truth, I was there as much to listen as to speak. The true gift of that gathering wasn't the microphone—it was the people I met, and the connections made.

One of those connections led to a profound insight at a follow-on meeting. With her permission, I share it here anonymised, but unaltered in essence.

Maria (not her real name) is an Iranian Christian who emigrated to Australia with her family about 14 years ago. Now a PhD candidate at a Sydney independent tertiary institution, she is articulate, perceptive, and courageous. Her doctoral research blends creativity, history, and lived experience. She remains closely connected to friends and family in Iran—many of whom despise the Islamic regime of the Ayatollahs, which has ruled since 1979 with brutality and repression.

And yet, Maria now finds herself in a bind—here in Australia.

In recent months, she has faced subtle but insidious academic pressure. Her thesis—factually referencing the Arab conquest of Persia—has drawn criticism from her supervisor. She has been advised, indirectly but unmistakably, to "soften," "alter," or omit that history. More troubling still, her supervisor reportedly expressed disbelief at the views of Maria's Iranian contacts—particularly their frustration that Israel agreed to a ceasefire ending the Twelve-Day War. "We wanted them to keep going," her friends said. "This regime—the Ayatollahs—has crushed us for decades. We wish someone would bring their rule to an end."

To her supervisor—purportedly a Progressive White Anglo-Saxon Atheist, or P-WASA if I may coin the term—such sentiments were simply inconceivable. Dismissed as implausible.

Treated, in effect, as untrue. The situation is causing Maria deep anxiety and costing her sleep.

An objective observer might describe Maria as a Persian Zionist—someone who believes in the political and cultural self-determination of the indigenous Jewish population in their ancient and ancestral homeland. That this view is held by an Iranian Christian woman who fled religious tyranny is not only intellectually consistent but morally coherent. And yet it stands in stark contrast to her supervisor, who—according to Maria—wears his hostility toward the Jewish state like a badge of honour.

What an inversion. And one that will no doubt provide rich material for scholars in decades to come—especially political psychologists and social theorists—studying ideological reversal, performative politics, and digital tribalism between 2023 and 2025 onward. What tomorrow's academics will make of movements like Queers for Palestine—whose slogans defy the lived realities of the regimes they claim to support—will make for fascinating, if tragicomic, reading.

Maria's experience speaks to a deeper crisis: passive-aggressive hostility to alternate viewpoints and the way both conscious and unconscious bias can distort academic freedom. Her supervisor likely believes he is acting from compassion. But compassion without curiosity—especially in institutions of learning—can become its own form of tyranny. It silences uncomfortable truths.

This is not a call to shame individuals, nor an attack on academia, which includes many brilliant and principled people. It is a call for humility. For educators to remember they, too, can be taught. And for students to recognise that lived experience can carry legitimate authority.

A former commanding officer in Australia's Special Air Service Regiment—Ben, one of the most grounded and intellectually humble men I've known—once shared a powerful metaphor. "The volume of a balloon," he said, "is what you know. The surface area is what you don't know. So paradoxically, the more you learn, the more you realise how much remains unknown."

Maria's supervisor—particularly given his overt anti-US sentiment, including visceral disdain for the forty-seventh President—would do well to reflect on that insight. The deeper one's learning, the more essential it is to meet the world with openness, not certainty.

This is especially urgent in Australia—a vibrant, multicultural democracy enriched by decades of thoughtful immigration policy. People like Maria, who fled tyranny and now contribute meaningfully to Australian society through study and service, deserve more than tolerance. They deserve to be heard. That they face pressure to dilute their truth to fit fashionable academic orthodoxy is disturbing.

My advice to Maria was simple, though not easy: When caught in a moral dilemma, choose the path you'll regret least. The "mirror test" has always served me. Can I look myself in the eye and say I acted with integrity? That I contributed—however modestly—to a future worthy of our unborn grandchildren? If the answer is no, then a course correction is needed.

That correction may require courage from students like Maria—but also humility from educators. Sometimes, the student becomes the teacher. And when that happens, the wise teacher listens.

Carl Jung once wrote: "The meeting of two personalities is like the contact of two chemical substances: if there is any reaction, both are transformed." What better aspiration for higher education? Not indoctrination. Not submission. But transformation—mutual, humble, and real.

At The 2023 Foundation, we champion lived experience—not to replace facts, but to enrich them. When people from different faiths, cultures, and histories come together with open hearts, prejudice dissolves. Minds open. Societies strengthen.

Maria's story reminds us that freedom must be defended not just on battlefields or at rallies—but in lecture halls, seminar rooms, staff offices, and in the private conversations between supervisors and PhD candidates. The quiet pressure to sanitise uncomfortable truths doesn't merely endanger one thesis—it corrodes the moral integrity of the academy itself.

And yet, there is hope. Each time someone like Maria finds her voice, hope grows. Each time a student respectfully challenges authority, the balloon expands. Each time a teacher truly listens, transformation begins.

That is what happened, in a small but meaningful way, in Parramatta that Sunday. I went to speak. But I left having learned.

Because sometimes, the quietest voice in the room is the one we most need to hear.

And yes—she deserves to be heard.

39

The Lioness Forgotten: Remembering Golda Meir in an Age of Historical Amnesia

Introduction

Societies that lose confidence in themselves often begin by losing confidence in their heroes.

Historical figures are not reassessed with seriousness, but reduced to caricature—judged not by the standards of their time, but by the ideological demands of the present.

This chapter returns to Golda Meir not as myth or saint, but as a case study in moral seriousness—and as a reminder of what leadership once required when survival, not virtue signalling, was at stake.

***

There is a small, unassuming house tucked away on the Auraria Campus in Denver, Colorado—and within it lives the legacy of a giant. Golda Meir, Israel's only female prime minister and one of the towering figures of the twentieth century, spent part of her adolescence in this very home after emigrating from Ukraine to the United States. Today, it stands as the Golda Meir House

Museum—a lovingly restored tribute to a woman who helped shape the modern world. If you are ever passing through Denver, I urge you to visit. What you'll find is not just a preserved residence, but a centre of memory, moral leadership, and enduring values too often forgotten in today's climate.

During my recent visit, I had the privilege of meeting Lena, the museum's Executive Director. Lena is far more than a curator—she is the embodiment of Meir's legacy. Steeped in the life and lessons of her heroine, Lena speaks of Golda not as a figure confined to history, but as a living example of strength, service, and conviction. Her quiet leadership, fierce intellect, and evident pride in stewarding Meir's legacy moved me deeply. It was a powerful reminder that the principles which built Israel—and indeed the free world—still reside in brave individuals today.

Golda Meir's legacy deserves more than reverence—it demands relevance. Born in Kyiv in 1898, raised in Milwaukee, and a pioneer in Mandatory Palestine, Meir was a founding signatory of Israel's Declaration of Independence and served in senior leadership from the 1940s through the turbulent 1970s. As Minister of Labour, she championed workers' rights and expanded Israel's social welfare system. As Foreign Minister, she steered Israeli diplomacy during its formative years. As Prime Minister, she led the nation through the Yom Kippur War with resilience and resolve. But it wasn't just what she did—it was how she did it: with dignity, moral clarity, and unwavering purpose. A socialist who believed in the dignity of labour. A feminist before the word had widespread currency. A mother, a fighter, and above all, a stateswoman.

It is one of the great ironies of our age that Meir—a lifelong champion of the poor, of women's rights, and of freedom—is now denounced by self-styled "social justice" activists who camp on university lawns claiming to speak for the oppressed. In the aftermath of the October 7 atrocities, when Hamas terrorists butchered, raped, and burned their way through Israeli communities, the contagion of campus protest swept across the West. Tent encampments appeared at Columbia, the University of Sydney, and indeed, at the University of Colorado—mere metres from the very home where Golda Meir once dreamed of a better world.

How quickly we forget.

The spectacle of hard-left agitators—alongside impressionable or misled students—chanting slogans against Israel, and by extension against the legacy of figures like Golda Meir, is a textbook case of historical amnesia. These are people who claim to support women's rights while flying the flag of Hamas. Who call themselves anti-colonialists while demonising one of the most extraordinary indigenous liberation movements in history—the return of the Jewish people to their ancestral homeland. Who say they fight for justice, while desecrating the memory of a woman who spent her life pursuing it.

It is not merely insulting. It is tragic. Because when we lose touch with our history, we lose our moral bearings.

Golda Meir once said: "We do not rejoice in victories. We rejoice when a new kind of cotton is grown and when strawberries bloom in Israel." She understood that peace, dignity, and human flourishing are not born of grievance, but cultivated through hard work, sacrifice, and love of country. She stood for values the Western Left once embraced—equality, labour, democracy, and national self-determination. That she is now reviled by some of its loudest voices is not an indictment of her character, but of their confusion.

Lena and her colleagues at the Golda Meir House Museum are doing heroic work to preserve and share this story. The museum is not only a place of remembrance, but a space for education, reflection, and leadership development—especially for younger generations hungry for authentic examples. It hosts events, runs programs, and fosters dialogue grounded in truth, not ideology.

We need more of that. In an era saturated with curated outrage and digital distortion, places like this—and people like Lena—are essential. They remind us that moral clarity is not obsolete; it is simply absent in those who have ceased to study the past.

To learn more about this remarkable institution, please visit: https://aurariacampus.edu/auraria/golda-meir-house/.

The Golda Meir House Museum is a must-visit for anyone coming to Denver—a hidden gem, a sanctuary of integrity, and a living tribute to one of the most important women of the last century. It belongs on the bucket list of every defender of democracy, decency, and historical truth.

40

A Very Dangerous Assumption

Introduction

There is a comforting belief that moments of violence represent rock bottom.

That once a line has been crossed, societies will correct themselves, authority will reassert control, and lessons will be learned.

History offers little support for this assumption.

This chapter examines why treating acts of hatred as anomalies rather than indicators is not merely naïve, but dangerous—and why waiting for "worse" is itself a form of abdication.

***

In the aftermath of the Bondi Beach massacre on 14 December 2025, one sentence captured the horror with devastating precision. Writing in *The Guardian*, Dean Sherr described the attack plainly: "At Bondi, every Jewish person's worst nightmare came true."

It was not rhetoric. It was recognition.

Jews were murdered in broad daylight, at one of Australia's most iconic public landmarks, in an ideologically motivated attack. Among the dead was a child. In a country that has long reassured itself that such atrocities are things that happen elsewhere.

The immediate temptation—already visible in public commentary—is to treat Bondi as rock bottom. To believe that this was the worst it could get, and that the system will now correct itself.

That is a very dangerous assumption.

I am unaware of any precedent in the history of our species in which prolonged political failure, moral evasion, and the erosion of public will produced a spontaneous and positive correction. History points in the opposite direction. When institutions hesitate, when leaders refuse to name causes clearly, and when intimidation is tolerated rather than confronted, societies do not stabilise. They deteriorate.

Bondi did not occur in isolation.

On 7 October 2023, as Israelis were being massacred in their homes, representatives of Hizb ut-Tahrir in Australia publicly declared themselves "elated." Two days later, on the steps of the Sydney Opera House—a national symbol—chants of "Gas the Jews" and "F*** the Jews" rang out without consequence. In the weeks that followed, terrorist flags and the image of Iran's Supreme Leader appeared brazenly near and across the Sydney Harbour Bridge.

At Bondi Beach itself, well before the massacre, mobs of terrorist sympathisers masquerading as "Palestine supporters" demonstrated openly. These were not fringe locations. They were landmarks.

This matters because extremist movements understand symbolism. They target places that represent belonging, normality, and shared civic life. They seek to shatter public confidence. They also go after a society's heroes—not because those figures are uniquely flawed, but because they anchor continuity and confidence. Rhodes. Churchill. Menzies. Tear them down, and the cultural immune system weakens.

We have fallen fast. And we have fallen far.

In December 2024, I wrote of the "baying mob"—crowds animated not merely by grievance, but by moral licence. That licence has only expanded. When hatred is contextualised, indulged, or excused rather than confronted, it grows bolder. When political leaders speak in abstractions instead of moral clarity, extremists hear permission.

What Bondi exposed was not just a security failure. It revealed a collapse of deterrence—social, cultural, and political.

Jewish Australians understand this instinctively. Fear is not abstract. It is learned. It is adaptive. And increasingly, lived experience teaches that protection cannot be assumed—even in broad daylight, even at the heart of mainstream Australia.

To call Bondi an aberration is comforting. To describe it as rock bottom is reassuring. Both are likely wrong.

Absent decisive leadership, honest language, and a restoration of consequences, this moment will not be remembered as a turning point. It will be remembered as a threshold—crossed.

Australia now faces a choice. Either we confront the forces that brought us here with clarity and resolve, or we continue the descent while reassuring ourselves, against all evidence, that things are about to improve.

History is not kind to that kind of denial.

41

Righteous Kings, Forgotten Lessons: A Persian and a Hindu Who Stood with the Jews

Introduction

History does not only warn. It also instructs.

"Righteous Kings, Forgotten Lessons" recalls figures who stood with the Jewish people across lines of empire, faith, and culture—not because it was popular, but because it was right.

In an age that struggles to recognise moral courage outside its own ideological categories, this essay reintroduces examples of leadership grounded in responsibility, restraint, and justice. It reminds us that alliance is not determined by identity, but by character.

This chapter examines what principled leadership looks like when convenience is set aside—and why such examples matter most when moral clarity is in shortest supply.

***

Adapted from a speech delivered by the author at a United Against Terror rally in Western Sydney on 6 July 2025, organised by Minority Impact and Never Again is Now.

At a time when the comfortable West is learning to hate—when institutions like Harvard, Columbia, Oxford, Sydney University, and The Australian National University have become breeding grounds for antisemitism and moral confusion—it is worth pausing to ask: Have we forgotten the examples we once revered?

Last month, as Israel conducted Operation Rising Lion—a decisive twelve-day campaign in June 2025 to dismantle Iran's nuclear program and ballistic missile capabilities—a familiar cast of performative radicals took to the streets. In city after city, cloaked in keffiyehs and echoing slogans they barely understand, they chanted genocidal rallying cries that call for the destruction of the world's only Jewish state. These self-styled activists and ideological opportunists—many of whom may struggle to locate Haifa or Beersheva on a map—chose, in their infinite self-assurance, to align themselves with the Ayatollahs of Iran, one of the most violent and regressive regimes on the planet.

Had they taken a moment to step outside their echo chambers, they might have noticed something telling: For nearly two years, proud Australian Iranians have been rallying in support of Israel and the Jewish Diaspora. These men and women, exiled by tyranny, know friend from foe. And they have been consistently, visibly, and courageously standing with Israel—against the terror state that continues to brutalise their homeland and threaten the civilised world.

The Islamic Republic of Iran is a state sponsor of terrorism. It funds Hezbollah in Lebanon, Hamas in Gaza, and death squads across Iraq, Syria, and Yemen. It jails artists, tortures dissidents, and murders its own citizens—teenage girls, minority faith leaders, LGBTQ individuals—with medieval cruelty. It executes people for speaking freely and sends drones and missiles across borders in pursuit of regional domination. It also provides ideological and financial cover to the broader Islamist terror ecosystem, which has brutalised parts of India for decades—through attacks on Hindu pilgrims, targeted bombings, and the ongoing infiltration of jihadist ideology across Kashmir and beyond.

This is the regime that Western protestors have chosen to celebrate—blind to its barbarity, or worse, complicit in it.

But history, thank goodness, offers us better models. Not all Persians were—or are—like Khamenei. Not all kings were butchers. If we are to reject the darkness, we must also embrace the light—and two figures shine brighter than most.

History is not short of villains. But if one knows where to look, it also offers giants of conscience—men who stood for justice across lines of ethnicity, religion, and empire. Two of them were a Persian emperor and an Indian king. And both stood with the Jewish people, not despite their identity, but because of their shared humanity.

Cyrus the Great: The Persian Who Freed the Jews

In the sixth century BCE, Cyrus the Great founded what would become the largest empire the world had yet seen: the Achaemenid Empire. But his greatness was not only in conquest—it was in compassion and wisdom.

After defeating the Babylonians in 539 BCE, Cyrus encountered the remnants of a broken people: the Jews, who had been exiled from Jerusalem and held captive for decades. Unlike so many rulers before him, he did not exploit them, enslave them, or erase their identity. Instead, he issued a decree: Return to your homeland. Rebuild your temple. Worship your God in peace.

The Hebrew Bible, written by the very people he freed, honours him as God's anointed—a title given to no other gentile king. The Book of Isaiah, written before his birth, proclaims: "This is what the Lord says to his anointed, to Cyrus…I will go before you and will level the mountains…I will raise up Cyrus in my righteousness." (Isaiah 45:1–3, 13, KJV)

What a stunning reversal: a Zoroastrian king of Persia becoming a divine instrument in Jewish eyes. Cyrus's example still echoes through time—of what it means to rule with justice, dignity, and tolerance.

And today, many brave Iranians—at great personal risk—continue that legacy. They revolt against the brutality of the ayatollahs and the terror of the IRGC. They resist not only on behalf of their own people, but in defence of the universal right to live free from tyranny and terror.

Maharaja Digvijaysinhji: The Hindu King Who Saved Jewish Children

Fast forward 2,500 years to World War II. Europe was burning. The Nazis were rounding up Jews and the gates of Auschwitz were open. And amid the horror, a Polish transport carrying over one thousand orphaned Jewish children somehow made its way to Iran—and then to the shores of British India.

There, a remarkable man intervened.

His name was Maharaja Jam Saheb Digvijaysinhji, the ruler of Nawanagar in Gujarat. The British colonial authorities were reluctant to help. But the Maharaja didn't hesitate. He opened his palaces. He gave the children food, shelter, schooling—and dignity.

When British officials protested, he replied: "They are like my own children. I will not throw them into the sea."

These were not his subjects. They did not share his faith. But they shared his humanity. He saw them not as Jews, not as foreigners, not as political burdens—but as children who needed saving.

Israel has not forgotten. A school in Tel Aviv bears his name. And for Jews around the world, the Maharaja remains a symbol of moral clarity in an age of moral collapse.

What Can We Learn?

What links Cyrus the Great and Maharaja Digvijaysinhji is not religion, geography, or political alignment. It is that, in their own times and ways, both exercised power with a degree of restraint and humanity that stood out—respecting the dignity of others, especially the vulnerable, when they could easily have done otherwise.

Contrast their legacy with the slogans shouted on university campuses today. The protesters chant "from the river to the sea," demanding the erasure of Israel. They pretend to fight for justice while justifying terrorism. They target Jews in shops, synagogues, and schools—then hide behind words like "decolonisation" and "resistance."

This is not justice. This is hatred wearing a mask.

Some might argue Cyrus acted out of pragmatic interest—the enemy of my enemy is my friend. And yet, whatever the motivations, his actions aligned with righteousness. He chose restoration over revenge, dignity over domination. His legacy—enshrined in Jewish scripture and global memory—remains a rare example of a conqueror who liberated rather than subjugated.

A Rallying Cry for Our Time

On 6 July 2025, I stood in Western Sydney alongside Iranian, Hindu, Jewish Australians and Christian and non-denominational allies—united not by uniformity of belief, but by a shared stand against terror.

We came together to say: We reject Hamas, Hezbollah, and all who glorify the murder of civilians. We reject those who excuse it. And we embrace the values of those who stood up when it mattered most.

Let our children learn the names of Cyrus the Great and Maharaja Digvijaysinhji—not because they were perfect, but because they were righteous. In an age where so many fail the test of courage, their memory reminds us: moral clarity is possible.

And it is urgently needed.

PART V
Conclusion

When hatred arrives at home, denial becomes a luxury.

It is no longer possible to pretend that language has no consequence, that narratives remain theoretical, or that indulgence is benign. The distance between rhetoric and reality collapses.

At this stage, societies face a choice.

They can continue to explain, contextualise, and defer—or they can confront the patterns they have allowed to take root. What they cannot do is claim ignorance.

The question that remains is not whether warning signs were present, but whether responsibility will now be accepted—and by whom.

Because once the threshold has been crossed, the cost of inaction rises sharply.

PART VI

THE UPWARD PATH

Agency, allies, and renewal

PART VI
Introduction

It would be easier to end this book with despair.

The evidence presented so far would justify it. Decay has been tolerated. Narratives have captured institutions. Hatred has returned home. Thresholds have been crossed that cannot be uncrossed.

But despair is not clarity. And resignation is not realism.

History does not move in straight lines. Periods of moral confusion are often followed—not automatically, but deliberately—by renewal, led by those willing to accept responsibility rather than outsource it.

This final part is about that responsibility.

It is about where agency still exists, where alliances still matter, and where courage—quiet, practical, and unspectacular—can still make the difference between fragility and failure.

42

Standing Up Starts Here

Introduction

Responsibility rarely announces itself with certainty.

It appears instead as a moment of choice—to speak or remain silent, to act or defer, to accept cost or preserve comfort.

This chapter begins not with institutions or movements, but with individuals. Because renewal does not start at scale. It starts at the point where someone decides that silence is no longer neutral.

***

Antisemitism in Australia is a national challenge—not just a Jewish concern.

On 10 July 2025, Jillian Segal AO, Australia's Special Envoy to Combat Antisemitism, released a comprehensive national strategy to address what she calls "an age-old hatred with deadly new energy." The forty-four-page plan, published by the Australian government's Advisory Group on Antisemitism, responds to a deeply troubling surge in antisemitic incidents across the country since the Hamas attacks of 7 October 2023.[7]

[7] Special Envoy's Plan to Combat Antisemitism, ASECA, July 10, 2025, https://www.aseca.gov.au/sites/default/files/2025-07/2025-aseca-plan.pdf.

But make no mistake: This is not just a plan for Jewish Australians. It is a plan for all of us.

Why does this plan matter to every Australian?

The data is stark. In the twelve months following the October 7 massacre, antisemitic incidents in Australia rose by more than 300 percent. We've seen swastikas defacing synagogues, students harassed for wearing a kippah, hate-filled graffiti on schools, and physical assaults in broad daylight.

Segal's message is clear: Antisemitism is not simply a problem for one community—it is a threat to the kind of nation we aspire to be. It undermines democracy, corrodes civil society, and paves the way for further bigotry. As she rightly notes, "Attacks on Jews have been the canary in the coal mine. They are the early warning signal that democratic values are under threat."

What are the key parts of the plan?

The strategy outlines thirteen urgent areas for national action. Some of the most significant include:

- Clear Definitions—Adopting the internationally recognised IHRA definition of antisemitism, drawing a vital line between legitimate criticism of Israeli policy and antisemitic tropes masquerading as activism.
- Education Reform—Mandatory Holocaust and antisemitism education in schools and universities, particularly targeting younger Australians who are vulnerable to online radicalisation and misinformation.
- Legal and Law Enforcement Reform—Stronger vilification laws, better hate crime tracking, and national training for police and judiciary to identify and respond to antisemitic conduct.

- Online and Media Responsibility—Greater accountability for digital platforms and media outlets in combatting antisemitic content and biased narratives that distort public understanding.
- Institutional Accountability—Linking government funding for universities, NGOs, and arts bodies to their efforts in combating antisemitism and maintaining safe environments for Jewish Australians.
- Visa and Migration Controls—Enhanced screening of visa applicants with extremist backgrounds, and deportation powers for those who pose a risk—mirroring steps taken in Canada and the UK.
- Cultural and Interfaith Engagement—Supporting Jewish arts, festivals, and interfaith initiatives to foster empathy, dialogue, and cultural understanding.

Taken as a whole, the plan offers a sensible and measured way forward—a clear-eyed national reset that reaffirms the basic promise of a fair go for all. As General Sir Peter Cosgrove once put it, "We should be a country where people instinctively look out for one another." This plan helps make that instinct a reality.

How does Australia compare internationally?

Australia is not alone in this fight. Canada and the United Kingdom already have national antisemitism envoys and robust hate-speech laws. Germany bans Holocaust denial and Nazi imagery. The United States recently launched its own National Strategy to Counter Antisemitism. Argentina, in the wake of the 1994 AMIA bombing, reclassified antisemitism as a national security threat.

Segal's plan builds on these international examples while adapting them to Australian conditions. It is principled, pragmatic—and long overdue.

Antisemitism is not a Jewish problem. It's an Australian problem.

This cannot be said often enough: Antisemitism does not only concern Jews. It concerns all of us—teachers, students, parents, journalists, faith leaders, employers, and artists alike.

When Jewish Australians feel compelled to hide their identity, avoid public transport, or withdraw their children from school, that is not just a Jewish tragedy—it is a national disgrace.

Segal's plan recognises this. Jewish Australians cannot—and should not—be expected to stand alone. Every Australian has a role to play. Whether by challenging antisemitic comments, reporting hate online, or ensuring our institutions reflect the values we claim to uphold, we each have agency.

This plan is not radical. It is responsible.

It will only succeed if ordinary Australians—especially non-Jewish Australians—step forward. Antisemitism will not remain confined to the fringes. Left unchecked, it infects everything it touches. History makes that plain.

Now is the time to act—not just with words of solidarity, but with concrete steps to build a nation where Jewish Australians feel safe, valued, and fully at home. Because when they do, all Australians benefit.

If Not Us, Who?

Introduction

Responsibility is often deferred to scale.

Individuals wait for institutions. Institutions wait for consensus. Consensus waits for crisis. And by the time crisis arrives, responsibility has already dissolved into process.

This chapter rejects that logic. It argues that moral agency does not originate at scale, nor require unanimity. It begins with individuals willing to accept the discomfort of acting early—and the cost of standing visibly when silence would be easier.

***

"If I am not for myself, who will be for me? And if I am only for myself, what am I? And if not now, when?"

The words of Rabbi Hillel the Elder—spoken nearly two thousand years ago—were never intended as a slogan. They were a moral challenge: a call to responsibility, a warning against passivity, and an antidote to the false comfort of silence. They speak not only to Jews, but to any society that imagines its values will endure without effort, articulation, and defence.

That challenge came to mind recently as I walked through the Sydney Jewish Museum.

I am a friend of this important institution. Over time, I have come to know members of the board, the executive, and many volunteers who give their time and energy to its mission. The Museum is undergoing a significant expansion, and I was invited to attend a VIP tour designed to showcase the redevelopment as part of a fundraising effort. It was an honour to be included among leaders from Australian Jewish life and broader civil society.

I had visited before. And as with my visits to Yad Vashem in Israel, the Holocaust galleries again brought tears to my eyes. They always do. In part, this is why I have committed myself to the work of combatting antisemitism. "Never Again" cannot remain a sentiment. It must be operationalised.

Yet on this visit, something else struck me—more quietly, but no less forcefully.

Israel felt marginal in the existing exhibition, and largely absent in the planned redevelopment.

I raise this not as a criticism from the outside, but as a well-intentioned observation from someone who, along with my wife, regularly speaks with non-Jewish Australians who have profoundly distorted ideas about what Israel is and who Israelis are. Israel is not the sum total of Australian Jewish identity—but in recent years it has dominated our television screens, news feeds, and public debate to an extraordinary degree. I struggle to think of another nation so relentlessly present in Australian public consciousness.

Whether we like the hand we have been dealt or not, those are the cards on the table. We do not get to choose the terrain. We only get to decide whether we explain, educate, and compete—or whether we retreat and hope for understanding. We should act as though the safety of our children, and theirs, may one day depend upon it. Because it just might.

Complexity Is Not an Excuse for Absence

Jewish communal life is complex. As the saying goes: two Jews, three opinions. That plurality is a strength. But internal complexity must never become an alibi for silence—especially in the era we are now living through.

We are all participants, whether we like it or not, in an information war over narrative. Vacuums do not remain empty for long. When institutions step back from telling their own story with clarity, others step forward to tell it for them—rarely with goodwill, accuracy, or proportion.

The Sydney Jewish Museum remains a thoughtful, carefully curated, emotionally powerful institution. The Holocaust galleries are sobering and necessary. The personal stories of survival, resilience, and rebuilding are deeply moving. They should be required viewing for every Australian student.

But telling the story of the Holocaust alone is no longer sufficient.

Our opponents have learned to dress their bigotry in the language of human rights. Many well-meaning people have been persuaded that Israel is committing genocide in Gaza, that there is a deliberate famine, or that Israel is an apartheid state. None of this is true.

Israel, like Australia, is a liberal democratic society in which there exist monsters, zealots, and extremists—as Australians were brutally reminded at Bondi on 14 December 2025. That reality does not define the nation. It defines the threat it faces.

Yes, there is a security barrier between Israel and the Palestinian territories. The alternative was the continuation of the Second Intifada—an era of buses, cafés, and family gatherings turned into killing fields. Context matters. History matters.

Against that backdrop, Israel's near-absence matters.

Not as a footnote. Not as a passing reference. But as the living expression of Jewish self-determination—the continuation of history, not an afterthought to tragedy.

An Outsider's Perspective

I am not Jewish.

I am, however, a patriotic Australian. A former soldier. A father. Someone who has spent years living and working in the Middle East, including over two years resident in Jerusalem while seconded to the United Nations.

I am an unapologetic Zionist—not because of religion, but because I believe, as a matter of justice and historical fact, in the political and cultural self-determination of the indigenous Jewish people in their ancient and ancestral homeland.

I did not arrive at these views through family tradition or communal loyalty. I arrived at them through lived experience—by observing how Israel is spoken about when Jews are not in the room, and how Jews are spoken about when Israel is placed on trial. Earlier in my career, a non-Jewish military mentor encouraged me to study the IDF at war—introducing me into the history, the politics, the repeated peace attempts, and the brutal moral asymmetries of the conflict.

That distance gives me a perspective that is sometimes clearer, sometimes more confronting, and often less constrained by internal communal dynamics. Disagreement is healthy. But when fear of division leads to Israel being quietly downplayed in spaces where it should stand confidently, something has gone wrong.

Israel Is Not a Political Hobby

Support for the Jewish state is not a matter of partisan politics. It is not an aesthetic preference. It is not a discretionary add-on to be bracketed off for comfort.

Israel exists because Jews learned—through centuries of persecution culminating in industrialised genocide—that moral appeals alone do not protect minorities. Sovereignty matters. Security matters. Power, responsibly exercised, matters.

And yet Israel is subjected to obsessive scrutiny and moral exceptionalism unmatched anywhere else.

Those who rage about Israel's wars against Hamas, Hezbollah, the Houthis, or Iran's terror apparatus rarely summon comparable outrage for Vladimir Putin's war in Ukraine, the gulags of North Korea, the repression of Uyghurs in China, or the mass atrocities in Syria.

This is not primarily about human rights. It is about double standards—and double standards have long been the preferred dialect of antisemitism.

I proudly support the only liberal democracy in the Middle East—not because it is perfect, but because it is real; because its flaws are contested in courts and parliaments; because its minorities vote, protest, serve, and dissent; because it shares the moral architecture of the West while surrounded by forces that do not.

Leadership Matters: Unity Versus Fracture

The discomfort around Israel within Western institutions reflects a broader moral shift—away from unity and shared obligation, and toward grievance and segmentation.

The contrast between John F. Kennedy and Barack Obama is instructive.

Kennedy's language was civic and unifying: "Ask not what your country can do for you—ask what you can do for your country." Citizenship came first.

From 2012 onward, Obama's politics increasingly leaned into intersectional logic—dividing society into ranked identity blocs, treating power as something to be redistributed rather than responsibly exercised. It was politically effective. It was also socially corrosive.

That framework travelled—into universities, bureaucracies, and cultural institutions—eventually shaping how Israel itself would be framed: not as a nation among nations, but as an illegitimate outlier. Jewish sovereignty became an irritant because it refused the role of permanent moral petitioner.

Institutions absorb the moral language of their age, even when they believe they are being neutral.

Museums Are Moral Educators

Museums are not neutral warehouses. They shape memory. They teach visitors what matters and why.

To tell the story of Jewish suffering without telling the story of Jewish sovereignty is to leave the narrative unfinished—and to risk reinforcing the idea that Jewish safety depends on the goodwill of others.

Israel is not separate from Jewish history. It is its continuation.

Belonging Without Qualification

I am uneasy with the habit of singling out "great Jewish Australians." Not because those individuals are undeserving, but because the framing subtly reinforces separation.

Sir John Monash was one of the greatest Australians—full stop.

Sir Isaac Isaacs embodied the Australian state.

Jessica Fox wins medals as an Australian.

Ron Castan shaped human-rights law for everyone.

Jewish Australians are not guests. They are co-owners of the national story.

Israel fits the same moral logic.

If Not Us, Who?

This is not a call for propaganda. It is a call for confidence.

Israel's story is complex—but complexity is not an argument for absence. It is an argument for education, clarity, and courage.

If we are not prepared to tell Israel's story in Jewish spaces—spaces dedicated to memory and truth—then we should ask ourselves a hard question:

If not us, who?

And if not now, when the consequences of silence are becoming unmistakably clear—when?

History does not pause while we deliberate. It moves forward, indifferent to hesitation.

The choice before us is not between controversy and comfort.

It is between truth and timidity.

And it cannot be deferred forever.

44

Reclaiming Tikkun Olam: Healing the World Doesn't Mean Ignoring Its Monsters

Introduction

Moral language shapes moral action.

When concepts intended to guide repair are stripped of boundaries and discipline, they become tools of evasion rather than healing.

This chapter reclaims the idea of tikkun olam from those who have hollowed it out—and restores it to its original moral seriousness: the obligation to confront evil as a prerequisite for repair.

***

There was a time I found the Hebrew phrase *tikkun olam*—"to heal or repair the world"—charming, even inspiring. That was before I understood how ruthlessly it had been appropriated. Before I saw it descend from spiritual aspiration to political cudgel. Before it became a sanctimonious catchcry for self-anointed activists and self-serving ideologues who see no difference between screaming in shopping centres and blocking highways, even as working families try to get their children to school and themselves to jobs that keep our complex societies functioning.

They yell, disrupt, and accuse—declaring their acts righteous under the banner of *tikkun olam*. But I've come to believe they are not healing the world. They are press-ganging us into imbibing their ideological snake oil.

My understanding of this ancient idea has evolved—and sharpened—in recent years. I am not Jewish. But I am the founder and CEO of The 2023 Foundation, a nascent international organisation committed to combating antisemitism through lived experience and truth-telling. I had earlier spent three decades as a professional Australian soldier. I have walked the war-scarred roads of Iraq, Afghanistan, the Middle East, and elsewhere. I have studied the human condition at its best—and at its worst.

And I have come to believe that *tikkun olam* does not mean utopia. It does not mean placard activism or mass virtue-signalling. It means confronting evil. Repairing the world, at times, may mean defending it—decisively and even violently—against monsters.

Because there are monsters.

This fact has always been true. But for many, it took events like Russia's illegal invasion of Ukraine in February 2022—or the atrocities of October 7, 2023, when Hamas terrorists butchered, raped, and incinerated 1,200 innocent people in southern Israel—for the veil to fall. To many Israelis, that day crystallised what should already have been obvious: history had not ended. Civilisation is not inevitable. Francis Fukuyama's 1992 thesis *The End of History*—once so seductive in its optimism—now rings dangerously naïve.

The monsters never left. It is my judgment that we simply lost our instinct for danger.

Some people—early adopters of clarity—recognised this reality long ago. Others followed more recently, shaken into awareness by unmistakable evil. Friends of mine have referred to themselves as October 8 Jews and October 8 Gentiles—those who awoke the day after the massacre with a renewed sense of moral purpose and unshakable solidarity.

But there remains a stubborn cohort of laggards—ensconced on the campuses of Columbia, Harvard, in London, Sydney, and Melbourne—who still cling to outdated paradigms, moral relativism, and intellectual vanity. They are not simply behind the curve. They are the white noise of our civilisation—deluded, distracting, and dangerously irrelevant in a world that demands moral courage and practical resolve. These are not the kinds of people we want teaching—or indoctrinating—tomorrow's generation. Having recently completed my third master's degree, with studies in both Sydney and New York, it gives me no pleasure to report that these types are dug in like paralysis ticks in our centres of higher learning—tenacious, toxic, and in urgent need of exposure, challenge, and replacement.

In truth, *tikkun olam* originates in rabbinic Judaism as a call to sustain society—particularly through justice and fulfilment of divine commandments. Over centuries, it acquired a more mystical and moral dimension. The Kabbalistic tradition described the world as shattered at creation, and humanity's role as assisting in its repair. This isn't soft sentiment. It's a duty that demands courage, clarity, and confrontation with chaos.

The Talmud teaches, *"If someone comes to kill you, rise early and kill him first"* (*Sanhedrin 72a*). This is not a celebration of violence—it is a tragic acknowledgement of the human condition.

Jewish tradition does not glorify war. But neither does it flinch from the moral imperative to resist annihilation. *tikkun olam* can mean many things, but in a world of genocidal ideologies and fanatical regimes, it may at times mean confronting evil—decisively—before it strikes.

Consider the Islamic Republic of Iran. Since the fall of the Shah in 1979, Iran's leaders have made no secret of their genocidal intent. "Death to Israel" and "Death to America" are not rhetorical flourishes. They are the regime's ideological backbone. Iran's Supreme Leader and the IRGC have long dreamt of a world without Jews, without Americans, without Western civilisation. That dream was dangerously close to being realised through a clandestine nuclear program—until recent joint kinetic actions by Israel and the United States began to dismantle it. These operations were not acts of aggression; they were acts of necessity. When the threat is existential, preemption is not only justified—it is morally required.

To ignore this is not idealism—it is delusion.

And yes, I care about the environment. We all should. Climate change is serious—perhaps one of the top twenty challenges confronting responsible governments. But to imagine that environmental collapse is the greatest existential threat to humanity is to fundamentally misread history. A third world war, ignited by unrestrained autocracies armed with weapons of mass destruction, would not only dwarf our emissions concerns—it could bring civilisation to an end. A nuclear, biological, or chemical winter is no longer just a scientific hypothesis. It is a looming possibility we edge toward every time tyrannical state and non-state actors are allowed to go unchecked.

Einstein once said that if he had an hour to save the world, he'd spend fifty-five minutes understanding the problem and five minutes solving it. My evolving understanding of *tikkun olam* has followed a similar arc. The problem is not simply carbon, inequality, or historical injustice—though all are real. The deeper problem is moral clarity. And the solution, I believe, lies in cultivating the kind of resilience, responsibility, and realism that too many modern societies have abandoned.

Maybe Ronald Reagan said it best: "Freedom is never more than one generation away from extinction." It is not inherited. It must be fought for, protected, handed on. As a father—and in the wake of October 7—I have thought long and deeply about the world I hope to one day bequeath to my unborn grandchildren. Not putting off until tomorrow what ought to be done today, nor making "hope" my method, are now pillars of my worldview. These convictions have driven me to act.

To combat antisemitism—that oldest and most enduring hatred—in its most modern and insidious manifestation: anti-Zionism disguised as virtue. Today's antisemitism doesn't wear a swastika; it wraps itself in progressive slogans while calling for the destruction of the world's only Jewish state.

From the vantage point of June 2025, as Iranian missiles strike family homes in Tel Aviv, and Israel—supported by the United States—moves to dismantle a genocidal materiel threat forty-six years in the making, I reflect on the real meaning of *tikkun olam*. The Iranian regime's Jew-hatred has long gone unanswered. At last, wrongs are being righted.

For too long, many in the West—especially in the comfortable, post-Cold War decades—thought we had reached some pinnacle of enlightened stability. We lost sight of the lower rungs of Maslow's famous hierarchy: safety, security, survival. These are not solved problems. They are the foundation upon which all higher ideals rest. When those rungs collapse, the entire pyramid crumbles.

To heal the world, then, is not to utopianise it. It is to protect it, to steward it, and in time, to bequeath it. And at times, that means having the moral strength to call evil by its name—and the strategic resolve to act accordingly.

If that means rising early to fight—metaphorically or literally—then so be it. That, too, is tikkun olam. The alternative is Auschwitz. That must never happen. Ever again.

And perhaps, just perhaps, reclaiming this ancient idea for what it truly is—an obligation to confront chaos, not decorate it—will help us all see more clearly in an age darkened by confusion, cowardice, and compromise.

45

The Druze, My Friends—Facing Mortal Danger

Introduction

One of the most persistent myths of our time is that solidarity must be ideological.

In reality, the most enduring alliances are forged through shared risk, mutual obligation, and lived experience.

This chapter tells the story of an often-overlooked community whose courage and loyalty offer a model of coexistence grounded not in slogans, but in responsibility.

***

I first came to know the Druze through a family I befriended in Canberra in 2018. Our children attended the same school, and our friendship has endured across continents. That family now lives once again on Mount Carmel in northern Israel—loyal citizens, guardians of tradition, and people of quiet strength. In August 2019, I joined them in their home for an Eid al-Adha celebration—a time of faith, generosity, and deep family bonds. They live in peace and with full rights as citizens of Israel. Just

140 kilometres to the east, however, their co-religionists in Syria face mortal danger.

The Druze are a proud, tight-knit community found across northern Israel, southern Lebanon, and southwestern Syria. In recent months—and especially in the past few days—Druze villages in Syria's Suwayda Province have come under sustained and violent assault. The perpetrators appear to be a mix of Bedouin tribal fighters and militias aligned with Syria's interim government, led by Ahmed al-Sharaa, better known as Abu Mohammed al-Jolani—a former al-Qaeda commander and the country's de facto ruler. His so-called transitional government is proving to be as lawless as it is violent.

Since late April 2025, more than two hundred Druze civilians have been murdered in coordinated raids around Suwayda. Reports describe extrajudicial executions in guesthouses, armed attacks on places of worship, looting, arson, and widespread terror. In just three days in mid-July, Jolani-aligned units escalated operations in Suwayda and Sahnaya. While some claims—such as the forced shaving of Druze men's moustaches—remain unverified, there is no doubt that the intent has been to humiliate, intimidate, and break the Druze will to resist.

Israel responded with rare force. On July 16, the Israel Defense Forces launched precision airstrikes deep into Syrian territory, targeting military and intelligence sites in Damascus, including the Defense Ministry and state television headquarters. Israeli officials made clear that the strikes aimed to deter further attacks against the Druze and prevent enemy entrenchment near Israel's northern border.

The Druze are an ancient ethno-religious minority with deep roots in the Levant. Their monotheistic faith emerged in the 11th century and combines elements of Islam, Gnosticism, and Neoplatonism. They revere a spiritual lineage that includes Jethro (Shu'ayb), Moses, Jesus, John the Baptist, and Muhammad—alongside a pivotal figure in their own tradition, the Fatimid Caliph al-Hakim bi-Amr Allah, who is believed to be a divine manifestation. Their theology is also shaped by classical Greek philosophy; Druze spiritual texts draw on the teachings of Plato and Pythagoras, especially regarding the soul, the pursuit of truth, and reincarnation.

Their religion is closed—there are no converts—and its teachings are reserved for an initiated class known as the uqqāl. But Druze values are well known: loyalty, honour, self-discipline, and service. In Israel, they are full citizens who serve with distinction in the IDF and have risen to senior ranks in public life. In Lebanon, they have long played a pivotal role in politics and society. In Syria, they have often been caught in the crossfire—respected, yet vulnerable.

Their efforts to remain neutral in Syria's many conflicts have not spared them. In early 2025, amid increasing attacks and lawlessness, Druze leaders in Suwayda established the Suwayda Military Council—a secular, community-based self-defence force. Rather than being welcomed as a stabilising presence, the force has been labelled a threat by Jolani's regime. That pretext has been used to justify the current campaign of violence.

The toll is staggering. Thousands have been displaced. Medical and food supplies have been cut off. Religious leaders have pleaded for international assistance. The United Nations has acknowledged the crisis, but its response has been mostly rhetorical.

A ceasefire brokered in mid-July by the United States, Turkey, and Arab states has temporarily paused the bloodshed. Syrian troops reportedly began withdrawing, with local Druze taking over security. But the ceasefire remains fragile—and many fear that once the world's attention moves on, the killing will resume.

The Jolani regime has tried to present itself as a transitional authority. In truth, it remains rooted in the same extremist ideology from which it sprang. Its actions in Suwayda—silencing dissent, attacking minorities, and consolidating control through fear—are a grim echo of its past. Syria cannot build a future on such foundations.

The Druze are not insurgents. They are not revolutionaries. They are a people of faith, family, and restraint. Their history is long. Their honour is deep. Their only demand is to live in peace and dignity. To stand by while they are hunted and humiliated is not just a political failure—it is a moral one.

What is happening in Suwayda is not an isolated skirmish. It is a test of principle. A test for those who speak loudly of human rights but hesitate when the victims are unfashionable or forgotten. I say this especially to Western audiences who have been overwhelmed by one-sided narratives about Gaza: look again. Israel is not the villain it is so often made out to be. It is a liberal democracy—imperfect, yes, but committed to the rule of law and human rights. And when the Druze called for help, it was Israel—not the UN, not the Arab League—that responded.

Let us not look away. Let us see clearly. And let us stand with the Druze—not because they are strategic allies or part of some broader conflict, but because they are human beings facing mortal danger. And because standing with them is the right thing to do.

46

A Non-Jewish Australian Army Veteran Standing with Israel

Introduction

Support is often dismissed as tribal.

But solidarity grounded in principle is not allegiance to a people alone; it is allegiance to values tested under pressure.

This chapter explains why standing with Israel is not an act of identity, but of moral alignment—and why non-Jewish allies have a particular responsibility to speak plainly.

***

As a non-Jewish career officer in the Australian Army, I never imagined that my service to country would one day lead me to the frontlines of a very different battle—a fight against the world's oldest hatred. But the atrocities of October 7, 2023, and the chants of "Gas the Jews" outside the Sydney Opera House just two days later compelled me to act.

It was morning in Israel—just after dawn—when Hamas launched its barbaric assault. At that same moment, it was

Saturday evening in Australia. My eighteen-year-old daughter was at a music festival in Sydney, dancing in celebration of life. I had lived in Israel for more than two years. Close friends were personally involved. One dear friend still has a loved one held hostage in Gaza. It could have been my daughter. I could not be a bystander.

That moment marked the beginning of what is now *The 2023 Foundation*—a nascent global charity dedicated to combatting antisemitism. Inspired by the Fulbright model of cultural exchange, our approach is rooted in lived experience. We identify, invite, and immerse non-Jewish influencers in Israeli society. Our aim is to build enduring cross-cultural understanding. But unlike Fulbright, we focus specifically on connecting gentiles—especially those from the silent majority who rarely engage with these issues—to the people and reality of Israel.

Our immersive experiences in Israel are a powerful catalyst—but the deeper purpose is to foster empathy, understanding, and connection as a gateway to something greater: our *Alumni Program*. This long-term initiative will cultivate a growing network of non-Jewish advocates who stand up for the Jewish people and the values we share. Not because I ask them to—but because they feel compelled to, after seeing Israel in all its perfect imperfections and realising they've been victims of Orwellian levels of gaslighting and projection.

I have committed educators, psychologists, and professionals helping refine the Alumni Program, which will be piloted and improved through trial visits.

Our vision is ambitious but achievable: seventy influencers in the first year, 750 within five years, and ultimately eight thousand annually matching the scale and impact of Fulbright. We begin in Australia and the United States and will expand to other

Western democracies with large Jewish diasporas. I spent the first four months of 2025 in New York completing my MBA at NYU's Stern School of Business while socialising this vision with prospective collaborators. The interest has been extraordinary. A grassroots initiative led by an apolitical former soldier, motivated by personal experience and conviction, has resonated—especially at a time when the world needs non-Jewish champions of change more than ever.

While serving with the United Nations, I met officers from around the world who, like me, are appalled by the behaviour of antisemites and social Marxists in the media, on campuses, and in Western schools. The problems we are seeing in the United States and Australia are replicated across the West. Our challenges are global—so too must be our response. Conversations are already underway in the UK, New Zealand, Germany, and South Korea.

In my judgment, there is no more effective antidote to antisemitism than involving non-Jews in the lived reality of Israel. Importantly, most of our program funding will be spent in Israel—supporting communities, rebuilding an economy wounded by an existential war, and appealing to values-aligned donors.

In September 2024, I returned to Israel as part of a senior international delegation. I entered Gaza alongside the IDF. What I witnessed reaffirmed what I already knew: the IDF is the most educated, ethical, and lawful military force in modern history—operating under constant scrutiny in a diabolically complex environment. They face not only terrorists with rifles, but terrorists with press and "health ministry" credentials—armed with cameras instead of guns, but equally committed to the cause of destruction.

To Jewish readers: be proud of your sons and daughters. I've served in war. I am confident these young Israelis will reintegrate into society as extraordinary citizens, spouses, and parents. They fight with love in their hearts—not hate. They understand the stakes. Their generation—the *Iron Swords Generation*—may one day be remembered as Israel's finest.

It is my assessment that things may get worse before they improve. But improve they will—on the shoulders of those who choose to stand up and share the burden. Together, we will build a legacy our grandchildren can inherit with pride.

Together, we will prevail.

47

The Strength We Share

Introduction

Shared values are not slogans.

They are revealed under strain—in the willingness to defend one another, to speak across difference, and to accept cost on behalf of principles that outlast comfort.

This chapter examines where that shared strength still exists, and why it remains the West's most underutilised asset.

***

Solidarity. Strength. Stewardship. These are not abstract slogans—they are lived virtues, forged in fire and refined in fear. A friend of mine—an Israeli father—recently shared a haunting image: his young children in a safe room as rockets rained down on Tel Aviv. Sirens blared. Explosions thudded. Yet earlier, he had quietly ushered them there with a smile—his soul steeled by necessity, his courage masked by calm. That moment wasn't just about survival. It was moral leadership under fire.

These scenes may not be isolated. They may be previews of a far darker future—one in which our own children in Western democracies face similar threats if we continue to look away.

Imagine if those explosions had carried chemical or nuclear warheads. First fired at Israel. Then at other nations across the Middle East, Europe, or beyond. A genocide—not the imagined one falsely screamed by zealots about Gaza, but a real one. A strike at the heart of the West: free markets, rule of law, women's rights, pluralism—and the bitter irony of a society that platforms and tolerates those who seek its destruction.

The horror is unspeakable—and may have been realised but for pre-emptive actions taken in June 2025, consistent with Article 51 of the UN Charter, which affirms every nation's inherent right of self-defence.

We live in momentous times. As Lenin observed, *"There are decades where nothing happens, and there are weeks where decades happen."* This is one of those weeks.

But I don't want to dwell on geopolitics or meta-trends. The cogs of history are always turning. Instead, I want to focus on individuals—on Israelis I feel a deep kinship with: Jews, Druze, Muslims, and Christians I met while living in Israel from 2019 to 2021. They are in my thoughts—they are my brothers and sisters in their time of need.

They are not merely surviving. They are stewarding a civilisation—rooted in ancient faith and modern vitality. They shelter not just themselves, but values the West once held dear: family, responsibility, discipline, pluralism, truth. If we fail to defend those values in Israel, we risk losing them everywhere.

I've been reflecting on *tikkun olam*—to repair the world. Not in the soft, performative tone favoured by celebrity activists, but in the real, faithful work of building, protecting, and persevering. While Greta Thunberg performs outrage for the cameras—making reckless, dishonest claims—others are quietly leading by example. There are leaders in every Israeli town, in every diaspora community, guiding families, supporting neighbours, standing for truth. They don't appear on television. But they are the moral backbone of our time.

C.S. Lewis once wrote, *"Hardships often prepare ordinary people for an extraordinary destiny."* And history reminds us: *"Hard times create strong men, strong men create good times, good times create weak men, and weak men create hard times."* We appear to be entering hard times again. But I believe the strength, leadership, and moral courage required to meet this moment will rise—even from the innocent eyes staring back into their parents' camera from a *mamad.*

To our Jewish Australian community: Now is the time for your light to shine. You carry the strength of the Maccabees in your DNA. And together with right-minded non-Jews who stand beside you, we carry the ANZAC spirit—a legacy of moral grit, mateship, and honour in the face of adversity. Just as our grandparents rose to the challenges of their time, we too must rise—beyond our self-imposed limits—in ways future generations will look back on with pride.

Now is not the time to ask, "Who will hide me in their attic if things get worse?" Now is the time to act—to make things better. Wear your Magen David with pride. Speak with your non-Jewish friends—not to lecture, but to connect. Share your story. Let them see the beauty of Jewish life—not through argument, but through candles, songs, stories, and warm bread. Each week, invite someone different—especially non-Jewish friends—to your Friday night table. Let them witness the strength, warmth, and grace of your tradition.

In my earlier military career, I made mistakes and have known failure. Once, I got so far ahead of my soldiers during a leadership challenge that when I turned around—no one was there. I had outrun my own team. And I wonder if that's not also a metaphor for what has happened across Western civilisation. Jewish communities have preserved traditions and moral disciplines for millennia. In my judgment, this—together with faith—is the source of your strength and success. It's no accident that Jews have risen to the apex of music, the arts, medicine, law, business, and innovation. Meanwhile, much of the wider West—once grounded in the wisdom of Jerusalem, Athens, and Rome—has forgotten. We can help them remember. One conversation, one Shabbat meal at a time. From drops come ripples. From ripples, waves. Where institutions like the ABC and the UN have failed us, community and human connection will recover us.

Let us be lights in this world. Let us be proud of who we are. Let us lead with courage, not retreat in fear. Let us rebuild bridges—across faiths, communities, and generations. Because this isn't just Israel's struggle. It's a struggle for truth. For goodness. For the soul of the West.

As rockets fall, we rise.

As sirens wail, we speak.

As others equivocate, we stand.

Together, we can and will prevail! יחד ננצח

48

Lighting the Way: How Lived Experience Can Defeat the World's Oldest Hatred

Introduction

Hatred thrives in abstraction.

It weakens when confronted with reality—with people, places, and experiences that resist caricature.

This chapter outlines a model grounded not in argument alone, but in lived experience—one that replaces distance with understanding and converts allies not through persuasion, but through exposure.

It is offered not as a theory, but as a practice.

***

Shalom. My name is Michael Scott. I am an Australian who served over thirty years in the Army, with deployments to East Timor, Bougainville, Iraq, and Afghanistan. From 2019 to 2021, I was based in Jerusalem as a senior UN peacekeeper. That experience changed me. It revealed the strength, resilience, and moral clarity of Israel and its people.

I've seen conflict up close. I've seen how narratives shape minds and how propaganda twists truth. I believe the only force more powerful than propaganda is personal witness.

I came to Zionism not through ideology, but through service. As a soldier, I admired the IDF's historical achievements, discipline, and ethics. As a father and humanist, I was moved by the courage and dignity of Israeli society. My Zionism is not inherited—it is earned.

On October 7, 2023, my then eighteen-year-old daughter was at a music festival in Australia. At the same moment, young Israelis were being massacred at Nova. That horror could have been hers. Two days later, I watched in disbelief as crowds outside the Sydney Opera House chanted "Gas the Jews." That moment made the stakes unmistakably clear: I resolved not to be a bystander.

In July 2024, I founded *The 2023 Foundation*—a grassroots, non-Jewish-led initiative to combat antisemitism through immersive education no propaganda can undo. Inspired by the Fulbright model of cultural exchange, our approach is rooted in first-hand experience. We identify, invite, and immerse non-Jewish influencers in Israeli society. Our focus is the silent majority: reasonable, open-minded individuals increasingly vulnerable to Orwellian gaslighting from extremists and their enablers in media and academia.

The Foundation operates on a simple yet strategic model: referral, immersive experience, and enduring connection. We don't advertise or cast a wide net. We prioritise depth over breadth. Participants are selected through trusted, name-based referrals to maintain mission integrity and prevent infiltration. This isn't for activists or ideologues—it's for people of character with the potential to grow into authentic voices for truth. Nurturing tomorrow's righteous gentiles.

Once selected, participants engage in a curated Israeli experience designed to foster empathy, challenge assumptions, and replace misinformation with insight. Each placement is thoughtfully tailored to align with personal and professional interests—"multiple birds with one well-aimed stone." For example, an emergency physician from New York might attend a seminar at Hadassah Hospital alongside peers from across the West. After witnessing Jewish, Muslim, Christian, and Druze staff working hand in glove to save lives, it becomes untenable to claim Israel is an apartheid state. These doctors return to their home countries and workplaces not just with memories, but with insight—and they will speak. From drops come ripples, from ripples, waves.

Military veterans might attend the Beersheba commemoration on October 31. LGBTQ+ participants may take part in Tel Aviv Pride in June as part of a wider program. A recent graduate could pursue their MBA at Tel Aviv University's Coller School of Management, supported by a 2023 Foundation scholarship. Entrepreneurs focused on sustainability may connect with Israeli leaders in water conservation and clean energy. Find the interest, make the connection—and through that connection, forge enduring allies.

As Albert Einstein put it, "Everything should be made as simple as possible, but not simpler." That's our approach: simple, but never simplistic.

I've long believed that a love of Israel cannot be taught—it must be caught. And it is best caught by walking its streets, meeting its people, and grappling with Israel's perfect imperfections. This is Fulbright-style soft power: personal, high-trust, and transformational.

But the journey doesn't end in Israel—it only then begins. Our alumni program will forge long-term impact, connecting participants into a global network of thoughtful, principled advocates. Pilot programs have been developed, and we are now seeking partners and donors. I share the conviction behind Victor Hugo's timeless insight: "There is nothing more powerful than an idea whose time has come."

Our goals are ambitious yet achievable: seventy influencers in year one, 750 by year five, and eight thousand annually within a decade. I'm forty-nine years of age with a lot of petrol in the tank. It is my judgment that my journey as leader and public face of The 2023 Foundation will span twenty years—by which time this model will be effectively scaled to many nations possessing Jewish diaspora communities.

Much of our spending will occur in Israel—generating economic, reputational, and diplomatic dividends. The work of The 2023 Foundation is not only a moral mission; it is a smart investment in Israel's future.

The urgency is real. Antisemitism is resurging across the West. The United States, Australia, and other democracies are facing levels of hostility not seen in generations. Meanwhile, Jews make up just 0.2 percent of the global population—a percentage expected to shrink further in the coming years due to higher birth rates in other ethnic and religious groups. The outreach tools that served before October 7 are no longer sufficient. I didn't see the world's reaction to the October 7 pogrom coming—where the victims were blamed. But the world's response has been unmistakable. We need fresh ideas and new means of reaching audiences that have eluded Jewish and Christian Zionist groups.

That's where I come in—because silence is not an option.

I am an apolitical former military officer with a lifetime of service in the profession of arms. I have no institutional baggage. What I do have is conviction, strategic clarity, and a deep sense of duty. Like Senator J. William Fulbright in the 1940s, I believe bold, strategic educational exchange can shape civilisations and safeguard freedom.

We are finalising our 501(c)(3) registration in the United States and replicating our structure in other Western democracies. We are not in competition with Jewish organisations—we are complementary. We reach those who are currently out of reach. We speak to those who do not yet know they care. And we do so with focus, integrity, and resolve.

Through The 2023 Foundation, I am building a scalable, high-trust model grounded in service, truth, and lived experience. Because those who threaten Jewish children threaten mine too.

There is no greater moral dilemma today than how we respond to antisemitism. I will not sit it out. I will shoulder my share.

And now, I am seeking others who will walk with me: partners. Collaborators. Donors. Visionaries.

Help me amplify the message. Help me build something that lasts.

Because when light is shared, it not only illuminates the way—it multiplies.

Together, we will prevail. יחד ננצח

PART VI
Conclusion

Renewal is rarely dramatic.

It does not arrive with slogans or guarantees. More often, it begins quietly—with individuals who refuse to surrender moral language to distortion, who choose responsibility over comfort, and who understand that standing with others is not an act of sentiment, but of obligation.

The essays in this part have not offered easy solutions. They have pointed instead to something more durable: agency. The capacity to act without waiting for permission. To form alliances grounded in shared values rather than shared grievances. To repair what is damaged without pretending that nothing is broken.

Fragility, properly understood, is not an accusation. It is a warning. It reminds us that what matters most requires care—not just defence, but attention. Not just conviction, but stewardship.

The question, then, is no longer whether the light still burns. It does.

The question is whether enough people are willing to tend it—deliberately, consistently, and before neglect becomes irreversible.

CONCLUSION

What Remains When the Light Is Tested

This book began with a rupture—the moment when illusion collapsed and what had long been rationalised, minimised, or explained away arrived without warning in a place that symbolised safety, normal life, and national ease. It ends somewhere quieter, but more demanding: with the recognition that what happens next is neither inevitable nor abstract, but contingent on choice.

The four quotations that open this book were chosen deliberately. They were not intended as decoration, but as orientation—a framework for understanding what has been examined here, and what now confronts us.

Arnold Toynbee's warning that civilisations die from suicide rather than murder speaks to the central diagnosis of these pages. The gravest threats faced by free societies today are not limited to external enemies, however real those may be. They lie in internal erosion: the quiet surrender of moral language, the normalisation of evasion, and the gradual substitution of comfort for responsibility. Will Durant sharpened this insight further, reminding us that no civilisation is truly conquered from without until it has first participated in its own undoing from within.

This book has traced that process—not as theory, but as lived experience. Unease ignored. Drift tolerated. Institutions captured. Language inverted. Violence contextualised until explanation itself became a form of indulgence. None of this occurred overnight. None of it required malice. It required only fatigue, moral hesitation, and the widespread belief that consequences could always be deferred.

G.K. Chesterton's insistence that a person's view of the universe is the most practical thing about them explains why these failures matter. Societies do not rise or fall primarily on policy alone, but on what they believe to be true—about good and evil, about agency and responsibility, about what is worth defending even when defence carries cost. When that worldview becomes distorted, when clarity is treated as cruelty and judgement as intolerance, the structures built upon it begin to weaken.

Václav Havel named the final stage with particular precision. The tragedy of modern man, he warned, is not ignorance, but indifference—the moment when meaning itself begins to matter less. That indifference is not loud or dramatic. It presents as sophistication, as weariness, as moral neutrality. But it is there, in that quiet withdrawal from seriousness, that the ground is prepared for catastrophe.

The Foreword offered by Chavi Israel, Lissy Abrahams and Larry anchors these ideas in human reality. Their accounts are not an argument. They are testimony. They give voice to what abstraction conceals: the lived cost of moral failure borne by families, by parents, by children who inherit the consequences of decisions they did not make. Their experiences—of warnings unheeded, of vulnerability exposed, of trauma followed by the deeper question of whether anything has truly been learned—reflects precisely the stakes this book has sought to clarify.

What emerges from their words, and from the essays that follow, is not despair. It is seriousness.

Renewal, when it comes, is rarely theatrical. It does not arrive with guarantees or slogans. More often, it begins quietly—with individuals who refuse to surrender moral language to distortion, who choose responsibility over comfort, and who understand that standing with others is not an act of sentiment, but of obligation.

The essays in this book have not offered easy solutions. They have pointed instead to something more durable: agency. The capacity to act without waiting for permission. To speak plainly when euphemism is rewarded. To correct course before catastrophe forces the issue. To understand that fragility is not an accusation, but a warning—and that warnings still allow for choice.

What remains, in the end, is exactly that: choice.

Not the dramatic kind, but the daily, cumulative kind. The choice to speak or remain silent. To name danger honestly or soften it for social ease. To stand with those targeted, or to retreat into the illusion that someone else will act first. Every civilisation reaches moments where its future is shaped less by what it claims to value than by what its citizens are prepared to defend.

History shows that delay is never neutral. The cost of indulgence is rarely paid by those who practice it, but by others—often the most vulnerable—who are left exposed when meaning collapses and permission is granted. Yet history also shows something else: that when enough people choose clarity over comfort, responsibility over abstraction, and courage over conformity, trajectories change.

Drift can be arrested. Damage can be repaired. What has dimmed can be strengthened again—not perfectly, not instantly, but deliberately.

The question, then, is no longer whether the light still burns.

It does.

The question is whether enough people are willing to tend it—consciously, consistently, and before neglect becomes irreversible. Civilisations are not sustained by grand gestures alone, but by ordinary people who refuse to abandon seriousness when it would be easier to do so.

Bondi was not the end of the story. It was a test.

What follows is not predetermined. History has not closed its ledger. The future remains responsive to courage exercised in time.

Light does not fail because it is weak.

It fails when it is ignored.

And when it is shared—protected, tended, and passed on—it does more than illuminate the way forward.

It multiplies.

APPENDICES

APPENDIX A
Definitions That Matter

Language does not merely describe reality; it shapes how we respond to it. When words are stretched beyond meaning, selectively applied, or emptied of precision, moral judgment becomes difficult and accountability elusive. This appendix is offered not to close debate, but to anchor it.

The definitions that follow are not ideological claims. They reflect established usage in law, history, ethics, and security analysis. Their purpose is simple: to preserve distinction where confusion has become fashionable, and clarity where euphemism has displaced responsibility.

Antisemitism

Hostility, prejudice, or discrimination directed at Jews as Jews.

Historically, antisemitism has adapted to the language of its age. Where it once appeared as religious accusation or racial theory, it now frequently presents indirectly—through conspiracy narratives, double standards, moral inversion, or the denial of Jewish legitimacy as a people entitled to collective rights.

Its adaptability is not evidence of disappearance, but of persistence.

Zionism

The belief that the Jewish people have the right to self-determination in their historic homeland.

Zionism does not assert moral perfection, immunity from criticism, or exemption from international law. It asserts only that Jews—like every other people—possess the right to collective existence, security, and political agency.

Opposition to specific Israeli policies is not antisemitic. Denial of Jewish self-determination alone, among all nations, is.

Genocide

A legal term defined by the intent to destroy, in whole or in part, a national, ethnic, racial, or religious group.

Genocide is not determined by casualty figures, emotional response, or media imagery. It hinges on demonstrable intent. Casual or rhetorical use of the term diminishes both its meaning and the historical atrocities it was created to describe.

Intent

In law and ethics, intent refers to the purpose or objective motivating an action, not merely its outcome.

Intent distinguishes accident from atrocity, negligence from malice, and tragedy from crime. Identical outcomes can arise from radically different intentions.

Proportionality

In the laws of armed conflict, proportionality refers to the relationship between a legitimate military objective and anticipated incidental harm to civilians.

It does not require equality of suffering, symmetry of casualties, or equivalence of loss. Proportionality is assessed before action, not imposed retroactively as a moral verdict.

Civilian

A person who is not a member of an armed force and does not take a direct part in hostilities.

Civilian status may be lost when an individual actively participates in combat or deliberately embeds military activity within civilian settings. The intentional blurring of this distinction places civilians at risk and constitutes a war crime in itself.

Collective Punishment

The intentional penalisation of civilians for actions they did not commit.

The term is frequently misused to describe the consequences of warfare rather than deliberate policy. Harm resulting from military action does not constitute collective punishment unless civilians are targeted because of group identity rather than military necessity.

Terrorism

The deliberate use of violence against civilians for political, ideological, or religious purposes.

Terrorism is defined by method and target, not grievance, popularity, or scale. The intentional targeting of civilians is terrorism regardless of who carries it out or what cause is claimed.

Incitement

Speech or conduct intended to encourage, legitimise, or provoke violence against a person or group.

Incitement does not require explicit instruction. Repeated dehumanisation, glorification of violence, or framing harm as justified can function as incitement even when indirect or euphemistic.

Radicalisation

The process by which individuals or groups adopt increasingly extreme beliefs that justify coercion, violence, or the rejection of coexistence.

Radicalisation is rarely sudden. It is typically cumulative, reinforced by grievance narratives, moral inversion, and social reinforcement.

Moral Equivalence

The treatment of unequal actions, intentions, or responsibilities as though they were morally identical.

Moral equivalence obscures accountability by flattening distinction, replacing judgment with false balance.

Moral Inversion

The reversal of moral categories such that virtue is recast as vice and vice as virtue.

Moral inversion allows restraint to be framed as cruelty, aggression as justice, and self-defence as wrongdoing.

Narrative Capture

The condition in which institutions responsible for truth adopt a predetermined narrative that constrains interpretation of evidence.

When narrative capture occurs, facts are filtered, omissions become systematic, and contradiction is treated as deviance rather than inquiry.

Silence as Permission

The phenomenon by which failure to challenge intimidation or falsehood is interpreted as acceptance.

Silence is not neutral in environments shaped by fear or power imbalance. Where authority retreats, escalation follows.

Restraint

The deliberate limitation of force despite legal or operational permission to do more.

Restraint is often invisible. It is measured by what does not occur rather than what does.

Social Cohesion

The degree to which members of a society share trust, norms, and a sense of mutual obligation.

Social cohesion depends on shared standards and credible enforcement of boundaries, not enforced agreement.

Civilisational Confidence

A society's belief in the legitimacy, durability, and worth of its own values and way of life.

Civilisational confidence expresses itself through reproduction, boundary-setting, and moral clarity. Its absence is often visible first in demographic decline and institutional hesitancy.

Why These Definitions Matter

These terms recur throughout this book because they shape how events are interpreted, justified, or excused. When definitions blur, responsibility follows. When language collapses, moral judgment soon does as well.

This appendix exists to hold the line—not against debate, but against erosion.

APPENDIX B
Australia: From October 7 to Bondi

This appendix is not an argument. It is a record.

It documents a sequence of events, responses, and omissions in Australia following the Hamas atrocities of 7 October 2023, tracing how overseas ideology translated into domestic intimidation, targeted violence, and ultimately mass murder.

7 October 2023

Hamas carries out coordinated mass murder, rape, torture, and abduction of Israeli civilians in southern Israel. The atrocities are filmed by perpetrators and publicly celebrated by aligned groups.

9 October 2023—Sydney Opera House

A protest on the steps of the Sydney Opera House becomes a national flashpoint. Chants threatening Jews are reported by witnesses and recorded on video. Subsequent police analysis confirms threatening anti-Jewish rhetoric, though wording is disputed publicly.

No significant charges are laid. Early official responses emphasise ambiguity.

November—December 2023

Jewish schools, synagogues, and community centres across Sydney and Melbourne increase private security. Posters of kidnapped Israeli civilians are torn down or defaced. Jewish students report harassment on university campuses.

6 December 2024—Ripponlea, Melbourne

The Adass Israel Synagogue is attacked in a deliberate arson in the early hours of the morning. Authorities later treat the incident as terrorism-related. The attack occurs at a prominent Jewish communal site.

Early January 2025—Sydney

- **10 January 2025**: Antisemitic graffiti, including swastikas, is found at Allawah Synagogue.
- **11 January 2025**: Newtown Synagogue is targeted with antisemitic vandalism and an attempted arson.
- **21 January 2025**: police announce charges in relation to the Newtown incident.

29 January 2025—Dural, NSW

Police uncover a caravan containing explosives amid fears of a mass-casualty antisemitic attack.

In March 2025, authorities announce the plot was fabricated and linked to organised crime rather than terrorism. The episode nonetheless heightens community fear.

4 July 2025—East Melbourne

The East Melbourne Hebrew Congregation is targeted in an arson attack during evening services. Worshippers evacuate. The attack occurs while the building is occupied.

Media and Institutional Response (2023—2025)

Throughout this period:

Arson and targeted attacks are often reported as isolated incidents rather than part of a pattern.

Euphemistic language and emphasis on uncertainty diminish perceived seriousness.

National broadcaster reporting frequently contextualises antisemitic incidents within overseas conflict, creating moral equivalence.

Condemnations are issued; deterrence remains limited.

14 December 2025—Bondi Beach

During a Jewish community Hanukkah gathering at Bondi Beach, attackers launch a coordinated assault involving firearms and explosives. Fifteen people are murdered, including a ten-year-old child.

One alleged attacker is killed at the scene. Another is charged with terrorism-related offences.

Aftermath

Public commentary frequently describes the attack as unforeseeable. The record suggests otherwise.

Why This Record Matters

Escalation rarely announces itself clearly. It proceeds through tolerated rhetoric, minimised threats, and delayed consequence.

Bondi was not an aberration. It was an inflection point—the moment when cumulative warning signs became impossible to deny.

APPENDIX C
What Standing Actually Looks Like

Standing is not a single act. It is a pattern of judgment exercised over time.

In periods of moral clarity, standing requires little courage. In periods of confusion, capture, or intimidation, it becomes costly—and therefore revealing. This appendix does not prescribe heroism. It outlines the ordinary, repeatable actions through which responsibility is either upheld or quietly surrendered.

What follows is not exhaustive. It is practical.

1. In Conversation

Standing begins privately, long before it becomes public.

It looks like:

- Speaking plainly when euphemism obscures reality.
- Refusing to repeat claims you would not defend if challenged.
- Naming antisemitism when it appears, rather than substituting safer abstractions.

- Listening to those affected without minimising, contextualising, or competing with their fear.
- Recognising when "just asking questions" functions as a shield for prejudice.
- Silence in conversation is rarely neutral. It teaches others which statements will pass without resistance.

2. In Professional Settings

Workplaces are often where moral boundaries erode first—quietly, incrementally, and under the guise of process.

Standing looks like:

- Challenging distortion presented as "balance" or "nuance."
- Declining to endorse statements that flatten responsibility.
- Asking who bears the cost of institutional caution.
- Accepting that reputational comfort is not the highest good.
- Understanding that neutrality toward intimidation is not professionalism; it is abdication.
- Professional standing is rarely rewarded. It is, however, remembered.

3. In Institutions

Institutions confer legitimacy. When they hesitate, the signal travels far beyond their walls.

Standing looks like:

- Insisting that standards apply consistently, regardless of cause or identity.
- Resisting the temptation to trade clarity for cohesion.

- Recognising when process is being used to delay judgment indefinitely.
- Refusing to outsource moral responsibility to committees, reviews, or future reports.
- Remembering that enforcement delayed is often enforcement denied.
- Institutions fail not when they err, but when they stop distinguishing.

4. In Media and Public Discourse

Words shape perception. Repetition shapes reality.

Standing looks like:

- Questioning framing, not just facts.
- Noticing what is omitted as carefully as what is included.
- Rejecting false equivalence that obscures intent.
- Distinguishing explanation from justification.
- Understanding that platforming without challenge is endorsement by another name.
- Media neutrality is not achieved by flattening truth. It is achieved by refusing distortion.

5. In Civic Life

Democratic societies rely not only on laws, but on norms that citizens are willing to defend.

Standing looks like:

- Rejecting conditional solidarity.
- Understanding that timing matters—delayed clarity often fails.

- Recognising when neutrality ceases to be neutral.
- Supporting those who speak early, not only those vindicated later.
- Accepting that moral responsibility does not require certainty of outcome.
- Civic courage is usually quiet. Its absence is not.

6. In Moments of Escalation

When rhetoric hardens and threats accumulate, early action matters more than perfect information.

Standing looks like:

- Treating intimidation as a warning, not a provocation.
- Acting on pattern recognition rather than waiting for catastrophe.
- Understanding that arson, vandalism, and harassment are not endpoints, but tests.
- Refusing to reassure prematurely.
- Naming escalation while it is still reversible.
- History is unkind to those who mistake restraint for delay.

7. What Standing Is Not

Standing is not:

- Online performance or symbolic outrage.
- Retrospective condemnation once costs have shifted.
- Adopting a posture without accepting consequence.
- Replacing judgment with slogans.
- Assuming that good intentions compensate for inaction.

Standing is not purity. It is responsibility.

8. Why Standing Matters

Free societies do not fail all at once. They erode when too many people decide that clarity is inconvenient, that judgment can wait, and that someone else will act first.

Standing interrupts that process.

It does not guarantee success. But without it, failure becomes predictable.

9. A Final Measure

The most reliable test of standing is simple:

Would you say this:

- if the target were different?
- if the room were less sympathetic?
- if the cost were higher?

If the answer is no, the issue is not complexity. It is courage.

APPENDIX D
A Note on Lived Experience

This book is shaped by proximity.

That does not mean it claims authority by virtue of suffering, nor that it dismisses the value of scholarship, law, or distance. It means something narrower and more defensible: Ideas behave differently when they are no longer abstract.

When concepts are debated at a remove, they are often treated as intellectual exercises. Language becomes flexible. Consequences are theoretical. Moral trade-offs can be postponed. Lived experience interrupts that comfort. It introduces friction—not emotion in place of reason, but reality into analysis.

This book does not argue that lived experience replaces evidence. It argues that it *tests* it.

Why Proximity Matters

Proximity changes perception in ways that are difficult to replicate through secondary sources alone.

Threat is not experienced as a headline.

Intimidation is not encountered as a statistic.

Escalation is not recognised all at once.

Those living within a pressured environment often notice pattern before proof. They adapt behaviour before policy responds. They recognise shifts in tone, posture, and restraint that are invisible to those observing from afar.

This does not make them infallible. It makes them early.

The Limits of Abstraction

Many of the terms examined in this book—restraint, proportionality, radicalisation, antisemitism, escalation—are frequently discussed at a high level of abstraction. In that setting, meaning drifts.

Abstraction allows:

Intent to be collapsed into outcome.

Threat to be minimised until violence occurs.

Language to be softened in the name of balance.

Responsibility to be deferred without consequence.

Lived experience reintroduces constraint. It forces questions to be answered sooner, with less room for rhetorical manoeuvre.

Experience Is Not Immunity

This book does not claim that proximity confers moral superiority or analytical immunity. Experience can mislead. It can narrow perspective. It can harden judgment if left unexamined.

For that reason, lived experience here is treated not as verdict, but as evidence—subject to the same scrutiny as any other source.

What it does provide is context that abstraction often lacks, and urgency that distance tends to dilute.

Why This Matters for Judgment

In democratic societies, decision-making often relies on delayed certainty. Reports are commissioned. Reviews are conducted. Language is moderated. In many contexts, this is prudent.

But when dealing with escalation, intimidation, and ideological violence, delayed judgment carries cost. Those closest to the threat tend to recognise this first—not because they are alarmist, but because they are exposed.

The question is not whether lived experience is perfect. It is whether ignoring it is safe.

The Reader's Role

This appendix exists not to ask the reader to defer to experience, but to account for why this book insists on clarity earlier than is comfortable.

Readers are free to disagree with conclusions. What this book asks is something more modest and more demanding: to consider whether distance has softened judgment, whether abstraction has replaced responsibility, and whether warnings have been dismissed because they arrived before catastrophe made them respectable.

A Final Distinction

Experience does not grant certainty.

Distance does not guarantee objectivity.

Wisdom lies in knowing which limits apply—and when.

This book is offered in that spirit.

ABOUT *A LIGHT STILL BURNS: ISRAEL AND THE VALUES WORTH DEFENDING* (2025, WICKED SON)

"In any moment of decision, the best thing you can do is the right thing, the next best thing is the wrong thing, and the worst thing you can do is nothing."
—Theodore Roosevelt
Twenty-sixth President of the United States

Throughout history, civilisations have risen and fallen based on their ability to defend themselves—not just with swords and shields, but with ideas, principles, and moral clarity. Today, we find ourselves in an era where Western values, once considered unshakable, are being systematically undermined. The resurgence of antisemitism, the erosion of historical truth, and the rise of ideological movements that seek to dismantle the foundations of democracy and civilisation are all symptoms of this broader decline.

This book is a call to arms—not with weapons, but with words, facts, and unwavering moral conviction. It is a collection of essays that I have written since October 7, 2023, each grappling with the stark realities facing Israel, the Jewish people, and the broader Western world. Through these pages, I seek to expose the lies, challenge the false narratives, and provide a framework for understanding the existential battle in which we are engaged.

Why I Wrote This Book

I have spent three decades in the Australian Defence Force, serving in some of the world's most volatile regions. My experiences in Timor-Leste, Bougainville, Iraq, and Afghanistan have given me a deep appreciation for the complexities of war, peace, and national survival. However, nothing shaped my worldview more profoundly than the years I spent in Israel.

From July 2019 to September 2021, I lived in Jerusalem while seconded to a United Nations peacekeeping mission. My role required me to travel extensively across the region—Israel, Lebanon, Syria, Jordan, and Egypt—engaging with military, diplomatic, and non-government officials together with citizens of the Levant. I witnessed firsthand the challenges Israel faces: the relentless existential threats from terrorist organisations, the moral dilemmas of asymmetrical warfare, and the absurd double standards imposed by the international community.

Yet, what struck me most was not just Israel's capacity for self-defence, but its resilience, ingenuity, and profound sense of humanity. It is a nation that has not only survived against all odds but has thrived, despite unrelenting hostility. It is a people who have turned deserts into gardens, persecution into perseverance, and adversity into strength.

In the aftermath of that atrocious display at the Sydney Opera House on October 9, 2023, I resolved to not be a bystander. To combat antisemitism, defend Israel's rightful place in the world, and fight for the preservation of Western civilisation. In July 2024, I founded The 2023 Foundation with my wife, Dracaena, to take this calling beyond words and into action. This book is part of that mission.

The Battle for Truth

Israel's struggle is not just military—it is informational, ideological, and existential. The war against the Jewish state is fought not only with rockets and terrorism but with lies, propaganda, and historical revisionism. The modern battlefield is as much in university lecture halls, media outlets, and on social media platforms as it is in the streets of Gaza or the hills of Judea and Samaria.

We live in an age where truth itself is under siege. The events of October 7, 2023, when Hamas terrorists launched the deadliest attack on Israel in decades, were a horrifying wake-up call. The massacre of innocent civilians, the widespread use of rape as a weapon of war, and the sadistic slaughter of entire families were met with a chilling response—not just from Hamas's apologists in the Arab world, but from left-wing activists, academics, and even Western governments who refused to unequivocally condemn the atrocities. Instead, they sought to "contextualise" the bloodshed, to justify the unjustifiable, and to place blame not on the perpetrators but on the victims.

This pattern is not new. The world has long been comfortable with Jewish suffering but intolerant of Jewish strength. When Jews are persecuted, the world issues solemn declarations of remembrance. When Jews fight back, they are called oppressors. This hypocrisy must be exposed and challenged.

This book is my contribution to that effort. It is a defence of Israel's right to exist—not merely as a political entity but as a moral necessity. It is a rejection of the poisonous ideologies that seek to erode Western civilisation from within. It is a challenge to the complacency, cowardice, and intellectual dishonesty that allow antisemitism to fester unchecked.

What This Book Offers

This book is structured into thematic sections, each addressing a critical aspect of the struggle for truth and civilisation.

- Section I—The Eternal Struggle: Examines the persistence of antisemitism, from historical pogroms to its modern resurgence in the West, exposing how hatred of the Jewish people evolves yet never truly disappears.
- Section II—The Iron Shield: Explores Israel's security challenges, the ethical dilemmas of warfare, and the double standards imposed on the Jewish state, revealing how Israel is condemned for doing what any other nation would consider self-preservation.
- Section III—The War of Perception: Dissects how misinformation, media bias, and academic corruption fuel the delegitimisation of Israel and Western values, turning propaganda into mainstream discourse.
- Section IV—The West at a Crossroads: Situates Israel's struggle within the larger decline of Western civilisation, warning against moral relativism, ideological subversion, and the erosion of democratic societies.
- Section V—Winning the Peace: Offers a strategic roadmap for Israel and its allies, outlining what must change

in policy, diplomacy, and global engagement to secure a just and lasting future.

Each essay is framed within a broader narrative, providing historical context, strategic analysis, and firsthand insight to help readers connect the dots between seemingly disparate events. Together, they form a mosaic of the ideological battle being waged today—one that will shape the future of our world.

Who This Book Is For

This book is for those who refuse to be bystanders. It is for those who understand that silence in the face of evil is complicity. It is for Jews and non-Jews alike who recognise that the fight against antisemitism is not merely about protecting one people—it is about defending the values that uphold free societies.

It is for those who are tired of media distortions, historical amnesia, and intellectual cowardice. It is for those who seek clarity in an age of deliberate confusion. It is for those who refuse to accept the false equivalence between democracy and terrorism, between civilisation and barbarism.

And above all, it is for those who understand that the battle for Israel's survival is inseparable from the battle for the survival of Western civilisation itself.

A Final Thought

In one of his final speeches, Winston Churchill warned that the greatest threat to civilisation was not external aggression but internal decay.

"To each there comes in their lifetime a special moment when they are figuratively tapped on the shoulder and offered the chance to do a very special thing, unique to them and fitted to their talents. What a tragedy if that moment finds them unprepared or unqualified for that which could have been their finest hour."

I have felt the tap on my shoulder. This book is my response.

The battle is far from over, but we are not powerless. We can push back against the tide. We can expose the lies. We can challenge the distortions. We can defend truth, justice, and civilisation itself. We have agency and ought to use it.

That is the mission of this book.

Together, we will prevail.

ACKNOWLEDGMENTS

Adrian Robertshaw
Alasha Volkov
Alana Kennedy & Michael Hendler
Alex Polson
Alexander Galanos
Alon Cassuto
Amanda Miller
Andrew Fox
Andrew White
Anna Pasternak
Arlen Wendt
Avi Cohen
Barry & Hilary Lazarus
Barry Smorgon
Ben Adler
Ben Klein
Ben Kresner
Brett Tooley
Carol Tannous Sleiman
Caroline Marcus
Chavi Israel
Colin Rubenstein
Daniel Aghion KC
Daniel Greengarten
Daniel Lewkovitz
Daniel Mendoza-Jones
Daniel Parasol
Danna Azrieli
Danny Beran
Danny Hakim
Danny Lamm
David & Caroline Lewis OAM
David Shein
Dean Rzecka
Deb & Anthony Meyer
Delia Burgess
Dionne Taylor
Dor Foundation
Dracaena Scott
Dr Robert Gregory
Effi Yaacobi
Elad Gur
Elahn Zetlin
Efrat Cohen, Yulia & Michael
Eli & Kim Alster
Elyse & Sam Schachna
Erdi Foundation
Esther Kubie

Ethy Levy
Evelynne & Jack Gance
Fred Linker
Gareth Narunsky
Gary Levin
Gavin Krawchuk
Gily Rosenberg
Ginnette Searle
Giora Levi
Grant McCorqoudale
Greg Fischer
Hamish & Rochelle Rotstein
Harlene Rubin
Ilan Rimer
Ilana Den
Inbal Costis
Jack Bolton
Jared Ziegler
Jerry Lissing
Jeremy and Roxanne Dunkel Jodi Samuels
Joel Burnie
John Ralph AM
John & Bridget Lockwood
John MacCullough
John Roth
Jonah Feiglin
Sagi & Yael Ben Yosef
Sam & Elyse Schachna
Sam Belfield
Sandy Tischman
Sara Tredler
Sarah Grunstein
Sarah Vanunu
Sean Plunket
Shai & Talila Lachman
Shari Lowe
Sharon & Mark Kuperholz
Sharri Markson
Sharonne Phillips
Shaul Costis
Shelly Freeman
Shoshana & Jason Eisner
Simona Weinstein
Simone Abel
Simone Szalmuk-Singer
Snir Pilus
Stanley Roth AM
Tali Shein
Tamar Shapira
Tanna Klevansky
Teneille Murray
Tony & Caroline Ziegler
Tony Scammer
Tony Surtees AM
Vivian Nassim
Will Nemesh
Yoash & Renee Dvir
Yosi Tal
Yossi Eshed
Zara Cooper
Zeke Solomon
Zoe Booth

ABOUT THE AUTHOR

Michael Scott CSC is an Australian author, strategist, and founder of The 2023 Foundation, a charity dedicated to combating antisemitism. A thirty-year veteran of the Australian Army, his operational experience includes deployments to Timor-Leste, Bougainville, Iraq, and two tours of Afghanistan.

From 2019 to 2021, Michael served as head of military for the United Nations Truce Supervision Organisation, based in Jerusalem, with a mission area spanning Israel, Lebanon, Syria, Jordan, and Egypt. For this service, he was awarded the Conspicuous Service Cross by the governor-general of Australia in the 2023 Australia Day Honours List. Michael holds multiple postgraduate qualifications, including an MBA from the Australian Graduate School of Management. Although not Jewish, he was made an honorary life member of Emanuel Synagogue in Woollahra, Sydney, in recognition of his service to the Australian Jewish community. Together, we will prevail. יחד ננצח

www.ingramcontent.com/pod-product-compliance
Lightning Source LLC
LaVergne TN
LVHW020520100826
845148LV00010B/1297

* 9 7 9 8 8 9 5 6 5 7 7 6 8 *